KT-549-818

Apples for Jam

RECIPES FOR LIFE

-TESSA KIROS-

PHOTOGRAPHY: MANOS CHATZIKONSTANTIS
STYLING: MICHAIL TOUROS   ART DIRECTION: LISA GREENBERG
ILLUSTRATIONS BY THE MICE

MURDOCH BOOKS

PUBLISHED IN 2006 BY MURDOCH BOOKS PTY LIMITED

MURDOCH BOOKS PTY LIMITED AUSTRALIA
PIER 8/9, 23 HICKSON ROAD, MILLERS POINT NSW 2000
PHONE: + 61 (0) 2 8220 2000 FAX: + 61 (0) 2 8220 2558
WWW.MURDOCHBOOKS.COM.AU

MURDOCH BOOKS UK LIMITED
ERICO HOUSE, 6TH FLOOR NORTH, 93/99 UPPER RICHMOND ROAD, LONDON SW15 2TG
PHONE: + 44 (0) 20 8785 5995   FAX: + 44 (0) 20 8785 5985

PHOTOGRAPHY: MANOS CHATZIKONSTANTIS
STYLING: MICHAIL TOUROS
ART DIRECTION: LISA GREENBERG

EDITOR: JANE PRICE
DESIGNER: SARAH ODGERS
FOOD EDITOR: JO GLYNN
PRODUCTION: MEGAN ALSOP

CHIEF EXECUTIVE: JULIET ROGERS
PUBLISHER: KAY SCARLETT

NATIONAL LIBRARY OF AUSTRALIA CATALOGUING-IN-PUBLICATION DATA:
KIROS, TESSA. APPLES FOR JAM. INCLUDES INDEX. ISBN 9 78174045 7484.
ISBN 1 74045 748 X. 1. COOKERY. 2. COOKERY, ITALIAN. I TITLE. 641.5

PRINTED BY 1010 PRINTING LIMITED. PRINTED IN CHINA.
FIRST PRINTED IN 2006. REPRINTED 2006 (FOUR TIMES).
COPYRIGHT © MURDOCH BOOKS
PHOTOGRAPHY COPYRIGHT © MANOS CHATZIKONSTANTIS
TEXT COPYRIGHT © TESSA KIROS

- FOR THE MAMMAS -

FOR GIOVANNI WHO HELPED ME MAKE THE MICE,

AND FOR YASMINE, CASSIA, ANAIS AND DANIEL

THE FOUR FAIRIES I KNOW BEST

- contents -

1   RECIPES FOR LIFE
12   RED
72   ORANGE
112 YELLOW
144 PINK
170 GREEN
208 GOLD
254 WHITE
286 BROWN
322 MONOCHROME
362 STRIPES
390 MULTICOLOUR
418 INDEX

recipes for life

I have collected these recipes over the years. This is food for families, for young people, for old people, for children, for the child in all... for life. Some are recipes I remember from my own childhood, others are the food I want to cook now for my family.

I have looked in the hide-and-seek places of children and tried to find four-leaf clovers; dug through the colouring boxes of summer and winter and found many treasures. This is about whispering advice to a sister, swapping recipes over fences, sharing crumbs on a train with a stranger. I am passing on those things that I wish to know from people — the very stuff that makes me smile and puts a twinkle in my eye. The things that we hold, together with emergency cookies, in our apron pockets — that we take to bed with us at night. The knowing and unknowing at that moment just before we close our eyes, when we wonder what we did all day, and if what we did do was right.

Feeding a family is about stitching all the bits together on a steady thread — between the tuck shop, your knowledge of nutrition, your own family's tastes, your capacity and how much you can give — and still leaving some space for spontaneity and the will of nature. And all this should still have the grace and honesty of a daisy chain.

Daisy chains, circuses, ice cream cones, fishing nets, dressing-up in mamma's clothes... we dreamed of reaching the stars. We knew it all, had solutions for everything and never got tired until they forced us to bed and we fell, exhausted, not wanting to miss a drop of anything. We had such dare in our glare, such things to get done, ideas that sprouted non-stop into our fertile minds, while our parents were trimming and weeding and, I am sure, at moments wishing the blossoms would stay still forever.

I love the collage of it all — a little bit like dancing together — the mixing of a child's soul and tastes with your own, and adding a squeeze of lemon and a dash of creativity. Step one, miss one, step one, miss one, don't step on that line or you'll marry a snake. And nod at every pillar on the way home from school.

As a child I wanted fizzy orange and special sandwiches held together with mystery. I wanted tiny coloured cakes and other things that I'd read about that impressed me — tubs of purity lying amongst fresh flowers in a field and wondering what the next password would be in our tiny club house. These are the things I want my children to have now — now, as I watch them lying in the grass hugging only this moment, while my mind is spinning with the washing machine and wondering what school lunch should be tomorrow.

For a lot of the time I feel as if we are in a relay race, swapping batons just in the nick of time, trying to get it all going a little smoother. But children are just so now, I try to take lessons from them — they want it now, to eat what they want now, to have fun now. No borrowing. No point.

I will not force them to like the smell of boiled cauliflower, but I will paint better pictures in their bowls, let them make their own sandwiches, have apple bread when they come home from school, ratty and ravenous, and tell stories while we eat, and love them all the same whether they like meat or not. I will try to compliment them on their differences and insight and hold them up to the light of other moons, and maybe hand-sew their marble sacks if they will have them in florals — just like the dresses I wanted to sew for my dolls, while I made mud pies and dreamed of being part of the circus. I wanted to somersault my way through life and fly gracefully through the air, all glittery and well-composed. I wanted to be confided in by the other girls, wanted the teacher to love me, wanted to eat home-churned butter and cream and have my sandwiches made from farmy things. And I wanted braces on my teeth — just like all the others had — so that I could blend in and be part of the flock.

And now I carefully weave things into lunchboxes so that they, too, can belong in the flock. I give them chocolate bread with butter, fish pie and bright-coloured fruit salad, roast chicken and crumpets, all with an air of no fuss and no importance, as if they just happened to be there. I will give them the things I dreamed about on my walks with my brother and sister. It is what I can give them from the depth of me... because I want to give them my best. My BEST chocolate cake.

I want to wash their sheets so they smell of tumbling hills and blossoms, and roll out crisp beautiful pastries; boil up bright floral and strawberry jams. Wrap their dreams up beautifully, and set them down on stable stones — with some big wholewheat breadcrumbs dropped down in case they lose their way.

Let me forget and just giggle with them, and leave apples lying around the house with just a couple of bites taken out, and fly with the winds of now as I collect the pearls that spill from their mouths. Let me scatter some inspiration onto them and hope to see it in their drawings — hope their suns are smiling, and that I am always drawn next to them. Let me sprinkle more cinnamon sugar on their paths, and hold hands as we collect apples and bright berries and watch them all joining together in the pot for jam.

Have I added to their building blocks, shoring them up with strength and their own magnificence? Have I shown them enough colour? Did I let them have enough ice cream and leave them alone enough without my anxieties? How can we know which is the right way? We have to go with our inner instincts and the feeling in our bones. But I can contribute to their growing cells, show them some foods that are better than others, walk with them and encourage their own tastes. I can teach them to love and appreciate food, help them treat their bodies like gold, listen to them wanting more or less. The rest I have to trust.

May I just get to the end of my road and say, I have done this important thing in my life and I have done it well.

So here are some of my recipes to add to yours. Leave out the wine and use unsweetened grape juice, if you like. Grind pepper over whoever's plate will appreciate it, and add your own favourite ingredients, or just use them as they are.

Tessa

red

Cranberry syrup
Vermicelli soup with tomato & basil
Vermicelli soup with lemon & butter
Penne with tomato, eggplant & ricotta
Pasta with tuna, tomato & olives
Spaghetti with meatballs
Pasta with prosciutto, tomato & oregano
Pasta with tomato sauce
Tomato lasagne
Meat lasagne
Tomato risotto
Fried risotto balls
Rice & vegetable pilaf
Chicken casserole
Chicken escalopes with tomatoes & capers
Veal involtini
Hamburger patties
Sautéed tomatoes in olive oil & rosemary
Ripe tomato salad
Cannellini beans in tomato
Eggs in tomato
La pizza rossa
Raspberry sauce
Berry & buttermilk cake
Chocolate & cranberry biscuits
Strawberry sorbet
A coloured fruit salad
Meringue with strawberries & chocolate
Rosehip jam
Rosehip semolina puddings
Strawberry jam
Quince jam
Jam shortbread

- memory -

I am scrambling everything into a basket for
a picnic, wondering what should go with
the red peppers on the sandwiches, and if
we have enough drinks and paper towels.
They are bickering about which toys to
take and how many books. The wonder of it all.
I'd like to keep them this way — just hopping,
scar-free, from one moment to the next.
I remember those moments, too, when long
playful days skipped onto rainbow-streaked
colours through the sky, as if a flutter of
fairies had just danced across, and we could
smell the night air beginning to settle. But
we still had some adventure left in us, so we
carried it into the dark and shone torches to
illuminate it. We fell asleep to the colours of
pompoms, still counting out the numbers of
our badly-drawn hopscotch. Every day was
like a holiday. We fell into our clothes after
leap-frogging out of bed and marched our
way through the house, demanding early
morning answers to our curiosities.
I would love a moment of that back — that
excitement at being allowed to leave the table,
just to fly through a field of long grass and
find a nest.

150 G (5½ OZ) CRANBERRIES
140 G (5 OZ) CASTER (SUPERFINE) SUGAR OR
VANILLA CASTER SUGAR

Cranberry syrup

Here are two ways to make a cranberry syrup: one for drinking with ice and the other for dribbling over vanilla or mango ice cream. This second version is also good drizzled over crumpets, pancakes or waffles, with some whipped cream or vanilla ice cream. I love starting from scratch with this type of thing — it really makes me feel as if I am doing something special. Add more or less sugar according to your personal taste and you can use fresh or frozen cranberries. I like to use vanilla-infused caster sugar if I have some in the cupboard.

Rinse the cranberries well. Put them in a deep non-aluminium bowl, sprinkle the sugar over the top and squish it through your fingers to break up the cranberries (children might like to help you with this). Pour in 125 ml (4 fl oz/½ cup) of just-boiled water and leave it to mingle for a bit. Crush the cranberries more now with a wooden spoon (or a potato masher works well). Strain through a sieve that is fine enough to eliminate all the seeds and skins, pressing down with your wooden spoon to extract all the juice. Cool completely, then chill.

Pour into glasses and top up with as much sparkling or still water as you like and a few ice cubes, or even just ice cubes, depending on how strong you like it.

For a thicker syrup to serve over ice cream, put the cranberry syrup into a small pan and simmer over medium heat until it reduces and thickens. If necessary, skim the surface with a slotted spoon to remove any foam. The syrup will turn ruby red and cling a little to the spoon. Cool completely.

Makes 375 ml (13 fl oz/1½ cups) of drinking syrup or a scant 250 ml (9 fl oz/1 cup) of pouring syrup.

1.75 LITRES (61 FL OZ/7 CUPS) WATER OR BROTH
1 TABLESPOON TOMATO PASSATA (PUREED
   TOMATOES)
4 BASIL LEAVES
120 G (4¼ OZ) VERMICELLI OR ANGEL HAIR
   PASTA, BROKEN UP
OLIVE OIL, TO SERVE
GRATED PARMESAN CHEESE, TO SERVE

Vermicelli soup with tomato & basil

This is very simple, quick and memorable when it's properly cooked. It really is my crisis-saver. If you use vegetable or chicken broth, your soup will have a stronger taste — but with just plain water like this, it is quick and beautiful and means you can present a meal in no time. Serve this immediately or the pasta just swells in the soup. If you're not feeling fantastic, or are down in the dumps with a bit of a cold, this is the thing to lift your spirits.

Put the water, passata and basil leaves in a pan and add 1½ teaspoons of salt (this shouldn't be necessary if you're using broth). Bring to the boil, then simmer over low heat for 6-7 minutes before adding the pasta. Cook the pasta until a few seconds before the packet says it should be ready (it will continue cooking in the hot broth) and then immediately remove the pan from the heat. Ladle out into bowls, diving to the bottom of the pot each time to make sure everyone has a fair helping of pasta and broth. Drizzle a little olive oil over each bowl if you like, but definitely give a good sprinkling of parmesan (about 1 very heaped tablespoon for each bowl). Serve immediately.

Serves 4-6

1.75 LITRES (61 FL OZ/7 CUPS) WATER OR BROTH
JUICE OF HALF A LEMON
30–40 G (1–1½ OZ) BUTTER
120 G (4¼ OZ) VERMICELLI OR ANGEL HAIR PASTA,
  BROKEN UP
FINELY GRATED HALOUMI OR PARMESAN CHEESE,
  TO SERVE
BLACK PEPPER, TO SERVE
3–4 MINT LEAVES, TORN (OR A LITTLE CRUSHED
  DRIED MINT), TO SERVE

Vermicelli soup with lemon & butter

Here is a version of vermicelli soup that they tend to make in Greece and Cyprus. If you have a light chicken, fish or meat stock, then use that, but I love this even just with water… a soup in moments. You can leave out the mint, if you'd prefer.

Put the water, lemon juice and butter in a pan and add 1½ teaspoons of salt (this shouldn't be necessary if you're using broth). Bring to the boil, then simmer over low heat for 6–7 minutes before adding the pasta. Cook the pasta until a few seconds before the packet says it should be ready (it will continue cooking in the hot broth) and then immediately remove the pan from the heat. Ladle out into bowls, sprinkle with haloumi or parmesan and give a good grinding of pepper and a scattering of mint for those who'd like it. Serve immediately.

Serves 4–6

The thing that every Italian person, in Tuscany at least, has told me when I ask what they remember from their childhood is a piece of white bread, rustic country bread, quite thickly cut, hand-splashed with red wine and then scattered with white sugar. Served just like that to the waiting children. They all remember it well.

150 G (5½ OZ) SMALL EGGPLANT (AUBERGINE)
4 TABLESPOONS OLIVE OIL
1 LARGE GARLIC CLOVE, PEELED AND SQUASHED
  A BIT
400 G (14 OZ) TINNED DICED TOMATOES,
  OR 400 ML (14 FL OZ) TOMATO PASSATA
350 G (12 OZ) PENNE
50 G (1¾ OZ) SALTED MATURE RICOTTA
  OR PARMESAN CHEESE, FINELY GRATED
2 TABLESPOONS CHOPPED PARSLEY

Penne with tomato, eggplant & ricotta

This has just a dash of eggplant (aubergine) but you could add more if you like. A nice, mild and still very Italian pasta.

Cut the eggplant into slices about 5 mm (¼ inch) thick and 2–3 cm (about 1 inch) across. Toss them into a colander, sprinkle with a teaspoon of salt and leave them for about 30 minutes to drain off any bitter juices.

Heat half the olive oil with the garlic clove in a smallish pan over medium-low heat until you can just smell the garlic. Add the tomatoes and season with some salt and pepper. When it comes to the boil, lower the heat and simmer uncovered for 15–20 minutes, until it all melts into a sauce. Break up any bits of tomato with a wooden spoon as you stir. Keep warm.

Rinse and drain the eggplant pieces and pat them dry with kitchen paper. Heat the remaining oil in a non-stick frying pan and sauté the eggplant over medium heat until it is crusty and golden in places on the outside, but still soft inside.

Meanwhile, cook the penne in a large pan of boiling salted water, following the packet instructions. Drain, keeping a cupful of the water.

Put the pasta in a large serving bowl. Tip in the eggplant, the tomato sauce, ricotta and parsley and mix together thoroughly, adding some of the pasta cooking water if it seems dry. Serve immediately.

Serves 4

My Greek friends remember coming home from school to a piece of white bread, lightly grilled and splashed with olive oil, then sprinkled with some beautiful oregano, crushed between their mamma's fingers.

2 TABLESPOONS OLIVE OIL
2 GARLIC CLOVES, PEELED AND SQUASHED A BIT
25 G (1 OZ) LEAFY CELERY STALKS, FINELY CHOPPED
400 G (14 OZ) TINNED DICED TOMATOES
185 G (6½ OZ) TUNA IN OIL, DRAINED
3 BASIL LEAVES, TORN
1½ TABLESPOONS FINELY CHOPPED PARSLEY
8 PITTED KALAMATA OLIVES, HALVED
400 G (14 OZ) PASTA (PENNE, FARFALLE
  OR SPAGHETTI)
OLIVE OIL, TO SERVE

Pasta with tuna, tomato & olives

Olives may or may not be appreciated by young ones, so I just add a few, leaving them in big chunks so the grown-ups can fish them out. I like to use penne, farfalle or spaghetti with this sauce. Adults can also sprinkle a little chopped chilli or chilli oil over theirs.

Heat the oil and garlic in a wide saucepan. When you can smell the garlic, add the celery and sauté over gentle heat until it softens and turns pale gold. Add the tomatoes, season with salt and a twist of pepper and simmer for 10–15 minutes, breaking up the tomatoes with a wooden spoon. Add the tuna, breaking up the chunks with your wooden spoon. Add 3 tablespoons of hot water, let it come to the boil and then stir in the basil, parsley and olives. Simmer for a few minutes before removing from the heat. The sauce should not be too dry, so add a few more drops of water if necessary.

Cook the pasta in a large pan of salted water, following the packet instructions. Drain, keeping a cupful of the cooking water. Toss the pasta with the sauce, adding a little of the cooking water if necessary to help the sauce coat the pasta. Serve immediately, with a drizzle of olive oil and a little black pepper for the adults.

Serves 4

MEATBALLS:
40–50 G (1½–2 OZ) SOFT CRUSTLESS WHITE BREAD,
    TORN INTO CHUNKS
4 TABLESPOONS MILK
400 G (14 OZ) MINCED (GROUND) PORK AND BEEF
2 TABLESPOONS CHOPPED PARSLEY
½ TEASPOON GROUND CINNAMON
½ TEASPOON GROUND CUMIN
½ SMALL RED ONION
ABOUT 4 TABLESPOONS LIGHT OLIVE OIL, FOR FRYING

SAUCE:
2 TABLESPOONS OLIVE OIL
2 GARLIC CLOVES, PEELED AND SQUASHED A BIT
400 G (14 OZ) TINNED DICED TOMATOES
3 OR 4 BASIL LEAVES, TORN
2 TABLESPOONS OLIVE OIL

350 G (12 OZ) SPAGHETTI
30 G (1 OZ) BUTTER
GRATED PARMESAN CHEESE, TO SERVE

Spaghetti with meatballs

If you're organized, you could make the meatballs in tomato sauce
the day before and just heat them up while you're cooking the pasta.
Once you have fried the meatballs, you will have some nice tasty oil with
meaty bits in the saucepan. I like to sauté some just-parboiled spinach
or even potatoes in this until they have mingled with the pan oil and
drunk up the flavour. Serve the spinach as a side dish and then all
you need is a couple of small scoops of ice cream for dessert and
you're settled.

For the meatballs, soak the bread in the milk in a small bowl, squishing it through
your fingers so that it breaks up completely.

Put the mince in a large bowl with the parsley, cinnamon, cumin, the bread
mixture and ½ teaspoon of salt. Grate in the onion (it is easier to do this holding
the whole onion and then keeping the unused half for another time). Mix
everything together thoroughly, kneading it with your hands as though it were a
bread dough. Form about 25 small meatballs the size of large cherry tomatoes,
rolling them between your palms so they are compact and smooth. Keep the made
ones on a plate while you finish rolling the rest. Depending on their age, kids
might like to help you with the rolling.

Heat the light olive oil in a non-stick frying pan and fry the meatballs in
batches, making sure they are golden before you turn them. You should be able to
shuffle them by holding the handle of the pan and giving a good flick with your
wrist. If not, use tongs to turn them.

Meanwhile, make the sauce. Heat the oil in a large saucepan which will
eventually also hold the meatballs. Add the garlic cloves and, when you can smell

them, add the tomato. Season with salt, add the basil and simmer for 10 minutes or so. Break up the tomatoes with a wooden spoon as you stir from time to time.

When all the meatballs have been fried, add them to the tomato sauce and stir in about 250 ml (9 fl oz/1 cup) of water. Simmer uncovered for another 20-25 minutes, until the meatballs are soft and there is a fair amount of thickened sauce to toss into your pasta. Taste for salt, adjusting if necessary.

Cook the spaghetti in boiling salted water, following the packet instructions. Drain, return to the cooking pot and gently but thoroughly toss the butter through. Serve the pasta in individual bowls with a good ladleful of the tomato sauce, a few meatballs and a scattering of parmesan on top.

Serves 4

---

4 TABLESPOONS OLIVE OIL
2 GARLIC CLOVES, FINELY CHOPPED
400 G (14 OZ) TINNED DICED TOMATOES
1 TEASPOON DRIED OREGANO, CRUSHED BETWEEN
   YOUR FINGERS
350 G (12 OZ) SPAGHETTI
100 G (3½ OZ) SLICED PROSCIUTTO CRUDO,
   CUT INTO STRIPS
GRATED PARMESAN CHEESE, TO SERVE

Pasta with prosciutto, tomato & oregano

This is my friend Mariella's spaghetti — it is so easy and a good variation on tomato pasta. I sometimes use ham and sometimes prosciutto crudo, and for adults I scatter in a bit of chopped chilli at the last minute.

Heat half the oil in a saucepan and sauté the garlic over medium-low heat until you start to smell it. Add the tomatoes, oregano and some salt, lower the heat a little and simmer for 15-20 minutes, crushing up the tomatoes with your wooden spoon every now and then as you stir so that it all melts into a sauce.

Meanwhile, bring a large pot of salted water to the boil and cook the spaghetti, following the packet instructions. When both the sauce and the pasta are ready, add the prosciutto to the sauce and cook briefly to heat through. Drain the spaghetti, return it to its pot and add the sauce and the rest of the oil. Toss lightly to coat the spaghetti.

Spoon into bowls and serve with grated parmesan all round, and some chopped chilli for those who like it.

Serves 4

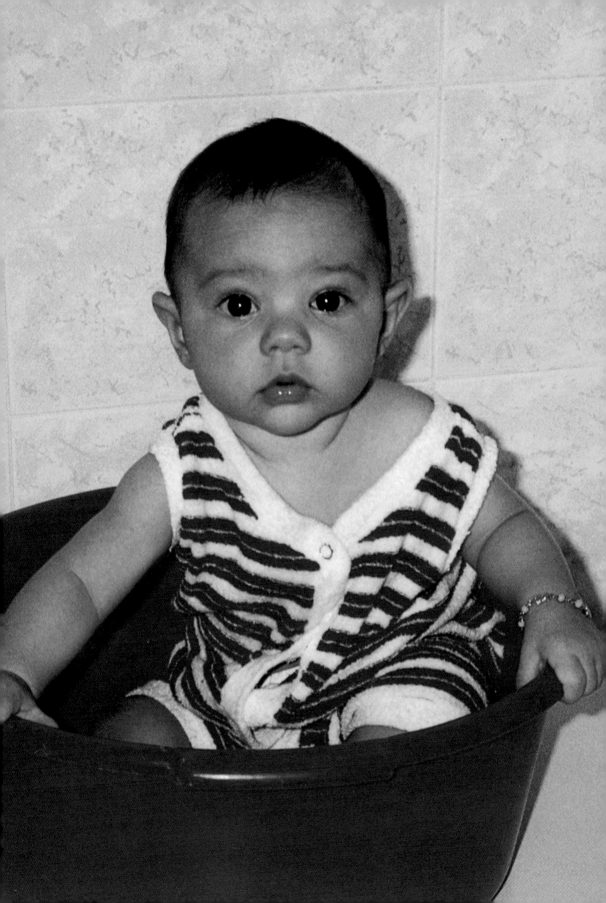

2 TABLESPOONS OLIVE OIL
1 GARLIC CLOVE, PEELED BUT LEFT WHOLE
400 G (14 OZ) TINNED DICED TOMATOES
ABOUT 4 BASIL LEAVES, TORN
350 G (12 OZ) SPAGHETTI, OR YOUR FAVOURITE PASTA
OLIVE OIL, TO SERVE
FRESHLY GRATED PARMESAN CHEESE, TO SERVE

Pasta with tomato sauce

My family love tomato sauce on pasta. Of course, other ingredients can be added but this is a quick base sauce to make. If you prefer a totally smooth sauce then you can quickly whiz it with a hand-held blender. If you aren't going to use the sauce immediately, let it cool completely and then freeze it. Otherwise, keep it in a glass jar in the fridge, completely covered by a layer of olive oil.

Put the oil and garlic in a saucepan over medium heat. When you can smell the garlic and it has flavoured the oil, add the tomatoes. Add a good pinch of salt and some pepper and bring to the boil. Lower the heat and cook uncovered for about 15-20 minutes, until the tomatoes have all merged with the oil into a sauce. Add the basil and a few drops of hot water towards the end of the cooking time if it looks as if it needs it. If you like, purée the sauce until smooth, taking out the garlic clove first.

Meanwhile, cook the pasta in boiling salted water, following the packet instructions. Drain the pasta and stir through most of the sauce. Divide among four serving bowls and spoon the rest of the sauce on top. Drizzle with a little olive oil, if you like, and serve with grated parmesan.

Serves 4

TOMATO SAUCE:
125 ML (4 FL OZ/½ CUP) OLIVE OIL
3 GARLIC CLOVES, PEELED BUT LEFT WHOLE
1.2 KG (2 LB 12 OZ) TINNED DICED TOMATOES
ABOUT 12 BASIL LEAVES, TORN

BÉCHAMEL SAUCE:
120 G (4¼ OZ) BUTTER
80 G (2¾ OZ) PLAIN (ALL-PURPOSE) FLOUR
1 LITRE (35 FL OZ/4 CUPS) MILK, WARMED
FRESHLY GRATED NUTMEG

ABOUT 350 G (12 OZ) LASAGNE SHEETS
80 G (2¾ OZ) GRATED PARMESAN CHEESE

Tomato lasagne

This is a straightforward recipe to which you can add a few blobs of goat's cheese, some dollops of pesto, a little cooked spinach or grilled long slices of zucchini (courgette) between the layers. This is just lasagne sheets, a good tomato sauce and béchamel, and my children love it. The easiest thing is to buy dried 'ready-cook' pasta sheets that can be put directly into your dish but they do absorb quite a lot of liquid so you need to keep your sauces fairly runny. If you prefer, use the sheets that require boiling first.

For the tomato sauce, heat the oil and garlic in a large pan. When you begin to smell the garlic, add the tomatoes and a good pinch of salt and bring to the boil. Lower the heat and cook uncovered for about 20-25 minutes, until it has all merged into a sauce. Add the basil and 250 ml (9 fl oz/1 cup) of hot water towards the end of the cooking time. Purée until smooth, minus the garlic if you'd prefer.

To make the béchamel, melt the butter in a small saucepan. Whisk in the flour and cook for a few minutes, stirring constantly, then begin adding the warm milk. It will be immediately absorbed, so work quickly, whisking with one hand while adding ladlefuls of milk with the other. When the sauce seems to be smooth and not too stiff, add salt, pepper and a grating of nutmeg and continue cooking, even after it comes to the boil, for 5 minutes or so, mixing all the time. It should be a very thick and smooth sauce.

Preheat the oven to 180°C (350°F/Gas 4) and grease a deep 22 x 30 cm (8½ x 12 inch) baking dish. Drizzle some béchamel over the bottom of the dish to cover it very thinly. Put a slightly overlapping layer of lasagne sheets on top. Dollop a thin layer of tomato sauce over that, spreading it with the back of the ladle. Add about two ladlefuls of béchamel in long drizzles and then cover with a sprinkling of parmesan. Add another layer of lasagne sheets, then tomato, béchamel and parmesan as before, and then repeat the layers one more time. You should have about 3 tablespoons of tomato sauce and a good amount of béchamel left. Make a final layer of lasagne sheets and cover with all the remaining béchamel. Dollop the tomato sauce here and there and sprinkle with any remaining parmesan. Bake for about 30 minutes, or until it is bubbling and golden on top.

Serves 6-8

MEAT SAUCE:
125 ML (4 FL OZ/1/2 CUP) OLIVE OIL
3 ONIONS, CHOPPED
2 GARLIC CLOVES, FINELY CHOPPED
1 KG (2 LB 4 OZ) MINCED (GROUND) BEEF
2 BAY LEAVES
1 CINNAMON STICK
2 TABLESPOONS WORCESTERSHIRE SAUCE
1 TEASPOON DRIED MINT
2 TEASPOONS SWEET PAPRIKA
375 ML (13 FL OZ/1 1/2 CUPS) WHITE WINE
800 G (1 LB 12 OZ) TINNED DICED TOMATOES
1 SMALL BUNCH PARSLEY, CHOPPED

BECHAMEL SAUCE:
120 G (4 1/4 OZ) BUTTER
80 G (2 3/4 OZ) PLAIN (ALL-PURPOSE) FLOUR
1 LITRE (35 FL OZ/4 CUPS) MILK, WARMED
FRESHLY GRATED NUTMEG

ABOUT 350 G (12 OZ) LASAGNE SHEETS
80 G (2 3/4 OZ) GRATED PARMESAN CHEESE

Meat lasagne

My mother makes a good lasagne — and she isn't Italian. She mostly uses the dried 'ready-cook' sheets and sometimes adds chopped celery, peppers and mushrooms to the meat sauce. The ready-cook sheets do absorb quite a lot of liquid, so it's important to keep your sauces fairly runny. If you prefer, just use the sheets that need boiling beforehand. The meat sauce and béchamel can be made in advance. I often make huge pots of the minced meat sauce and freeze it; then when I want to make lasagne it doesn't seem much of a job at all.

For the meat sauce, heat the olive oil in a large saucepan and sauté the onions over medium heat until they are quite golden. Stir in the garlic and then add the mince, bay leaves, cinnamon stick, worcestershire sauce, mint and paprika. Sauté over high heat for 8–10 minutes until the meat starts to brown, stirring often to prevent sticking. Add the wine and cook for 5 minutes or so until it evaporates. Add the tomatoes, cook for a few minutes and then add 750 ml (26 fl oz/3 cups) of water. Season with salt. Bring to the boil, lower the heat and simmer uncovered for 1 hour. Add the parsley for the last 10 minutes.

APPLES FOR SAM

To make the béchamel, melt the butter in a small saucepan. Whisk in the flour and cook for a few minutes, stirring constantly, then begin adding the warm milk. It will be immediately absorbed, so work quickly, whisking with one hand while adding ladlefuls of milk with the other. When the sauce seems to be smooth and not too stiff, add salt, pepper and a grating of nutmeg and continue cooking, even after it comes to the boil, for 5 minutes or so, mixing all the time. It should be a very thick and smooth sauce.

Preheat the oven to 180°C (350°F/Gas 4) and grease a deep 22 x 30 cm (8½ x 12 inch) baking dish. Drizzle some béchamel over the bottom of the dish and rock it from side to side so that the béchamel more or less covers the bottom very thinly. Put a slightly overlapping layer of lasagne sheets on top. Ladle on a thin layer of meat sauce, spreading it with the back of the ladle. Add about two ladlefuls of béchamel in long drizzles and then cover with a sprinkling of grated parmesan cheese.

Add another layer of lasagne sheets, then meat sauce, béchamel and parmesan, as before, and repeat this layering twice more. Use up all the meat sauce in a last layer, then top this with a final layer of pasta. Scrape out the last of the béchamel to thinly cover the lasagne sheets and sprinkle the top with any remaining parmesan. Put in the oven with a tray underneath to catch the drips and bake for 30-40 minutes, until it is crusty in parts, golden and bubbling.

Serves 6-8

I watch them playing in the moment. I think about their stickers — the ones I save in the drawer for when they are exceptional and lay out on the rug for them to choose.

They take the first one that grabs their young and cheerful eyes and don't give it another thought. They stick it in their book, askew, in whatever way it lands, and that's that. Then they flip their books shut and lie back and think of what to do next. If I said 'let's go and live in China,' they'd believe me and pack with the most enthusiasm I'd ever seen, and tag along, not even wanting any big details, until we got all the way to China — as long as they had one or two toys to play with.

BROTH:
½ RED ONION, PEELED
1 SMALL CARROT, PEELED
½ LEAFY CELERY STALK
3 PARSLEY STALKS
½ SMALL TOMATO

3 TABLESPOONS OLIVE OIL
½ RED ONION, FINELY CHOPPED
2 GARLIC CLOVES, PEELED BUT LEFT WHOLE
PINCH OF DRIED CHILLI FLAKES (OPTIONAL)
200 G (7 OZ) RISQTTO RICE
250 ML (9 FL OZ/1 CUP) TINNED TOMATOES, PUREED
2 LARGE BASIL LEAVES, TORN
20 G (¾ OZ) PARMESAN CHEESE, GRATED
100 G (3½ OZ) FRESH MOZZARELLA CHEESE,
    CUT INTO 1-2 CM (½ INCH) BLOCKS
2 TABLESPOONS OLIVE OIL, TO SERVE
GRATED PARMESAN CHEESE, TO SERVE

Tomato risotto

This is lovely with the little cubes of mozzarella stirred through near the end but, if you think you're going to have some leftover to make fried risotto balls (opposite), put that to one side before you add the mozzarella. Leave out the chilli when you're feeding youngsters. Use arborio or carnaroli rice.

For the broth, put the onion, carrot, celery, parsley and tomato in a pan with 1.25 litres (44 fl oz/5 cups) of water. Add salt and bring to the boil. Reduce the heat to low and simmer for 30 minutes, then turn down the heat as low as it will go and leave the pan over the heat.

Heat the olive oil in a wide heavy-based pan. Sauté the onion and garlic over low-medium heat for about 5 minutes, or until lightly golden. Stir in the chilli flakes and rice and cook for another minute. Add half the tomato purée, half the basil and 375 ml (13 fl oz/1½ cups) of the hot broth.

Reduce the heat to low and simmer for 10 minutes, stirring now and then. Add the rest of the tomato purée and the remaining broth and simmer for 10 minutes or until the risotto is cooked (if it needs another few minutes or a little more liquid, just use hot water). Fish out the garlic cloves and throw them away. Stir in the parmesan, mozzarella and remaining basil. Serve as soon as the mozzarella starts to melt, drizzled with olive oil and with a good grating of black pepper for the adults. Pass around the extra parmesan.

Serves 3

400 G (14 OZ/ABOUT 3 CUPS) COLD RISOTTO
(½ BATCH TOMATO RISOTTO, OPPOSITE)
3 TABLESPOONS GRATED PARMESAN CHEESE
2 EGGS
75 G (2½ OZ) FRESH MOZZARELLA CHEESE, CUT INTO
SMALL CUBES
150 G (5½ OZ) DRY BREADCRUMBS
OLIVE OIL, FOR FRYING
LEMON WEDGES, TO SERVE

Fried
risotto balls

My kids love these. You can use any leftover risotto but they are
particularly good made with the tomato risotto (opposite).

Mix the risotto and parmesan together in a bowl. Lightly beat one of the eggs and
gradually stir into the risotto, stopping when the risotto is damp but still firm
enough to be shaped. Moisten your hands with a little water, take a heaped
tablespoon of mixture and roll it into a ball. Make a tunnel into the centre with
your finger and push a mozzarella cube into it. Squeeze the ball to close the
opening and seal in the mozzarella. Do this with the rest of the mixture.

Lightly beat the other egg in a flat bowl. Put the breadcrumbs on a plate. Roll
the balls in the egg and then the breadcrumbs and put on a tray or large plate.
Chill for at least 30 minutes.

Pour 2–3 cm (about 1 inch) of olive oil into a frying pan and heat until hot
but not smoking. Fry the balls in batches, gently moving them around in the oil
and turning them often so that they brown evenly. Each batch will take about
2 minutes, then you can lift them out onto a plate lined with paper towels to
absorb the excess oil. Fried risotto balls are best served warm with a squeeze of
lemon juice, but are also fine eaten at room temperature.

Makes about 36 balls

30 G (1 OZ) BUTTER
2 TABLESPOONS OLIVE OIL
1 SMALL RED ONION, CHOPPED
1 TEASPOON SWEET PAPRIKA
2 GARLIC CLOVES, CHOPPED
1 SMALL RED PEPPER (CAPSICUM), DICED
1 SMALL LEAFY CELERY STALK, DICED
150 G (5½ OZ) BUTTON MUSHROOMS, DICED
4 TABLESPOONS CHOPPED PARSLEY
2 TABLESPOONS WORCESTERSHIRE SAUCE
2 TABLESPOONS SOY SAUCE
250 G (9 OZ) TINNED DICED TOMATOES
300 G (10½ OZ/1½ CUPS) LONG-GRAIN RICE

Rice & vegetable pilaf

Adults can add a few shakes of Tabasco sauce to this tasty rice. It can be made in advance and served warm or at room temperature, alone or with a dollop of thick, natural yoghurt. This could nicely accompany a grilled chicken dish, or fish. Once all the vegetables are chopped up finely no-one will be at all suspicious of them, but if you think you won't get away with serving these to your children, then leave out the mushrooms and peppers.

Heat the butter and oil in a heavy-based pan. Sauté the onion over low heat for a few minutes, until it is softened and golden. Add the paprika, sauté for half a minute or so and then add the garlic, pepper, celery and mushrooms. Increase the heat and continue cooking and stirring until all the juice has evaporated and the vegetables become soft and golden and look almost gooey. This is important so that they don't taste steamed at the end. Add the parsley, worcestershire sauce and soy sauce. Let it bubble up and then pour in the tomatoes. After a few minutes, when the tomatoes surrender and collapse, add the rice, stirring to coat it well. Season with salt (remembering you have added soy sauce already) and pepper, then cover with 750 ml (26 fl oz/3 cups) of hot water.

Bring to the boil and cook for a couple of minutes to get it going. Give it a stir, cover the pan and lower the heat to an absolute minimum. If you have a simmer mat, then you can use it here. Cook for 15 minutes or so, until holes appear on the surface and the rice is cooked. Take care not to burn it, but it's fine to have a few nice crusty patches on the bottom. Remove from the heat and fluff it up a bit with a fork. Cover with a tea towel, replace the lid and leave to steam for 10 minutes or so before serving.

Serves 6 as a side dish, or 4 as a main meal

3 TABLESPOONS OLIVE OIL
1 LARGE CHICKEN, CUT INTO 8 PORTIONS
1 RED ONION, CHOPPED
1 SMALL LEAFY CELERY STALK, CHOPPED
3 GARLIC CLOVES, FINELY CHOPPED
2 TEASPOONS SWEET PAPRIKA
400 G (14 OZ) TINNED DICED TOMATOES
2 LARGE ROSEMARY SPRIGS

Chicken casserole

This is a simple casserole to which you can add any other vegetables that you like. I sometimes get a small cauliflower, break it up into florets and boil them in lightly salted water for a few minutes, just to soften. I pat them dry, sauté in olive oil over high heat until golden and add them to the casserole just towards the end so they don't collapse — they go well with the tomato. Zucchini (courgette) and carrot chunks or mushrooms can also be added here. Serve with bread, brown rice or boiled potatoes with parsley (page 233).

Preheat the oven to 180°C (350°F/Gas 4). Heat the oil in a large flameproof casserole. Fry the chicken in batches over medium-high heat so that it is golden all over. Lift the pieces out onto a plate as they are done and sprinkle them with salt.

Add the onion to the casserole, reduce the heat and sauté until quite golden. Add the celery and continue cooking until it is all a bit sticky looking and well cooked. Stir in the garlic and paprika and, when you can smell the garlic, add the tomatoes. Season with salt and pepper. Let it bubble up for a bit then add 500 ml (17 fl oz/2 cups) of hot water and the rosemary and return the chicken to the casserole. Bring to the boil.

Cover the casserole and move it to the oven. Bake for an hour, then take off the lid and spoon the juices over any exposed bits of chicken. Cook uncovered for another 30 minutes so that the sauce reduces and the chicken pieces brown a bit. Put the lid back on, turn the oven off and leave the casserole in the oven until you are ready to eat. If that is a long time off then you can gently reheat the pot on the stovetop.

Serves 4

ABOUT 4 TABLESPOONS OLIVE OIL
2 GARLIC CLOVES, PEELED AND SQUASHED A BIT
150 G (5½ OZ) CHERRY TOMATOES, HALVED
4 CHICKEN ESCALOPES
PLAIN (ALL-PURPOSE) FLOUR, FOR DUSTING
2 SAGE SPRIGS
3 TABLESPOONS WHITE WINE OR WATER
1 TABLESPOON DRAINED CAPERS IN VINEGAR,
   RINSED
1 TABLESPOON CHOPPED PARSLEY

Chicken escalopes with tomatoes & capers

This is the kind of dish my mother-in-law has taught me to make — she is such an inspiration. You can add a couple of olives or anything else you think might be appreciated. I like to serve this with some pan-fried chips with rosemary and sage (page 245) or even just my favourite bread. Buy chicken escalopes from your butcher, or buy one chicken breast and thinly slice it horizontally into four escalopes.

Heat half the oil with the garlic in a large non-stick frying pan. Add the tomatoes with a little salt and fry over high heat until they are just starting to pucker. Lift them out onto a plate.

Add the remaining oil to the pan. Lightly dust the chicken with flour on both sides. Put into the pan, add the sage and fry over medium-high heat until the underside is golden. Turn over and season with salt. Put the garlic cloves on top of the chicken if they look in danger of burning. Cook until the new underside is golden brown, then turn the chicken again and season with salt. Add the wine, put the tomatoes on top of the chicken escalopes and throw in the capers and parsley. Let it bubble up and evaporate a bit, then put on the lid and leave for a couple of minutes before serving.

Serves 2

APPLES FOR SAM

TOMATO SAUCE:
2 TABLESPOONS OLIVE OIL
1 GARLIC CLOVE, PEELED AND SQUASHED
    A BIT
400 G (14 OZ) TINNED DICED TOMATOES
3 BASIL LEAVES, TORN

8 THIN VEAL ESCALOPES, ABOUT 2 MM
    ($^{1}/_{16}$ INCH) THICK
8 THIN SLICES HAM, ROUGHLY THE SAME SIZE
    AS THE VEAL
125 G (4$^{1}/_{2}$ OZ) FRESH MOZZARELLA CHEESE,
    CUT INTO 8 THIN SLICES
40 G (1$^{1}/_{2}$ OZ) PARMESAN CHEESE, GRATED
4 TABLESPOONS PLAIN (ALL-PURPOSE) FLOUR
3 TABLESPOONS OLIVE OIL

Veal
involtini

The veal for this should always be best quality. I usually ask the butcher for four long slices that each weigh about 90 g (3 oz), then cut them in two and bash them out even thinner.

For the tomato sauce, heat the oil in a pan with the garlic. When you can smell the garlic, add the tomatoes and 1 teaspoon of salt. Mash up a little with a wooden spoon and simmer for about 15 minutes, or until the tomatoes and oil have melted into each other. Add the basil leaves and simmer for another couple of minutes.

Meanwhile, put the veal slices flat on a board. Lay a piece of ham on top of each one, then a slice of mozzarella over the ham. Scatter a teaspoon of parmesan over each one and roll up securely. Stitch them closed with toothpicks, so that the toothpicks lie flat and don't stick up. Don't worry if they all look different. Put the flour on a plate and lightly roll the involtini in it to coat them on all sides. Shake off the excess flour.

Heat the oil in a large frying pan and fry the involtini for just a few minutes, turning them often so that they are golden brown all over. Scatter them with a little salt when they are done, remembering that the tomato sauce is well salted. Leave them in the pan and add the tomato sauce, making sure they are coated. Cover with a lid and simmer for a minute or so. The mozzarella will have softened and started to melt. Remove from the heat but leave the lid on for a minute longer to cook the meat all the way through. Serve immediately, whole or sliced up, with extra toothpicks to use as forks.

Serves 4

4 SLICES WHITE BREAD
ABOUT 125 ML (4 FL OZ/½ CUP) MILK
500 G (1 LB 2 OZ) MINCED (GROUND) PORK AND BEEF
2 TABLESPOONS CHOPPED PARSLEY
2 TABLESPOONS OLIVE OIL
JUICE OF 1 LEMON

Hamburger patties

These are my friend Didi's. Her mum, Helen, often made these for us when we went to their house after school. This will make about eight delicious soft patties. I like mine more oval-ish than round and love them with the sautéed tomatoes (overleaf) and some bread, although chips are good, too. You can easily add some extra spices to the mixture — cumin, ground coriander or paprika would be nice. And you could make these all beef, if you prefer. The patties can also be eaten on a roll with a few slices of ripe and sweet tomato, a bit of lettuce, cheese or other fillings. You will need a good non-stick frying pan as no oil is used for the cooking here.

Tear the bread into pieces and put it in a small bowl. Add the milk and leave it to soak for a while, turning the bread over a few times with a spoon until it has completely collapsed.

Put the meat and parsley in a bowl and season well with salt. Add the bread and milk mixture and then knead and squish the mixture through your fingers until it is completely smooth. Divide into 8 portions and shape into balls or ovals (your mixture might be quite soft and wobbly to shape but that's what makes the cooked patties so good).

Heat a non-stick frying pan on the stovetop. Put the patties into the hot pan and flatten them to about 1 cm (½ inch) thick. Fry them over medium heat until they are deep golden brown and crusty underneath, then gently flip them over with a spatula. Cook until the new underside is crusty and deep golden brown, then check that the inside is cooked through. Lift out onto a serving plate.

Mix the oil and lemon juice together, add some salt and pour over the patties while they are still warm.

Makes 8

700 G (1 LB 9 OZ/ABOUT 6) RIPE AND FIRM BUT
  JUICY TOMATOES
3 TABLESPOONS OLIVE OIL
2 GARLIC CLOVES, PEELED AND SQUASHED A BIT
2 SMALL ROSEMARY SPRIGS

Sautéed tomatoes in olive oil & rosemary

These are simple and good and are great on grilled bread (particularly olive bread) or served with a main course such as hamburger patties (previous page) or any other grilled meat or fish. You can also dress a pasta with them. I prefer to use tomatoes that are slightly longer than they are round. Whatever shape you use, your tomatoes must be ripe and juicy to make the finished dish sticky, sweet and tasty rather than watery. Try to keep the tomatoes more or less in their shape and not too collapsed. You might like to add some anchovies and capers to the pan.

Cut the tomatoes into quarters from top to bottom. Heat the oil in a large non-stick frying pan and add the tomatoes, garlic and rosemary sprigs. Cook over quite high heat at first, until the undersides of the tomatoes are deep golden. Turn them gently. The skins may be loosening a bit, which doesn't matter — just try to keep them as intact as possible. Sprinkle with some salt and pepper if you like. Lower the heat and cook for about 10 minutes, or until the juice from the tomatoes mingles with the oil and makes a syrup in the bottom of the pan. If the garlic cloves seem to be getting too dark just sit them on top of one of the tomatoes. Cook until the tomatoes have a lovely colour and look roasted rather than boiled. Serve warm or even at room temperature.

Serves 5

400 G (14 OZ) VERY RIPE BUT FIRM TOMATOES
1 GARLIC CLOVE, PEELED AND SQUASHED A BIT
3 TABLESPOONS OLIVE OIL
½ TEASPOON DRIED OREGANO

Ripe
tomato salad

You need the best and sweetest tomatoes (cherry tomatoes are also good).
Make this in advance so the flavours have time to mingle (later on you
can dip bread into the juice that collects at the bottom of the tomato bowl).
If you're feeding adults, this is wonderful with a chopped fresh red chilli
tossed through just before serving. Or you could tear up a few basil leaves
and toss them in. It is sometimes just the simplest of things that you need
to accompany a meal like hamburger patties, but this is also perfect for
lunch with bread and a good piece of cheese (I like mozzarella or feta).

Cut the tomatoes into chunks and put them in a serving bowl. Add the garlic, olive
oil and salt to taste. Crush the oregano between your fingers and add to the bowl.
Toss together gently and then leave to marinate for an hour or so before serving.

Serves 5

500 G (1 LB 2 OZ) DRIED CANNELLINI BEANS, SOAKED
    IN COLD WATER OVERNIGHT
1 SAGE SPRIG
1 BAY LEAF
4 TABLESPOONS OLIVE OIL
1 SMALL RED ONION, FINELY CHOPPED
2 TABLESPOONS CHOPPED PARSLEY
1 TABLESPOON CHOPPED CELERY LEAVES
2 GARLIC CLOVES, FINELY CHOPPED
1 TEASPOON SWEET PAPRIKA
600 G (1 LB 5 OZ) TINNED DICED TOMATOES

Cannellini beans in tomato

My family seems to like any version of white beans in tomato sauce. I make quite a lot so we can have it over two days. I like the beans soft and creamy. Serve them with grilled sausages or another meat, or just on their own on toast with a great heap of grated parmesan on top. These are cooked first on the stovetop for an hour and then finished in a casserole dish in the oven for another hour or so. Leftovers are great for throwing into a soup.

Put the beans in a large pan, cover with plenty of cold water and bring to the boil. Skim the surface, lower the heat and add the sage sprig and bay leaf. If the bay leaf is fresh, add it towards the end of cooking. High simmer for about an hour, uncovered, topping up with hot water if it seems necessary. Add about a teaspoon of salt towards the end. Preheat the oven to 180°C (350°F/Gas 4).
    Meanwhile, heat the olive oil in a large casserole dish over medium heat. Sauté the onion for a few minutes until it is golden and a bit sticky. Add the parsley and celery leaves, cook for a few moments and then stir in the garlic and paprika. When you can smell the garlic, add the tomatoes and simmer for about 15 minutes or until they melt into a sauce. From time to time stir and squash them with your wooden spoon. Season well with salt and a couple of grinds of pepper. Drain the beans and add to the casserole with 500 ml (17 fl oz/2 cups) of hot water. Bring to a fast boil and boil for a few minutes. Put the dish, uncovered, in the oven for about 45 minutes, or until it looks golden on the top. It's not necessary to stir, but check a couple of times that nothing is sticking. Turn down the heat to 150°C (300°F/Gas 2), add a little hot water if it looks too dry and bake for 15-20 minutes more. Taste for salt, put the lid back on and turn off the oven. Leave the beans in the oven to cool down a bit before serving.

Serves 8

2 TABLESPOONS OLIVE OIL
1 GARLIC CLOVE, PEELED AND SQUASHED A BIT
200 G (7 OZ) TINNED DICED TOMATOES
2 BASIL LEAVES, TORN UP
2 EGGS

Eggs in tomato

You can also make this in individual egg pans, if you like, and take them straight to the table. If your children are old enough to cope with the heat, that's a lovely way to serve them — mine enjoy dipping the bread into their own pan. If not, use a bigger frying pan and cook the two eggs together, as in this recipe. You could easily pop another egg into the larger pan, too. Take the eggs out of the fridge a while before you cook them. Serve with thick slices of rustic white bread, toasted and cut into dipping soldiers.

Heat the olive oil and garlic in a 20 cm (8 inch) frying pan. When it begins to sizzle and you can smell the garlic, add the tomatoes. Season with salt, add the basil and cook for a few minutes over medium heat, until the tomatoes start to melt together.

Reduce the heat and carefully break the eggs into the pan, leaving a little space between them. Cook until the whites just start to set, then make sure the bottoms aren't sticking to the pan. Cover the pan with a lid and cook for about half a minute until the whites are milky-set. Sprinkle a little salt over the soft yolks. Adults will probably need a little freshly ground black pepper as well. Leave the eggs slightly undercooked and take the pan to the table with the lid on, rather than risk having the eggs hard and overcooked, as you need to be able to dunk your bread in the yolks.

Serves 2

DOUGH:
435 ML (15¼ FL OZ/1¾ CUPS) WARM (COMFORTABLE
  TO YOUR FINGERS) WATER
20 G (¾ OZ) FRESH YEAST, CRUMBLED, OR 10 G
  (¼ OZ) ACTIVE DRY YEAST
1 TEASPOON HONEY
1 TABLESPOON OLIVE OIL
600 G (1 LB 5 OZ/4¾ CUPS) PLAIN (ALL-PURPOSE)
  FLOUR

TOMATO TOPPING:
4 TABLESPOONS OLIVE OIL
1 LARGE GARLIC CLOVE, PEELED AND SQUASHED
  A BIT
800 G (1 LB 12 OZ) TINNED DICED TOMATOES
3 BASIL LEAVES, TORN

La pizza rossa

Many times we have this plain, but, if you like, you could coarsely grate up
250 g (9 oz) of mozzarella and strew it here and there over the pizza
about 10 minutes before the end of the cooking time. Often I do half red
and the other half with mozzarella. You could also scatter a few thin slices
of ham or Vienna sausages over the top. The dough must be sticky (this is
what gives a nice texture to the cooked pizza), so don't feel you've done
something wrong or be tempted to add any more flour. Mine is impossible
to knead on the table, so I just punch it around and bash it in the bowl
until it is smooth. It takes about 5 minutes to get the dough unstuck from
my hands and find my ring. It gets a bit easier to work with after the
rising. There should be quite an abundant amount of tomato sauce, which
is the way I like it. If you prefer, you can set a few spoonfuls aside to dress
pasta later or use for eggs in tomato (page 49).

Put the water, yeast, honey, olive oil and 3 fistfuls of the flour in a bowl. Mix with
electric beaters until smooth. Cover the bowl and leave for 20–30 minutes, until
the mixture froths up and looks foamy on top. Mix in the rest of the flour and
1½ teaspoons of salt. The dough will be very soft and sticky — don't be tempted to
add more flour. Now, using a dough hook, mix for about 4–5 minutes so everything
is completely incorporated. If you don't have a dough hook just mix it with your
hands, slapping it from one side of the bowl to the other as it will be too soft to
knead. Cover the bowl with a couple of cloths and leave it in a warm and draught-
free place for about 1½ hours, or until the dough has puffed up well.
  Very lightly oil a 28 x 38 x 4 cm (11 x 15 x 1½ inch) baking tray. Punch down
the dough with one firm blow to the centre. Spread the dough gently into the tray,
right out to the edges, working it with your palms to stretch it along the tray. If it
won't stretch easily, leave it to relax for another 5 minutes and then gently stretch
out the dough, starting from the centre and flicking your palms across it. Make
sure the dough doesn't break anywhere and that it is more or less evenly spread.
Put in a warm draught-free place. Arrange four glasses around the tray and drape
a couple of tea towels or a towel over them like a tent to completely cover the tray

75 G (2¾ OZ) BUTTER, SOFTENED
50 G (1¾ OZ) SOFT BROWN SUGAR
50 G (1¾ OZ) CASTER (SUPERFINE) SUGAR
1 EGG
A FEW DROPS OF VANILLA EXTRACT
160 G (5¾ OZ) PLAIN (ALL-PURPOSE) FLOUR
½ TEASPOON BAKING POWDER
110 G (3¾ OZ) DARK (SEMI-SWEET)
  CHOCOLATE, ROUGHLY CHOPPED
50 G (1¾ OZ) DRIED CRANBERRIES

Chocolate & cranberry biscuits

These I learned from my American friend, Sue. When I first made them my children said they were the best ever and I must definitely put the recipe in this book — so here it is. I also love them with dried strawberries instead of cranberries, and sometimes my girls prefer them without the cranberries, just chocolate. I like these small so I make them no bigger than a good teaspoon of dough, but you might like to make them larger. I also like to take them as a gift, packed in a lovely box and tied with a ribbon. Unless you have a huge oven, you will need to bake these in batches, so have the two trays ready.

Preheat the oven to 190°C (375°F/Gas 5) and line two baking trays with baking paper. Mash up the butter and sugar with a wooden spoon until well mixed, then whisk with electric beaters until smooth. Mix in the egg and vanilla. Sift in the flour and baking powder and add a small pinch of salt. Beat with the wooden spoon to make a soft sandy mixture. Stir in the chocolate and cranberries.
    Lightly moisten your hands and roughly roll teaspoons of the mixture into balls. Arrange them on the trays, leaving a fair space between for flattening and spreading. Bake for about 12-15 minutes, or until the biscuits are golden and darkening around the edges. Remove from the oven but leave them on the tray to cool and firm up. These will keep in a biscuit tin for a couple of days.

Makes 30 biscuits

500 G (1 LB 2 OZ) FRESH STRAWBERRIES, HULLED
ABOUT 180 G (6½ OZ) SUGAR
JUICE OF HALF A LEMON
ONE LONGISH STRIP OF LEMON PEEL WITH NO PITH
4 TABLESPOONS MILK

Strawberry sorbet

This is fresh, soothing, easy and just lovely for that time of year when strawberries show up. It works well both by hand or in an ice cream machine, but if do you use a machine you'll get a particularly smooth sorbet with no icy granules. I like this served with a small dollop of fresh cream or totally alone.

Purée the strawberries in a blender or processor until they are completely smooth, then tip them into a medium-sized bowl or container that has a lid.

Put the sugar, lemon juice and lemon peel in a pan with 375 ml (13 fl oz/ 1½ cups) of cold water. Bring to the boil and cook, stirring, for just long enough to dissolve the sugar. Remove from the heat and leave to cool for 10 minutes or so.

Fish out the lemon peel and pour the syrup into the strawberry purée. Add the milk and mix well, then put the lid on and put in the fridge until completely cooled. Now put the bowl in the freezer. After an hour give the mixture an energetic whisk with a hand whisk or electric mixer. Put it back in the freezer and then whisk again after another couple of hours. When the sorbet is nearly firm, give one last whisk and put it back in the freezer to set.

Alternatively, pour into your ice cream machine and churn, following the manufacturer's instructions.

Serves 5-6

We wanted sleepovers and midnight feasts and would insist on setting the alarm for five to midnight. My father would sit on the terrace those nights, quite silent in his dressing gown, until we had just about finished.

700 G (1 LB 9 OZ) WATERMELON
200 G (7 OZ) CHERRIES, STONED
200 G (7 OZ) SMALL STRAWBERRIES, HULLED
2 SMOOTH-SKINNED PEACHES OR
  NECTARINES, STONED AND SLICED
1 POMEGRANATE
JUICE OF 1 ORANGE
2 TABLESPOONS CASTER (SUPERFINE) SUGAR

A coloured fruit salad

I love serving bowls of colour. You could use all green fruits: say, kiwi, melon, green apples with some berries for contrast. Or golden mangoes, pineapples and oranges with a handful of strawberries thrown in. Figs are also lovely in here — you can add anything you like as long as you use beautiful juicy sweet fruit that smells gorgeous and is the freshest of the fresh. Serve this on its own or with a scoop of strawberry sorbet (previous page) or vanilla ice cream (page 374).

Cut up the watermelon into nice-sized chunky slithers and remove the seeds. Put in a bowl with the cherries, strawberries and peaches. Halve the pomegranate and squeeze the juice from one half into the bowl. Carefully pick out the seeds from the other half, making sure there is no white pith attached, and add to the bowl. Add the orange juice and sugar and mix together gently but thoroughly.

Serves 5

MERINGUE:
4 EGG WHITES
160 G (5½ OZ) CASTER (SUPERFINE) SUGAR
1 TEASPOON VANILLA EXTRACT
2 TEASPOONS APPLE CIDER VINEGAR
60 G (2¼ OZ/½ CUP) FINELY CHOPPED
   WALNUTS OR HAZELNUTS
60 G (2¼ OZ) UNSALTED CRACKERS, FINELY
   CRUSHED

TOPPING:
140 G (5 OZ) DARK (SEMI-SWEET) CHOCOLATE
250 ML (9 FL OZ/1 CUP) WHIPPING CREAM
1 TEASPOON VANILLA EXTRACT
150 G (5½ OZ) STRAWBERRIES
ICING (CONFECITONERS') SUGAR, TO SERVE

Meringue with strawberries & chocolate

This is my friend Sue's meringue. It's well-dressed, showy — quite over-the-top — and easy to make. You can add a little icing sugar to your cream as you whip it, if you like your sweet things very sweet. I whip it without and just shake a little sugar over the top of the cake to serve. This is lovely with strawberries, blackberries or raspberries, served in rough slices with a big cup of milky tea.

Preheat the oven to 120°C (235°F/Gas ½). Cover the base of a 24 cm (9½ inch) springform cake tin with a sheet of baking paper before clipping the side in place. The paper will stick out of the side, making it easier to remove the meringue later. Grease the side of the tin.

Whisk the egg whites in a bowl until they lose their foaminess and look like very thick, stiff shaving cream. Whisk in the sugar bit by bit until it is all incorporated, then whisk in the vanilla and the vinegar. Gently but thoroughly fold in the nuts and crackers. Spoon into the tin and level the surface, making a slight indent in the middle.

Bake for about 1¼–1½ hours, until the meringue is lightly golden and coming away from the side of the tin. Turn off the oven, prop the door just slightly ajar and leave the meringue inside until it is completely cool. Take the meringue out of the tin and put it on a serving plate, removing the baking paper.

Melt the dark chocolate in the top of a double boiler, making sure that the water doesn't touch the bottom of the bowl. Drizzle over the meringue in a criss-cross pattern and then leave to harden completely.

Whip the cream with the vanilla until it holds thickly on the beaters. Dollop onto the meringue, leaving a small border to show off the chocolate. Dot the berries on top and cover with a gentle shake of icing sugar to serve.

Serves 8

APPLES FOR SAM

200 G (7 OZ) ROSEHIPS
ABOUT 300 G (10 1/2 OZ/1 1/3 CUPS) SUGAR
JUICE OF HALF A LEMON

Rosehip jam

I love the deep reddy colour of this jam. Aunt Paola taught me the recipe
and makes it every year. Rosehips must be fully ripe and ideally should be
picked just after the first frosts, which soften them enough for jam
making. Aunt Paola says we should pick the berries and freeze them in
a plastic bag until we are ready to make the jam, because if you wait too
long they will spoil on the bush, and if you pick them and leave them lying
about in your kitchen they dry and harden. This is slightly thinner than
most jams, but still very easy to spread, and chock-a-block full of vitamin C.

Cut the black tips off the rosehips. If they are large, remove the tuft on the end.
Smaller ones may not have them and the tiny ones can be left whole (the jam is
later passed through a sieve that will catch any bits). Halve the rosehips
lengthways and scoop out all the seeds and hairy bits (throw these away). Put the
rosehips in a saucepan and cover with 375 ml (13 fl oz/1 1/2 cups) of warm water.
Put a lid on and leave to soak overnight.

Sterilize your jars for when the hot jam is ready to bottle. It is always best to
use several small jars, rather than one or two big ones. Wash the jars and lids in
hot soapy water, or in the dishwasher, and rinse well in hot water. Then put the
jars (and the lids) on a baking tray and leave in a 120°C (235°F/Gas 1/2) oven for
at least 20 minutes, or until you are ready to use them. (Don't use a tea towel to
dry them — they should dry thoroughly in the oven.)

Bring the pan of rosehips to the boil, then lower the heat, cover the pan and
simmer for 30 minutes. Add another 125 ml (4 fl oz/1/2 cup) of hot water and
purée thoroughly. Return to the cleaned pan. Add the sugar and lemon juice and
bring to the boil to melt the sugar. Remove from the heat and pour through a sieve
to collect any seeds.

Put the jam back in the pan and bring it back to the boil. Lower the heat and
simmer uncovered for about 8 minutes, stirring constantly so that nothing
sticks — the jam will start glooping a bit on the surface and look a bit syrupy.
Test if the jam is ready by dropping a heaped teaspoonful onto a plate. When you
slightly tilt the plate, the jam should not run off, but cling and slowly glide down
(it will thicken a little when it cools). If the jam seems too thick already, add a bit
more water and simmer for another moment. If it doesn't seem thick enough,
carry on simmering for a while longer.

Spoon into the warm sterilized jars and close the lids tightly. Turn the jars
upside down, cover with a tea towel and leave to cool (this creates a vacuum that
can be seen on the lid). Turn upright and store in a cool dark place. The jam will
keep for about 6 weeks before it is opened. After opening, keep it in the fridge.

Makes about 435 ml (15 fl oz/1 3/4 cups)

40 G (1½ OZ) DRIED ROSEHIPS
5 ROSEHIP TEA BAGS
30 G (1 OZ) PEELED PISTACHIOS
160 G (5¾ OZ) CASTER (SUPERFINE) SUGAR
80 G (2¾ OZ) FINE SEMOLINA
500 ML (17 FL OZ/2 CUPS) MILK
1 TEASPOON VANILLA EXTRACT
20 G (¾ OZ) BUTTER
1 EGG, LIGHTLY BEATEN

Rosehip semolina puddings

Fresh rosehips are best, but this version is just as delicious when they are out of season. Rosehip tea bags give a lovely colour and their flavour is good. Using all tea bags (use 10 instead of five) also makes good puddings with a lovely colour and subtle flavour.

Preheat the oven to 180°C (350°F/Gas 4) and grease six 125 ml (4 fl oz/½ cup) pudding pots. Put the rosehips and tea bags in a saucepan with 1.5 litres (52 fl oz/ 6 cups) of water and bring to the boil. Simmer over low heat for 20 minutes or so, until you have a good rich colour and flavour. Leave to cool for a while.

Meanwhile, spread the pistachios on a tray and toss with ½ teaspoon of the sugar. Roast in the oven for about 5-10 minutes until they are crisp, then let them cool before roughly chopping them.

Strain the rosehip liquid into a bowl and throw away the solids. You should have about 750 ml (26 fl oz/3 cups) of liquid. Put 250 ml (9 fl oz/1 cup) of it in a heavy-based saucepan over medium heat. Just before it comes to the boil, add the semolina in a fine steady stream, whisking constantly so that no lumps form. As it starts to thicken, stir in the milk, vanilla and 115 g (4 oz/½ cup) of the sugar. Lower the heat and simmer for about 10 minutes, whisking almost continuously, until thickened and smooth. Take the pan off the heat and stir in the butter. Sit the pan in a sink of cold water, stirring a few times to help it cool. Whisk in the egg.

Meanwhile, put 375 ml (13 fl oz/1½ cups) of the cooking liquid and the remaining sugar in a small saucepan and bring to the boil, stirring until the sugar has dissolved. Lower the heat and simmer for 15-20 minutes, stirring occasionally, until the syrup has thickened. Keep on one side.

Divide the semolina among the pudding pots (they won't be completely full). Cover each one with a circle of baking paper and put the pots in a roasting tin. Pour hot water into the tin to come halfway up the sides of the pots. Carefully move the tin to the oven and bake for about 30 minutes, until the puddings are puffed, set and slightly pulling away from the sides of the pots. Remove from the oven and the water bath and leave to cool a little (they will lose a bit of their height). Peel off the baking paper and unmould them onto serving plates. Drizzle with the syrup and scatter some pistachios on top. Serve warm or at room temperature.

Serves 6

500 G (1 LB 2 OZ) STRAWBERRIES, HULLED
200 G (7 OZ) CASTER (SUPERFINE) SUGAR
JUICE OF 1 LEMON

Strawberry jam

I like this with some bits of strawberry in, but you can easily decide that you want it all smooth. It is also incredibly easy to make with just this small amount of strawberries; it's not necessary to make a supply for the whole year and the whole neighbourhood — although wouldn't that be nice? This is great dolloped onto crumpets or home-made white or brown bread and can also be used to sandwich together a simple sponge. I love it spooned into tiny sweet tart cases with another miniature dollop of double cream on the top. I always try to find small strawberries, which I think have more flavour than those large ones. You can make raspberry jam like this, too (and pass it through a fine sieve to get rid of the seeds).

Quarter the strawberries, or cut them up even smaller if they are large. Put them in a non-aluminium bowl and add the sugar and lemon juice. Toss them around to distribute everything evenly. Cover and leave them overnight in the fridge to draw out the juices.

Sterilize your jars for when you have a panful of hot jam ready to bottle. It is always best to use several small jars, rather than one or two big ones. Wash the jars and lids in hot soapy water, or in the dishwasher, and rinse well in hot water. Then put the jars (and the lids) on a baking tray and leave in a 120°C (235°F/Gas 1/2) oven for at least 20 minutes, or until you are ready to use them. (Don't use a tea towel to dry them — they should dry thoroughly in the oven.)

Drain off all the liquid from the strawberries into a large heavy-based jam pan. Add half the strawberries and bring to the boil. Lower the heat and simmer gently for about 15 minutes, until thickened. Purée until smooth, then add the rest of the strawberries and bring back to the boil. Simmer over low heat for 10–15 minutes more, and then test if the jam is ready by dropping a heaped teaspoonful onto a plate. When you slightly tilt the plate, the jam should not run off, but cling and slowly glide down. If the jam isn't ready, put it back on the heat for a while. It should be a lovely red and look quite sticky.

Spoon into the warm sterilized jars and close the lids tightly. Turn the jars upside down, cover with a tea towel and leave to completely cool (this creates a vacuum that can be seen on the lid). Turn upright and store in a cool dark place. The jam will keep for about 6 weeks before it is opened. After opening, you need to keep it in the fridge and use it up fairly quickly.

Makes 375 ml (13 fl oz/1 1/2 cups)

2 KG (4 LB 8 OZ/ABOUT 6 MEDIUM-SIZED) QUINCES
JUICE OF 1 LEMON
ABOUT 700 G (1 LB 9 OZ) SUGAR

Quince jam

My mother-in-law taught me a love of this jam. I like having a few jars of this in the house to see us through those early cooler months just after the quinces have made their brief appearance.

Rinse the quinces, rubbing their skins well. Put into a saucepan with enough cold water to just cover them and add the lemon juice. Boil for 30 minutes. Take off the heat and leave the quinces in the liquid overnight.

Drain the fruit, keeping the liquid. Peel and core the quinces and then cut them into chunks. Put them in a large heavy-based pan and add the sugar. Measure the cooking liquid and top up with water until you have 2½ litres (87 fl oz/10 cups), then add this to the quinces. Bring to the boil and, when the sugar has dissolved, turn the heat to low and simmer for 1½ to 2 hours until the quinces have turned deep purply red and blended with the syrup.

Meanwhile, sterilize your jars for when you have a panful of hot jam ready to bottle. It is always best to use several small jars, rather than one or two big ones. Wash the jars and lids in hot soapy water, or in the dishwasher, and rinse well in hot water. Then put the jars (and the lids) on a baking tray and leave in a 120°C (250°F/Gas ½) oven for at least 20 minutes, or until you are ready to use them. (Don't use a tea towel to dry them — they should dry thoroughly in the oven.)

Test that the jam is ready by dropping a heaped teaspoonful onto a plate. When you slightly tilt the plate, the jam should not run off, but cling and slowly glide down. If the jam isn't ready, put it back on the heat for a while.

When the jam is ready, remove it from the heat. If you like your jam smooth, mash it with a potato masher or purée with a hand-held blender. Spoon into the warm sterilized jars and close the lids tightly. Turn the jars upside down, cover with a tea towel and leave to completely cool (this creates a vacuum that can be seen on the lid). Turn upright and store in a cool dark place. The jam will keep for 10–12 months before it is opened. After opening, you need to keep it in the fridge.

Makes 1.5 litres (52 fl oz/6 cups)

100 G (3½ OZ) BUTTER, SOFTENED
100 G (3½ OZ) CASTER (SUPERFINE) SUGAR
200 G (7 OZ/1⅔ CUPS) PLAIN (ALL-PURPOSE) FLOUR
½ TEASPOON BAKING POWDER
1 EGG, LIGHTLY BEATEN
A FEW DROPS OF VANILLA EXTRACT
ABOUT 200 G (7 OZ/⅔ CUP) OF YOUR FAVOURITE JAM

Jam shortbread

This is Jem's jam shortbread. I loved it straightaway: it's so simple and so good. I love it with any jam that's not too sweet but I usually use strawberry, raspberry or plum (it's very special with fig jam, too). It's my children's favourite kind of thing — a bit like those biscuits sandwiched together with raspberry jam that shows through the round window in front. You can use more jam if you like a lot.

Preheat the oven to 170°C (325°F/Gas 3). Have a 30 x 40 cm (12 x 16 inch) baking tray ready — you can line it if you like, to help you lift out the shortbread when it's cooked, but it's not absolutely necessary.

Put the butter and sugar in a good-sized bowl and work them together by hand or with a wooden spoon until combined. Add the flour and baking powder and work them in. Add the egg and vanilla and knead them in until it is all compact and smooth. Cover with plastic wrap and leave in the fridge for at least half an hour until the dough is firm enough to roll out.

Divide the dough in half. Roll out one half on a lightly floured surface so that it will fit into your tray. It should be 2-3 mm thick (about ⅛ inch). Fit it into your baking tray, making sure that it is a fairly even thickness all over. Spread the jam over the top, as if you were spreading it over a slice of toast. Roll out the other half of the dough and fit it as exactly as possible over the bottom one. If it is difficult to lift, roll it loosely over your rolling pin and carry it that way. It isn't essential that all your edges are exact; you can break off a bit from here and patchwork it in there. It will taste the same.

Bake for about 15 minutes, or until the shortbread is golden in places. The edges will start to turn golden brown first, followed by the top. Remove from the oven and cool for 5 minutes in the tray. Lift out of the tray, using the baking paper.

Cut into shapes with a cookie cutter, or just into squares or diamonds. Or you can leave it in one piece and keep cutting chunks out of it as you go past. It will keep in a biscuit tin for 5 or 6 days.

Makes 12-15 pieces, depending on the size you cut them

orange

Cream of pumpkin soup
Sausage & potato goulash
Chicken drumsticks & wings with orange tomato glaze
Pumpkin pizza
Roast veal with oranges & lemons
Turkey breast with dried apricots & pancetta
Roast rack of pork with fennel & honey
Cabbage salad with oranges & lemons
Beef stew with carrots
Sage & rosemary mashed potatoes
Carrot purée
Creamy carrots
Baked pumpkin with butter & brown sugar
Pumpkin fritters
Orange juice & olive oil cake with pine nuts
Greek yoghurt with condensed milk & oranges
Wholemeal apricot & apple pie
Mandarin jam
Apricot sauce
Mango sorbet

- memory -

At nursery school there was a long winding cobbly hill with a witch's house on the side. This hill gave us so many scratches and bruised knees. The wall outside had jagged, unfriendly bits of glass cemented on to keep away our swallows. The witch's house was very very dark and spidery inside, with old velvety wine-coloured curtains. We used to peep through where the window had a great big crack in it; the only place where you could see through the dust. The table was always a mess: plates used and piled up from ages ago, it seemed. We knew that a witch lived there, so we would creep up in groups of three or four and hover around as long as the scare in us could keep us there. The bravest would go right up and press their noses against the unbroken window pane. Sometimes we would even throw our orange peels through the crack and then, with adrenaline fizzing through our arms and legs, we would fly back down the cobbles, down the higgledy piggledy drive, our small hearts beating much faster than the clock that announced our break was over.

250 G (9 OZ/2 LARGE) CHICKEN WINGS
1 CARROT, PEELED AND HALVED
1 SMALL LEEK, TRIMMED AND HALVED
2 GARLIC CLOVES, PEELED BUT LEFT WHOLE
SMALL BUNCH OF PARSLEY
3 THYME SPRIGS
7 PEPPERCORNS
ABOUT 1.2 KG (2 LB 12 OZ) PUMPKIN
25 G (¾ OZ) BUTTER
150 ML (5 FL OZ) POURING (SINGLE) CREAM

Cream of pumpkin soup

This is a full-bodied soup on account of the chicken broth base. I use beautiful deep reddy-orange pumpkins. Serve with or without cream — it's nice both ways, although my kids like to see the swirls of cream through the orange pumpkin. When you scoop out the seeds, rinse them and bake them in the oven with a scattering of salt — they make a great snack.

Put the chicken in a large saucepan with 2.25 litres (79 fl oz/9 cups) of cold water and bring to the boil. Skim the surface well, then add the carrot, leek, garlic, parsley, thyme and peppercorns and season with salt. Bring back to the boil, skimming off any more froth that comes to the surface. Lower the heat, cover the pan and simmer for about an hour.

Strain the broth into a clean pan. (You won't need any of the solids here, but some chicken can be picked off and the vegetables can be chopped up, turned through some rice and served with parmesan.)

Peel and deseed the pumpkin, then cut it up into smallish pieces. You should have about 750 g (1 lb 10 oz). Heat the butter in a large non-stick frying pan and sauté the pumpkin over fairly high heat so that it turns quite golden in places and starts to get a little soft inside. Tip it into the broth and simmer over low heat for about 20 minutes until it is soft all the way through. Purée with a hand-held blender until it is completely smooth, and taste for salt. Add the cream, whisking it in a bit, and heat through, or swirl a little cream through each bowl. Serve with some brown bread and butter, and adults could add a small scattering of ground chilli powder if they want.

Serves 6

750 G (1 LB 10 OZ) GOOD-QUALITY SAUSAGES
2 TABLESPOONS OLIVE OIL
30 G (1 OZ) BUTTER
1 LARGE RED ONION, FINELY CHOPPED
1–2 TEASPOONS SWEET PAPRIKA
1 KG (2 LB 4 OZ) POTATOES, PEELED AND CUT INTO
    BITE-SIZED CHUNKS
250 G (9 OZ) TINNED DICED TOMATOES
A PIECE OF CASSIA BARK OR 1/2 CINNAMON STICK
1 BAY LEAF
2 TABLESPOONS CHOPPED PARSLEY

Sausage & potato goulash

This is a great, quick, tasty, meal-in-one that will serve quite a few people or leave you with enough leftovers for the next day. Adults can serve theirs with a twist of pepper. This can be completely prepared in advance and just warmed up to serve. It's important to use good-quality sausages — Italian sausages are also good.

Slice the sausages into rounds about 1 cm (1/2 inch) thick. Heat the oil and butter in a large heavy-based pan (cast iron is good) and sauté the onion for a couple of minutes over medium heat. Stir in the paprika, cook for 30 seconds or so and then add the sausages. Continue cooking, stirring fairly often, until the sausages turn golden in places. Add the potatoes, tomatoes, cassia and bay leaf and 500 ml (17 fl oz/2 cups) of hot water. Season with salt and bring to the boil.
  Lower the heat, cover and simmer for about 20 minutes until the potatoes are softened and the soup is thick and stewy. Stir with a wooden spoon from time to time and shuffle the bits at the bottom to make sure they don't stick. If the potatoes are not quite done after that time, take the pot off the heat and leave it with the lid on for the potatoes to continue steaming. Mix the parsley through and serve hot, or even at room temperature.

Serves 8

110 G (3³/4 OZ) LIGHT BROWN SUGAR
375 ML (13 FL OZ/1 ¹/2 CUPS) FRESH ORANGE JUICE
185 ML (6 FL OZ/³/4 CUP) TOMATO PASSATA (PUREED
   TOMATOES)
1 TABLESPOON SOY SAUCE
1 TABLESPOON WORCESTERSHIRE SAUCE
6 CHICKEN DRUMSTICKS
6 CHICKEN WINGS

Chicken drumsticks & wings with orange tomato glaze

This is my friend Alan's recipe. He is somebody I trust completely with food and wine and he says this recipe is also beautiful with pork, especially the parts which benefit from long cooking time.

Preheat the oven to 160°C (315°F/Gas 2-3). Put the sugar, orange juice, passata, soy sauce and worcestershire sauce in a pan and bring to the boil, stirring to dissolve the sugar. Simmer for 5 minutes.
   Spread the chicken drumsticks and wings in a baking dish just large enough to fit them in a single layer and pour the sauce over the top. Bake for 2-2¹/2 hours, basting and turning the pieces over every now and then, until the chicken is crispy and sticky and the sauce is a thick sticky glaze. Serve warm, or even at room temperature.

Serve 6

I loved the orange quarters at half-time in school netball matches. We would rip at them. We never minded having bits of orange stuck in our teeth for the rest of the game. And I liked them at home in the cooler afternoons, scattered with a smidgen of salt.

ABOUT 1.4 KG (3 LB 2 OZ/½ SMALL) PUMPKIN
4–6 TABLESPOONS OLIVE OIL
ABOUT 125 G (4½ OZ/1 CUP) PLAIN (ALL-PURPOSE)
    FLOUR, FOR DUSTING
200 ML (7 FL OZ) TOMATO PASSATA (PUREED
    TOMATOES)
1–2 TEASPOONS DRIED OREGANO
125 G (4½ OZ) MOZZARELLA CHEESE, GRATED

Pumpkin pizza

This is my friend Caterina's recipe and is something she often makes for her kids. It's not really a pizza, but they call it that. It is very important to make the pumpkin slices as thin and long as you can, and you can keep the seeds, rinse them and bake them in the oven to serve as a snack with a sprinkling of salt. Next time you make this you could even try adding a few dollops of leftover cooked mince between the layers of pumpkin.

Peel the pumpkin, cut out the seeds and cut the flesh into very thin, long slices about 2 mm (1/16 inch) thick. Put the slices in a colander, sprinkle with salt and leave for about 1 hour. Rinse them very well and pat dry. Preheat the oven to 180°C (350°F/Gas 4).

Drizzle 2 tablespoons of olive oil into a round 25–30 cm (10–12 inch) baking dish and spread it to coat the base of the dish. Put the flour on a plate and pat both sides of the pumpkin slices in it. Make a slightly overlapping layer of slices in the baking dish. Trickle the tiniest bit of olive oil over this layer, then repeat the layering and oiling until you have used up all the pumpkin (you should have four or five layers).

Mix a little salt into the passata and dot here and there over the top of the pumpkin. Put into the oven and bake for about 50 minutes, until the bottom is sizzling and the top is turning quite golden. Scatter the oregano over the top, crushing it between your fingers. Sprinkle with the mozzarella and return to the oven for 5 or 10 minutes, until the cheese melts and browns slightly. Cool a little before serving in wedges like pizza.

Serves 6

1 1/2 ORANGES
1 1/2 LEMONS
3 TABLESPOONS OLIVE OIL
30 G (1 OZ) BUTTER
ABOUT 700 G (1 LB 9 OZ) VEAL NUT, TIED
    WITH STRING TO KEEP ITS SHAPE
2 GARLIC CLOVES, UNPEELED
2 FRENCH SHALLOTS, PEELED AND
    HALVED LENGTHWAYS
4 CARROTS, PEELED AND CUT INTO THIRDS
2 ROSEMARY SPRIGS
4 THYME SPRIGS
125 ML (4 FL OZ/1/2 CUP) WHITE WINE

Roast veal with oranges & lemons

I made this with Luca and Luisa — my brother and sister-in-law who are fantastic cooks — and it left me incredibly happy. There is not too much orange and lemon, just a hint, but I love the citrus wedges and a roasted thyme sprig served on the plate with the veal so that you know exactly what has gone into the cooking. (If you want, you can add more orange and lemon wedges towards the end of the cooking time, although they could make the sauce a little more tart.) The meat should be deep golden on the outside and cooked but just slightly rosy inside. You will need a small roasting dish (mine is about 18 x 25 cm/7 x 10 inches) that fits the meat and vegetables quite compactly and can transfer to the stovetop.

Preheat the oven to 200°C (400°F/Gas 6). Cut the whole orange and lemon into quarters lengthways (or into 6 wedges, if they are large) and put to one side. Keep the halves for later.

Put the oil and butter in a flameproof roasting tin and put over medium heat until the butter melts. Add the veal, garlic, shallots and carrots, turn the heat to high and brown the meat, salting and peppering the done sides and turning the vegetables over when you turn the meat.

Add the rosemary and thyme and put the tin in the oven. Roast for about 20 minutes, or until the surface of the veal looks bubbling and golden, then turn it over. Squeeze in the juice from the orange and lemon halves, and add the wine. Roast for 10 minutes, then add the orange and lemon wedges. Reduce the temperature to 180°C (350°F/Gas 4) and roast for another 10 minutes. Turn the wedges, taking care not to pierce them and ruin their shape, then roast for a final 20 minutes. Remove from the oven and let the dish sit for about 15 minutes.

Remove the string before carving the meat into fine slices. Serve with the pan juices, some carrots and an orange and lemon wedge for each person.

Serves 4-5

500 G (1 LB 2 OZ) TURKEY BREAST IN ONE SLICE,
  LESS THAN 1 CM ($\frac{1}{2}$ INCH) THICK
9 DRIED APRICOTS
9 THIN SLICES UNSMOKED PANCETTA
1 EGG
2 TABLESPOONS PLAIN (ALL-PURPOSE) FLOUR
2 TABLESPOONS FINE POLENTA
4 TABLESPOONS OLIVE OIL
180 G (6$\frac{1}{2}$ OZ) LARGE FRENCH SHALLOTS,
  PEELED AND QUARTERED LENGTHWAYS
3 TABLESPOONS WHITE WINE

Turkey breast with dried apricots & pancetta

This is my sister-in law, Luisa's. Her kids loved this kind of thing when they were young. You can also make it with two chicken breasts, making two smaller bundles.

Heat the oven to 180°C (350°F/Gas 4) and lay the turkey breast flat on a board. Roll up each apricot in a slice of pancetta and sit them in a line along one long side of the turkey breast. Roll up the turkey and stitch the seam closed with a few metal skewers or toothpicks.

Break the egg into a large flat dish and whip with salt and pepper. Soak the turkey roll in the egg for 5 minutes or so, turning it over so that it is well coated. Hold it up so that the excess egg drips off and then pat the flour all over it. Dip it again in the egg, covering it well, then pat with the polenta, making sure that it is covered everywhere.

Heat half the oil in a non-stick frying pan and fry the turkey roll over medium heat to seal the crumbs. Turn over very gently, but only when the polenta crust is lightly golden and has set or it will stick to the pan and come away.

Put the shallots in a baking dish and drizzle with the wine and the remaining oil. Toss the shallots to coat them well and then put the turkey on top. Put in the oven for 40-50 minutes, turning the turkey when the top is golden and shuffling the shallots. Once the wine has almost evaporated, add about 3 tablespoons of water and finish cooking. Serve in slices with some shallots on the side and the pan juices spooned over the top.

Serves 4-5

2 FENNEL BULBS, TRIMMED
1 KG (2 LB 4 OZ) PORK LOIN RACK, PREPARED
  AS DISCUSSED BELOW
2 LONG ROSEMARY SPRIGS
4 POTATOES (ABOUT 800 G/1 LB 12 OZ),
  PEELED AND CUT INTO LONG WEDGES
5 FRENCH SHALLOTS, PEELED
2 OR 3 GARLIC CLOVES, UNPEELED
2 FRESH BAY LEAVES
150 ML (5 FL OZ) OLIVE OIL
125 ML (4 FL OZ/1/2 CUP) WHITE WINE
3 OR 4 SAGE SPRIGS
2 TABLESPOONS RUNNY HONEY
1 TEASPOON MUSTARD POWDER

Roast rack of pork with fennel & honey

This is really quite simple even though it may seem fussy. Ask your butcher to prepare the meat for you by cutting it away from the bone and leaving it attached just at the bottom. Then, to serve, all you have to do is detach the last bottom bit and slice it up. Roasting it with the bones just gives extra flavour to the dish and it looks good. But, if you prefer, you can cook it from the beginning deboned — a simple loin of pork. You can easily get a bigger piece than this, depending on how many you will be feeding. If you prefer, use unsweetened clear apple juice in place of the wine. And you can brush the pork with some mandarin jam and mustard instead of the honey, if you happen to have some. Or leave out the last step of brushing with honey mustard and serve a plain unsweetened roast instead.

Preheat the oven to 200°C (400°F/Gas 6). Cut the fennel bulbs lengthways into 4 or 6 wedges that are still attached at the base. Bring a large saucepan of salted water to the boil and simmer the fennel for about 7-8 minutes to soften it a little, then drain.

Put the pork in a roasting tin and tuck the rosemary sprigs between the bone and the meat. Secure it closed with a skewer, or tie it with string so that it stays in place while cooking. Season all over with salt and pepper. Scatter the potatoes, shallots, garlic, bay leaves and fennel around the meat. Sprinkle a little salt over the potatoes, drizzle the olive oil over the meat and potatoes and pour the wine and 125 ml (4 fl oz/½ cup) of water around. Put one sage sprig on top of the meat like a crown and tuck the rest under the vegetables.

Put the tin in the oven and roast for about 1½ hours, turning the potatoes, shallots and fennel over and basting them a few times. The meat won't need basting or turning over. By the end of the cooking time the potatoes should be juicy and crisp on the outside and the meat nicely golden and cooked through, but still soft inside. If something is ready before everything else, remove it from the tin and put it in an ovenproof dish. This can be put in the oven to heat through for a few minutes before serving.

Meanwhile, mix together the honey and mustard until smooth, pressing down with a spoon to squash out any lumps.

Preheat the grill (broiler) to high. Remove the roasting tin from the oven and move the vegetables to the ovenproof dish to keep warm in the oven. Brush the honey mustard over the meat and put it under the grill for about 5 minutes, until it crisps up and becomes nicely golden. Cut the meat completely off the bone and serve on a platter, carved up in slices as thin or thick as you like. Arrange the vegetables on the platter around the meat and drizzle some of the melted honey juices over the potatoes before serving.

Serves 5-6

400 G (14 OZ) FINELY SLICED CABBAGE
2 SMALLISH LEAFY CELERY STALKS, FINELY SLICED
2 WHOLE ORANGES (BLOOD ORANGES, WHEN
   IN SEASON)
GROUND CHILLI, TO SERVE

DRESSING:
3 TABLESPOONS OLIVE OIL
1 TABLESPOON LEMON JUICE
2 TEASPOONS BALSAMIC VINEGAR
1/2 TEASPOON DRIED OREGANO, CRUSHED
   THROUGH YOUR FINGERS

Cabbage salad with oranges & lemons

A soft cabbage like savoy is best here, as the dressing will happily cling to it. You can easily add other ingredients — sometimes I sprinkle in some crushed dried mint or freshly chopped parsley, ground coriander seeds or caraway seeds (although not for my children, who say they look like 'gogos' — a word we used in South Africa for something small and insecty). Finely sliced fennel and coarsely grated carrots are also good, and you could use some beautiful purple cabbage for extra colour. It is also lovely with a peeled, cored and chopped apple tossed through. Walnuts are great, too. I normally use blood oranges, but, when they are out of season, orange oranges are fine — just make sure that they are bright, sweet and at their very best.

Put the cabbage in a large bowl, sprinkle with 1 teaspoon of salt and cover with cold water. Leave to soak for an hour or so. This will help draw away any acid from the cabbage. Drain, rinse and put it in your serving bowl with the celery. Cut the skin and all the pith from the oranges. Slice the oranges into fine wheels (picking out any seeds) and add to the cabbage.

   For the dressing, lightly whisk the oil, lemon juice, balsamic vinegar and oregano together. Season with salt and pepper and pour over the cabbage. Mix through well. Let it settle, then mix through a few more times so that the cabbage is completely coated. Toss through a sprinkling of ground chilli just before serving, or pass it around separately for those who want it.

   Serve in winter (when cabbage is at its best) with roast pork or chicken, or in summer with barbecued meats.

Serves 6

3 TABLESPOONS OLIVE OIL
700 G (1 LB 9 OZ) TOPSIDE BEEF, CUT INTO 3 CM
 (1½ INCH) CUBES
1 RED ONION, FINELY CHOPPED
30 G (1 OZ) BUTTER
2 GARLIC CLOVES, CHOPPED
4 THYME SPRIGS
125 ML (4 FL OZ/½ CUP) LIGHT RED WINE
125 ML (4 FL OZ/½ CUP) PUREED TINNED TOMATOES
3 CARROTS, PEELED AND CUT DIAGONALLY INTO
 3 CM (1½ INCH) CHUNKS

Beef stew with carrots

This will be really soft and should have a nice amount of sauce after it has been cooking for a couple of hours. It is wonderful served with the sage and rosemary mash (overleaf). You decide if you want to leave a bit of fat on the meat or not — I like it sometimes with and sometimes without.

Heat the oil in a large flameproof casserole. Add the beef and brown it over high heat until it is deep golden on all sides, salting the done parts as you go. Add the onion and fry until it is lightly browned and looking a bit sticky. Add the butter, garlic and thyme and cook until you can smell the garlic. Add the wine, cook until it has evaporated and then add the puréed tomatoes.

Add 750 ml (26 fl oz/3 cups) of hot water and bring to the boil. Cover, turn the heat to minimum and simmer for 1½-2 hours, giving it a stir now and then. The meat should be soft and there should be a good amount of liquid.

Add the carrots and sprinkle them with a little salt. Cook uncovered for another 20-30 minutes, until the carrots are cooked all the way through but not collapsing, the meat is meltingly soft and the sauce fairly thickened. Remove from the heat, leave with the lid on for 10 minutes or so and then serve with mash.

Serves 4

1 KG (2 LB 4 OZ) POTATOES, PEELED AND CUT
   INTO CHUNKS
3 TABLESPOONS OLIVE OIL
1 LARGE GARLIC CLOVE, PEELED AND
   SQUASHED A BIT
2 SAGE SPRIGS
1 ROSEMARY SPRIG
60 G (2¼ OZ) BUTTER
125 ML (4 FL OZ/½ CUP) MILK
3 TABLESPOONS POURING (SINGLE) CREAM

Sage & rosemary mashed potatoes

You can make these plain without the herb-flavoured oil, if you like. This is easy and, once you get past the idea that there might be more dishes to wash, it's quick to make. There really is nothing to compare with a dollop of creamy mash on your plate, especially with a stewy saucy dish like the beef stew with carrots (previous page).

Bring a saucepan of salted water to the boil. Add the potatoes and cook them for about 20 minutes, until you can pierce right through them and they look frayed at the edges. Drain well.

Heat the oil in a non-stick frying pan. Add the garlic, sage and rosemary and cook over medium heat for just long enough to lightly flavour the oil. Add the potato chunks and sauté for a few minutes so that they are well coated in oil and absorb the flavours.

Heat the butter, milk and cream in a small saucepan just until the butter has melted. Pass just the potatoes through a potato mill into a bowl, or mash with a potato masher. Add the hot milk mixture and fluff it through with a wooden spoon, trying not to overmix but keeping it light and fluffy. Add a little extra milk and cream if it seems too stiff, and add salt if needed. Serve immediately.

Serves 4

1 KG (2 LB 4 OZ) CARROTS, PEELED AND ROUGHLY CHOPPED
1 BAY LEAF
2 THYME SPRIGS
1 SMALL LEAFY CELERY STALK, HALVED
2 PARSLEY STALKS
A FEW WHOLE PEPPERCORNS
60 G (2¼ OZ) BUTTER, DICED
GROUND CINNAMON, TO SERVE

Carrot purée

The colour of this is so very appealing. Serve in a small heap with roast pork, veal or chicken. Use sweet, bright orange carrots.

Put the carrots in a pan of boiling salted water with the bay leaf, thyme, celery, parsley and peppercorns. Simmer for about 20 minutes until the carrots are soft. Transfer just the carrots to a food processor, keeping about 125 ml (4 fl oz/½ cup) of the cooking liquid. Purée until completely smooth, adding teaspoonfuls of the cooking liquid if you need to. Add the butter and process just enough for it to melt. Taste for salt and pepper and serve warm, sprinkled with cinnamon.

Serves 6

1 KG (2 LB 4 OZ) CARROTS, PEELED AND CUT
    INTO 1 CM (½ INCH ROUNDS)
30 G (1 OZ) BUTTER
1-2 TABLESPOONS CHOPPED PARSLEY
100 ML (3½ FL OZ) POURING (SINGLE) CREAM

Creamy carrots

This is a very simple carrot sauté that renders them soft and sweet and easy to eat. Make sure your carrots are bright orange and sweet to start with — the kind that you would like to eat raw. Sometimes we like these with grated parmesan sprinkled over the top and sometimes just plain.

Simmer the carrots in salted water for 10–15 minutes until they are quite soft and almost fraying on the outside, but still just a bit firm inside. Drain and put them in a large non-stick frying pan with the butter and the parsley. Sauté over medium heat until the butter starts to sizzle and turn a little golden, then pour in the cream. Let the cream bubble up and reduce a little, then serve hot.

Serves 4

50 G (1³/4 OZ) BUTTER
ABOUT 1 KG (2 LB 4 OZ) UNPEELED PUMPKIN
50–70 G (1½–2½ OZ) LIGHT BROWN SUGAR
2 BAY LEAVES

Baked pumpkin with butter & brown sugar

This is lovely and sweet and goes very well with roast pork or chicken, and also game if you happen to be serving that. I use organic pumpkin which is a beautiful reddish orange outside and butternut orange inside. Make sure you start off with a lovely pumpkin, but if you suspect yours is not very ripe and tasty, you could add a little more sugar. You might like to add another vegetable here too, like turnips or other root vegetables. You can also add some ground cinnamon before baking. I use a 32 cm (about 12 inch) round baking dish, but you can work out how many you need to serve and what size dish will be right, as these are very easy amounts to adjust.

Preheat the oven to 180°C (350°F/Gas 4) and generously butter the bottom of a large round ovenproof dish with some of the butter. Peel the pumpkin by first cutting it in half, then scooping out the seeds with a spoon (save the seeds to toast in the oven for a snack, or to plant). Cut the pumpkin into long slices that are 2–3 cm (about an inch) thick. Using a small sharp knife, carefully cut away the skin, keeping the shape of the pumpkin slices and taking care that you don't cut yourself, as the skin is hard. You should have about 750 g (1 lb 10 oz) of pumpkin.

Scatter some of the sugar over the bottom of the dish and then lay the pumpkin slices flat, in a single layer. Scatter the rest of the sugar over the top, dot with the rest of the butter and sprinkle with a little salt. Pour 3 tablespoons of water around the side and add the bay leaves. Put into the oven for about 1 hour, or until the pumpkin is soft and golden, even dark in places, and there is some thick golden juice bubbling away at the bottom. Spoon the pan juices over the pumpkin a couple of times during the cooking — if it looks a little too dry, add a dribble more water. Serve warm. If you aren't serving it immediately, then reheat gently so that the butter melts again.

Serves 6

500 G (1 LB 2 OZ) PUMPKIN (ABOUT 310 G/11 OZ
    ONCE PEELED AND DESEEDED)
60 G (2¼ OZ/½ CUP) PLAIN (ALL-PURPOSE) FLOUR
A LARGE PINCH OF BICARBONATE OF SODA
2 EGGS, LIGHTLY BEATEN
4 TABLESPOONS CASTER (SUPERFINE) SUGAR
1 TEASPOON GROUND CINNAMON
BUTTER, FOR FRYING

Pumpkin fritters

I use beautiful organic pumpkins for this — they are small with reddish-orange skin outside and very bright autumny orange inside. This dish is best warm but also quite nice and stodgy when at room temperature (because we don't always get round to frying things and serving them immediately). If you have clarified butter, use that for frying because it doesn't burn so quickly. Otherwise, just use ordinary butter and throw in a few extra blobs from time to time to cool it down.

Cut the pumpkin into chunks and boil in a large pan of water for 15 minutes or so until very soft. Drain well and then leave on a plate for a few minutes for the excess water to evaporate. Put it into a bowl and mash very well. You should get about a cupful of mash.

Add the flour, bicarbonate of soda, eggs, ½ teaspoon of salt and a couple of grindings of pepper and mix it all together well. Mix the sugar and cinnamon together on a flat plate.

Heat enough butter in a non-stick frying pan to just cover the bottom. When it sizzles, turn the heat to medium and dollop in a few large tablespoonfuls of the pumpkin mixture, letting them settle into fritters. Don't touch them until they have set, with some holes appearing on their tops and their bottoms are golden brown. Swiftly flip them over with a metal spatula and cook until the new bottoms turn golden. Lift them out onto a plate lined with kitchen paper to soak up the oil, and then pat them richly on both sides in the cinnamon sugar. If the butter looks dark and as if it's starting to burn, wipe out the pan with kitchen paper and add fresh butter. Carry on frying the rest, adding fresh butter as needed.

Makes about 18 fritters

4 EGGS, SEPARATED
1 TEASPOON VANILLA EXTRACT
250 G (9 OZ) CASTER (SUPERFINE) SUGAR
50 G (1^3/$_4$ OZ) LIGHT BROWN SUGAR
200 ML (7 FL OZ) OLIVE OIL
400 G (14 OZ/3^1/$_3$ CUPS) PLAIN (ALL-PURPOSE) FLOUR
1 HEAPED TEASPOON BAKING POWDER
FINELY GRATED RIND OF 1 ORANGE
250 ML (9 FL OZ/1 CUP) FRESHLY SQUEEZED ORANGE
   JUICE (JUICE OF ABOUT 4 ORANGES)
40 G (1^1/$_2$ OZ) PINE NUTS

Orange juice & olive oil cake with pine nuts

I like making this in two small moulds — they look good together and you can take one to a friend. I just love what's in it and I love it when my kids eat things like this. You could dress it up for afternoon tea with a creamy yoghurt on the side or just serve it for what it is: an honest simple sponge.

Preheat the oven to 180°C (350°F/Gas 4). Brush two 22 cm (8^1/$_2$ inch) springform tins with olive oil and dust with flour. Whip the egg whites in a large bowl until they are firm and snowy white (keep them in the fridge in hot weather, and don't leave them too long or they could collapse). Whip the yolks with the vanilla until they bulk up and become foamy. Whisk in the caster and brown sugars, then add the olive oil bit by bit, mixing well after each addition. Add the flour, baking powder, orange rind and juice and beat well until you have a smooth batter. Gently fold in the egg whites.

Scrape out half the batter into each tin and sprinkle each cake with pine nuts. Bake for about 35 minutes, or until the tops are golden and crusty and a skewer poked into the middle comes out clean. Leave to cool before serving. This will keep well in a tin for 4 or 5 days.

Makes two 22 cm (8^1/$_2$ inch) cakes

APPLES FOR SAM

2 WHOLE ORANGES OR BLOOD ORANGES
100 ML (3½ FL OZ) SWEETENED CONDENSED MILK
FINELY GRATED RIND AND JUICE OF
  1 SMALL ORANGE
300 G (10½ OZ) GREEK-STYLE NATURAL YOGHURT

Greek yoghurt with condensed milk & oranges

The base of this recipe was given to me — thank you, Ioanna. I added the oranges, but you might like to add another fruit. I sometimes use blood oranges, sometimes ordinary. Whatever sort you use, make sure they are sweet as sweet. You could actually serve this with any other fruit you like, keeping the orange juice and rind for mixing into the yoghurt, and then draping this over any other cut fruit — bananas, mangoes, plums would be beautiful…

Use a small sharp knife to cut away the skin of the oranges, leaving no pith. Slice the oranges into substantial wheels, maybe 5 mm (¼ inch) thick, and then halve those. Put the cut slices in a bowl to collect their juice. If you don't think they're very sweet, sprinkle a tablespoon or so of sugar over them.

Put the condensed milk, half of the orange rind and 4 tablespoons of the orange juice in a jug (you can drink the rest of the orange juice). Slowly mix this into the yoghurt, bit by bit. Cover and put in the fridge for a couple of hours until it has set to a very soft and creamy pudding. Serve a few orange slices with a dollop of the yoghurt, some juice dribbled over the top and a tiny hill of left-over rind, just for extra colour.

Serves 4

These are the rabbits that my sister, Ludi, and I tucked tightly into our pockets. We never left home without our rabbits.

PASTRY:
200 G (7 OZ) WHOLEMEAL (WHOLEWHEAT) FLOUR
70 G (2½ OZ) LIGHT BROWN SUGAR
100 G (3½ OZ) CHILLED BUTTER, CUT INTO CUBES
1 EGG, PLUS 1 EGG YOLK
A FEW DROPS OF VANILLA EXTRACT

500 G (1 LB 2 OZ/ABOUT 3) APPLES
40 G (1½ OZ) BUTTER
30 G (1 OZ) LIGHT BROWN SUGAR
1 TEASPOON GROUND CINNAMON
600 G (1 LB 5 OZ/ABOUT 10) APRICOTS, HALVED
    (OR QUARTERED, IF LARGE), STONES REMOVED
ABOUT 2 TABLESPOONS CASTER (SUPERFINE) SUGAR

Wholemeal apricot & apple pie

You can use absolutely any fruit you like here; fresh figs are good. I use apple purée for the base and then put apricot halves on top, but you can stick to all apples, strawberries or nectarines, and plums are beautiful. You can serve this with half-and-half Greek yoghurt and lightly sweetened whipped cream with a couple of drops of vanilla extract stirred through. This is dripping with health, I feel — I love to have things like this in my kitchen when the kids ask for a snack.

To make the pastry, put the flour, sugar and butter in a bowl. Work it all together with your fingers until you have a sandy mixture. Add the egg, extra egg yolk and vanilla and carry on mixing until you have a smooth ball. Wrap it up in plastic wrap, flatten and put it in the fridge for about 30 minutes.

Meanwhile, peel and core the apples and cut them into chunks. Put half the butter in a non-stick pan and add the apple chunks, the brown sugar and a tablespoon of water. Put the lid on and cook over medium heat for about 15-20 minutes until the apples collapse and turn slightly golden on the bottom. Stir in the cinnamon and squash the apples into a purée with a wooden spoon. Remove from the heat.

Preheat the oven to 200°C (400°F/Gas 6). Roll out the pastry on a sheet of baking paper to a circle of roughly 32-34 cm (12-13 inches), dusting with a little plain flour if necessary. Using the baking paper, flip the pastry over into an ungreased 24 cm (9½ inch) springform tin. Let it settle in before peeling off the paper and pressing the pastry onto the base and side of the tin. Don't worry if the pastry tears, just patch it and press the gaps together.

Spread the apple purée over the base and put the apricots on top. Scatter with caster sugar, more or less, depending on the sweetness of your fruit. Dot with the rest of the butter, then fold the pastry edge in and over to cover the edge of the filling. Bake for about 40 minutes, or until the top of the fruit is golden brown in places and the pastry crisp. Serve plain or with yoghurt and whipped cream.

Serves 6-8

1.2 KG (2 LB 12 OZ) LARGE MANDARINS
600 G (1 LB 5 OZ) CASTER (SUPERFINE) SUGAR

Mandarin jam

It is a bit of a job peeling the mandarins, but you can't leave the skins on to make this beautiful jam. It is quite a quantity to get through, but if you have three or four friends over this will move really quickly while everyone catches up on news. Working alone you may well end up in a trance from the monotonous concentration. Use brightly coloured, sweet, no-pip mandarins if possible. You can add a piece of cinnamon or some cardamom for a different touch but I love this jam just simply on the breakfast table next to chocolate loaf, white loaf and strawberry jam. It makes me feel as if I'm strolling through a citrus grove. This is also great for using as a crust on pork. Roast a pork loin, spread it with mustard, this jam and some breadcrumbs and bake for another half an hour until the crust is crisp.

First of all, sterilize your jars for when you have a panful of hot jam ready to bottle. It is always best to use several small jars, rather than one or two big ones. Wash the jars and lids in hot soapy water, or in the dishwasher, and rinse well in hot water. Then put the jars (and the lids) on a baking tray and leave in a 120°C (235°F/Gas 1/2) oven for at least 20 minutes, or until you are ready to use them. (Don't use a tea towel to dry them — they should dry thoroughly in the oven.)

Rinse the mandarins in warm water and then peel them. Keep the peel from half of them, taking off the black eye where the stem connected to the fruit.

Divide all the mandarins into segments, then remove the skin from each segment. A small pair of scissors or a sharp paring knife will be useful in cutting the pith line, then gently pulling this up will help loosen the skin. Sometimes they come away easily, sometimes not. Try to keep some segments whole if possible, but it is not a problem if they break up (many of them will). Put the segments in a colander set over another bowl to catch the juice.

Roughly tear up the peel you have saved and put it in a large heavy-based pan with the sugar, the collected mandarin juice and 500 ml (17 fl oz/2 cups) of water. Bring to the boil, then lower the heat and simmer uncovered for 20 minutes or so, or until the peel starts to look glazed. Purée until it is as smooth as you can get it.

Add the mandarin segments, keeping a small handful back, and any further juice that has accumulated. Bring back to the boil and simmer for another 30 minutes or so, taking care that the jam doesn't colour and caramelize. Stir often with a wooden spoon to make sure that nothing sticks to the bottom. Test that the jam is ready by dropping a heaped teaspoonful onto a plate. When you slightly tilt the plate, the jam should not run off, but cling and slowly glide down. If the jam isn't ready, put it back on the heat for a while.

Add the handful of mandarins about 5 minutes before the jam is ready, to add a splash of brighter colour and some texture. Spoon into the warm sterilized jars and close the lids tightly. Turn the jars upside down, cover with a tea towel and leave to completely cool (this creates a vacuum that can be seen on the lid). Turn upright and store in a cool dark place. The jam will keep for 10–12 months before it is opened. After opening, you need to keep it in the fridge.

Makes 580 ml (20 fl oz/2⅓ cups)

100 G (3½ OZ) SUGAR
A FEW DROPS OF VANILLA EXTRACT
1 KG (2 LB 4 OZ/ABOUT 15) RIPE APRICOTS, HALVED, STONES REMOVED

Apricot sauce

I serve this over Greek yoghurt and it would be ideal on pancakes or ice cream. I also like it chilled as a summer drink, topped up with ice-cold sparkling water (two thirds sauce, one third water) in tall glasses. I don't like my sauces overly sweet, but you can add more sugar if your apricots seem a little sour, and if you prefer the sauce a little thicker, then simmer for a few moments more with the lid off. This makes quite a bit, so, when you have an abundance of apricots, make this and freeze some for an emergency future sauce.

Put the sugar and vanilla in a large saucepan with 375 ml (13 fl oz/1½ cups) of water. Bring to the boil, stirring until the sugar dissolves. Simmer for a few minutes and then add the apricots. Cover the pan and simmer over low heat for about 10 minutes until the apricots start to lose their shape. Purée until totally smooth and then chill, depending on how you're serving it. Serve over vanilla ice cream, or with pancakes or crumpets.

Makes about 750 ml (26 fl oz/3 cups)

ORANGE

2 LARGE RIPE MANGOES (ABOUT 1.2 KG/2 LB 12 OZ)
110 G (3¾ OZ /½ CUP) CASTER (SUPERFINE) SUGAR
FINELY GRATED RIND OF 1 LIME
JUICE OF 2 LIMES

Mango sorbet

This is pure frozen mango — wonderful, thick, plain and simple, yet a splash of colour. It looks fantastic served with a scoop of pomegranate or strawberry sorbet. Seek out the best-quality fruit — your sorbet will only ever be as good as the mangoes you start off with. You can also serve this unfrozen as a mango purée to pour over ice cream or yoghurt.

Peel the mangoes and cut as much flesh as possible from the stone. Cut the flesh into small chunks and put it in a bowl with the sugar, lime rind and lime juice. Stir, cover and leave overnight in the fridge to draw out the juice. Purée until smooth and, if necessary, pass through a sieve to extract the very pulpy and stringy bits. Taste for sweetness and add extra caster sugar, a teaspoon at a time, if you think it needs it. (This will depend on the variety and ripeness of your mangoes.) Top up the purée with water to give 500 ml (17 fl oz/2 cups).

Pour the purée into a bowl or container that has a lid. Put the lid on and put it in the freezer. After an hour give the mixture an energetic whisk with a hand whisk or electric mixer. Put it back in the freezer and then whisk again after another couple of hours. When the sorbet is nearly firm, give one last whisk and put it back in the freezer to set.

Alternatively, pour into your ice cream machine and churn, following the manufacturer's instructions.

Serves 4–6

We always saved our mango stones. We tore off every scrap with our teeth and then washed and scrubbed them carefully, running our nails first in one direction and then the other until they were clean of all mango. After they were towel-dried, we kept our mango pets and brushed their lovely hair with our old toothbrushes. They still needed a bath and looking after now and then.

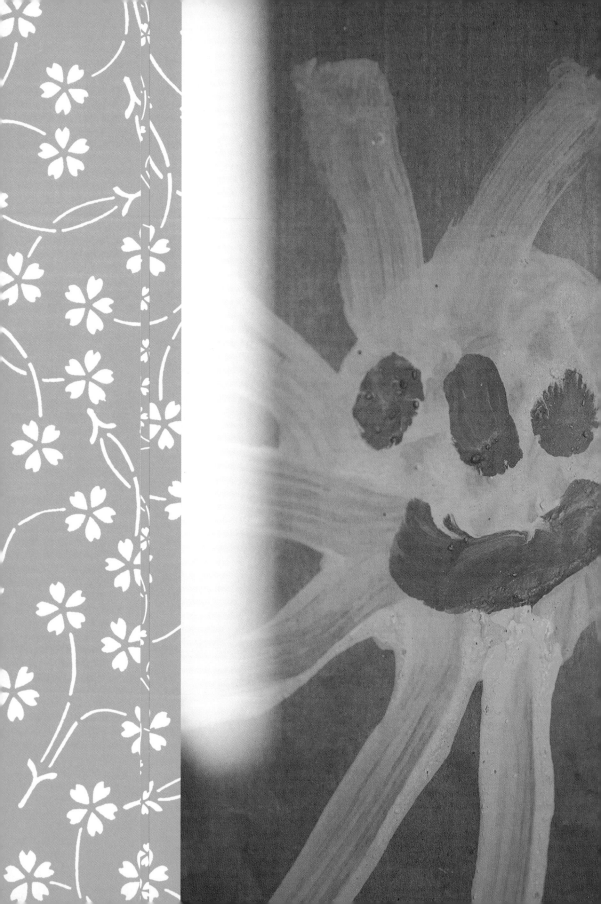

yellow

Lemonade & fizzy orange
Risotto with fried egg
Spaghettini with egg & toasted parsley
  breadcrumbs
Barbecued fish skewers
Barbecued mixed grill with corn
Chicken sautéed with cheese & milk
Ham & cheese omelette
Eggs with bread & butter
Sautéed potatoes with egg
Fun dough
Custard
Fried custard squares
Lemon sandwiches with raspberries & cream
Lemon curd ice cream
Lemon meringue ice cream cake

- memory -

There is children's laughter escaping out through the iron gates and past the oleander and daffodils, sprinkling onto the just-cut lawns that line the road and fluttering up to me through my open window, falling over my shoulders like fairy glitter. And that atmosphere of sleeping head to tail in trains and on holiday, and knocking on walls to see if others are awake.

70 G (2½ OZ) CASTER (SUPERFINE) SUGAR
ONE LONG STRIP OF LEMON RIND, PITH REMOVED
JUICE OF 2½ LEMONS (ABOUT 125 ML/4 FL OZ/½ CUP)
500 ML (17 FL OZ/2 CUPS) ICE-COLD SPARKLING WATER

Lemonade

This is a lovely basic to which you can add more or less sugar or lemons and double, halve or triple quantities as you like. If you and your children prefer, you can use still, not fizzy, water. On a hot summer day this always has been, and always will be, amazing. I like to put the sparkling water in the freezer so that it is really cold, make up the syrup (and leave it to cool) and then pour in the ice-cold water just before serving so that the bubbles don't disappear. I think you could probably make a lovely limeade in this way, too, and soon I might try it with pink grapefruits for a brunch.

Put the sugar, lemon rind and 3 tablespoons of tap water in a small pan. Bring to the boil, stirring so that the sugar dissolves completely, then boil for a few minutes so that the lemon rind flavours the syrup. Add the lemon juice (I like to leave in some fleshy bits that might get through, but no pips) and let that bubble up for a minute or two. Pour into a large jug and cover with a cloth or lid as you'll probably be making this in summer and there might be flies. Leave to cool completely. When you're ready to serve, pour in the sparkling water and mix well. Ladle out into glasses and add ice if you like.

Makes 625 ml (21½ fl oz/2½ cups)

We are all born to play a role, from our early days... remember the lemonade maker, the one who set up the stall on the side of the road, the passer-by?

60 G (2¼ OZ) CASTER (SUPERFINE) SUGAR
ONE LONG STRIP OF ORANGE RIND, PITH REMOVED
JUICE OF 4 ORANGES (ABOUT 330 ML/11¼ FL OZ/
   1⅓ CUPS)
500 ML (17 FL OZ/2 CUPS) ICE-COLD SPARKLING
   WATER

Fizzy orange

If lemons aren't readily available, or lemonade is slightly tart for your children, you can make up a jug of fizzy orange which, I find, always goes down well. If you like, you can strain the drink at the end. I prefer it with some bits in, personally — and so does one of my daughters, but the other will only drink it if I strain it. For adults, who might want a bit of extra pizzazz, you could make a jugful with added spices such as a vanilla bean or a small stick of cinnamon.

Put the sugar, orange rind and 3 tablespoons of tap water into a small pan. Bring to the boil, stirring so that the sugar dissolves completely, then boil for a few minutes so that the orange rind flavours the syrup. Add the orange juice (I like to leave in some fleshy bits that might get through, but no pips) and let that bubble for about 5 minutes, or until it looks slightly denser. Pour into a jug and cover with a cloth or lid to keep the flies out. Leave to cool completely.

    When you're ready to serve, pour in the sparkling water and mix well. Ladle out into glasses and add ice if you like.

Makes 830 ml (29 fl oz/3⅓ cups)

YELLOW

40 G (1 1/2 OZ) BUTTER
3 TABLESPOONS OLIVE OIL
2 FRENCH SHALLOTS, CHOPPED
320 G (11 1/4 OZ) RISOTTO RICE
125 ML (4 FL OZ/1/2 CUP) WHITE WINE
1 LITRE (35 FL OZ/4 CUPS) HOT VEGETABLE BROTH
FRESHLY GRATED NUTMEG
40 G (1 1/2 OZ) GRATED PARMESAN OR GRANA
    CHEESE
ABOUT 8 FRESH SAGE LEAVES
4 EGGS, AT ROOM TEMPERATURE
GRATED PARMESAN CHEESE, TO SERVE

Risotto with fried egg

These are all the things my family loves — white risotto, egg, parmesan — on one plate. The egg yolk must be soft when you serve it so that it can drip into the rice, and we like the white to be golden and frayed around the edge.

Heat half the butter and 2 tablespoons of oil in a heavy-based pan suitable for making risotto. Sauté the shallots over low heat until light gold and then stir in the rice with a wooden spoon. Stir for a few minutes to completely coat the rice and let it cook just a bit. Add the wine and when that has evaporated, add all of the broth. Add a few good grinds of nutmeg and taste for salt (your broth will probably be seasoned enough). Simmer uncovered over high heat for about 15 minutes, or until the rice has absorbed much of the liquid. If it seems as if it needs a bit more liquid, add some hot water. Remove from the heat and stir in the remaining butter and the parmesan. Taste for salt, adjusting if necessary. Leave with the lid on so that the steam continues to cook the rice.

Heat the remaining oil in a large non-stick frying pan and briefly fry the sage leaves until crisp. Remove with tongs. Gently break the eggs into the pan and sprinkle a little salt on the yolks. Cook until the edges of the white are a bit golden. Cover the pan with a lid and fry until the yolks are just slightly opaque on the surface but still soft inside (they are best when the undersides are golden and a bit crisp).

Scoop the rice onto serving plates and top each serving with an egg and a couple of sage leaves, being careful not to break the yolk just yet. Serve with a sprinkling of parmesan and a few grinds of black pepper for those who want it.

Serves 4

4 EGGS, AT ROOM TEMPERATURE
4 TABLESPOONS OLIVE OIL
300 G (10½ OZ) SPAGHETTINI
60 G (2¼ OZ) SOFT WHITE BREAD, BROKEN UP INTO
    COARSE CRUMBS
2 ANCHOVY FILLETS, FINELY CHOPPED
1 GARLIC CLOVE, FINELY CHOPPED
1 HEAPED TABLESPOON CHOPPED PARSLEY
FINELY GRATED ZEST OF ½ LEMON
OLIVE OIL, TO SERVE
GRATED PARMESAN CHEESE, TO SERVE

Spaghettini with egg & toasted parsley breadcrumbs

This is nice and simple. The anchovies and garlic can be left out, and you could also add baby capers or maybe some chopped olives. This could nicely precede a simple sautéed chicken breast or fish fillet.

Bring a large pot of salted water to the boil. Add the eggs and boil for 4 minutes. Fish out the eggs with a slotted spoon, run under cold water and peel off the shells. Put the eggs in a large serving bowl and mash up into small bits with a fork. Add a couple of tablespoons of olive oil and a little salt.

Add the spaghettini to the boiling water and cook, following the packet instructions. Meanwhile, heat 2 tablespoons of oil in a non-stick frying pan, add the breadcrumbs, anchovies and garlic and sauté over medium heat until the breadcrumbs are golden and crisp. Remove from the heat and stir in the parsley and lemon zest.

Drain the spaghettini, keeping some of the cooking water. Add the pasta to the egg with a few spoonfuls of the cooking water. Toss through very well and serve immediately. Drizzle each serving with some olive oil and scatter parsley bread-crumbs over the top. Pass around the parmesan, and some black pepper for those who like it.

Serves 4

APPLES FOR SAM

ABOUT 480 G (1 LB 1 OZ) SWORDFISH, ABOUT 2 CM
   (3/4 INCH) THICK
ABOUT 400 G (14 OZ) TUNA, ABOUT 2 CM
   (3/4 INCH) THICK
400 G (14 OZ) RAW PRAWNS (SHRIMP)
600 G (1 LB 5 OZ) SMALL CALAMARI
2 HEAPED TABLESPOONS CHOPPED PARSLEY
1 LARGE GARLIC CLOVE, FINELY CHOPPED
ABOUT 50 G (1 3/4 OZ/1/2 CUP) DRY BREADCRUMBS
OLIVE OIL, FOR THE BARBECUE

DRESSING:
125 ML (4 FL OZ/1/2 CUP) OLIVE OIL
2 GARLIC CLOVES, PEELED AND SQUASHED A BIT
JUICE OF 1 LARGE JUICY LEMON

Barbecued fish skewers

Your fish has got to be super-fresh with that almost-sweet smell. Tuna should be lovely and bright red; swordfish white. You can choose another type of fish here, as long as you can cut it easily into squares and thread it onto skewers. These are passed through a breadcrumb, parsley and garlic mix and then grilled so they turn golden dark and crispy in places. It is important that they are still soft and moist inside but cooked through. You could add some chopped herbs, or even finely chopped red chilli to the dressing.

Cut the swordfish and tuna into 2 cm (3/4 inch) blocks. Peel and devein the prawns, leaving the tails on. Clean the calamari and cut the bodies into thick rings (you won't need the wings or tentacles here, so save them for something else).

Using short metal skewers, or bamboo ones that have been soaked in cold water for an hour, thread a block of swordfish, a block of tuna, a calamari ring, then a prawn (spiking this through in two places), then another block of swordfish and finally tuna. You should have enough to make about 12 skewers, and you might need to juggle the order around a bit at the end depending on how much of each fish you have left.

Heat the barbecue to high. Mix the parsley, garlic, breadcrumbs and a little salt together on a large plate. Pat the skewers on all sides in this mixture so that they're lightly coated.

For the dressing, mix together the oil, garlic and lemon juice, and add some salt and black pepper.

Brush the barbecue rack with oil and barbecue the skewers until they are charred deep golden in some parts, but not for so long that they dry out. Reduce the heat or move the rack further from the coals if the crust starts to burn before the fish cooks through. Serve hot, with some dressing drizzled over and a sprinkling of salt.

Makes about 12 skewers

APPLES FOR SAM

125 G (4½ OZ) BUTTER, SOFTENED
1½ TABLESPOONS FINELY CHOPPED HERBS, (THYME, BASIL,
    PARSLEY, MINT)
6 POTATOES, SCRUBBED BUT NOT PEELED
6 SMALL RED ONIONS, PEELED
JUICE OF 1½ LEMONS
4 TABLESPOONS OLIVE OIL
1 TEASPOON DRIED OREGANO, CRUSHED BETWEEN YOUR FINGERS
1 X 350 G (12 OZ) VEAL FILLET
ABOUT 14 YOUNG LAMB CUTLETS, TRIMMED OF EXCESS FAT
6 CORN COBS, HUSKS REMOVED, HALVED IF LARGE
350 G (12 OZ) SOUR CREAM OR GREEK-STYLE NATURAL YOGHURT
BUTTER, TO SERVE

Barbecued
mixed grill with corn

I am crazy about mixed grills — they are something my mother always made for us and remind me of restaurants in Greece where you can just order lamb chops by the kilo and they come out barbecue-grilled with oregano and a squeeze of lemon. Here I make them with a whole fillet of veal, and potatoes and onions roasted amongst the coals. We love a dollop of sour cream or Greek yoghurt and an extra drizzle of olive oil over our potatoes. You might like a tomato salad and bread to finish off this display.

Beat the butter and herbs together. Put on a sheet of foil in a fat little sausage shape, roll up tightly and put in the fridge to firm up.

Preheat the barbecue or chargrill. Rinse the potatoes and prick the skins here and there. While they are still wet, lay each potato on a square of foil. Sprinkle quite generously all over with salt, then wrap up the foil parcels tightly. Do the same with the onions. Put the parcels directly into the coals, if that's the style of your barbecue, or over the flame on a rack. Cook for 10 minutes, turning a couple of times with tongs, before you add the meat.

Meanwhile, mix the lemon juice with the oil and add the oregano. Add a few grinds of black pepper and ½ teaspoon or so of salt. Put the whole veal fillet onto the barbecue rack and cook until the underside is deep golden. Turn, brushing the cooked side with the lemon dressing. Add the cutlets and corn to the rack and, when the undersides are golden, turn them over and brush the cutlets with the dressing. Keep turning the potatoes and onions, too. Turn the meat and corn again, brushing the meat with dressing. When the meat is golden and a bit crispy in places, put it on a serving platter and drizzle the remaining dressing over the top. The whole fillet should ideally be cooked through but still pink inside. Leave them to rest for a minute or so and then cut the fillet into fairly thick slices.

Check that the potatoes and onions are soft, then unwrap and add to the platter. Cut a deep slash in the potatoes, pinch their bottoms to fluff them up and then mash the tops a bit with a fork. Top with sour cream or yoghurt. Slice the herb butter and serve alongside some plain butter for people to have with their corn.

Serves 6

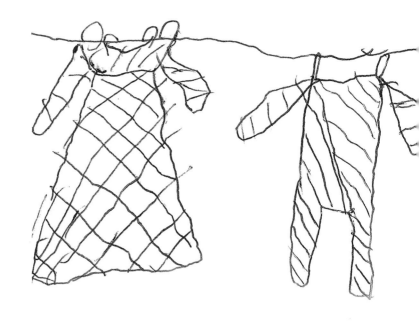
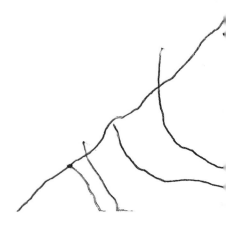

2 SMALL CHICKEN BREASTS
ABOUT 3 TABLESPOONS PLAIN (ALL-PURPOSE) FLOUR,
    FOR DUSTING
2 TABLESPOONS OLIVE OIL
4 LARGE THIN SLICES FONTINA CHEESE
125 ML (4 FL OZ/½ CUP) MILK

Chicken sautéed with cheese & milk

I find there is something really encouraging about serving this to my kids. It is warm and homely and the kind of thing I like to call them downstairs to after their bath... to have it sitting on that ready table, a small vase of flowers, some pan-fried chips with herbs (page 245) and maybe even a small pan of sautéed broccoli.

Slice each chicken breast horizontally to give two thin escalopes. Cover them with a sheet of plastic wrap and pound with a meat mallet until they are of an even thickness and a bit thinner. Dust in flour.

Heat the oil in a large frying pan. Add the four chicken escalopes and cook over medium heat until the underneaths are nicely browned. Turn over and season the cooked sides with salt. Cook until golden underneath and then turn them again and season. Put a slice of cheese over each escalope so that it covers the chicken completely. Add the milk to the pan, put the lid on and cook until the cheese has melted and there is a bubbly, thickened sauce. Check that the chicken is soft and cooked through but be careful not to overcook it. Remove from the heat and leave the lid on the pan until the very last second before serving so that the cheese carries on melting. Serve hot.

Serves 4

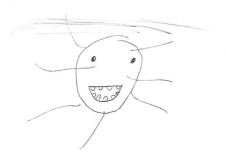

APPLES FOR SAM

1 EGG
1 TEASPOON BUTTER
1 THIN SLICE HAM, CHOPPED
1 TABLESPOON GRATED PARMESAN CHEESE

Ham & cheese omelette

We like this with a handful of pan-fried chips and saut ed zucchini (courgette). The quantities can be doubled and made in a larger pan.

Whip the egg with a touch of salt. Melt the butter in a 14 cm (6 inch) non-stick frying pan over medium heat until it is fizzling. Pour in the egg and swirl it around the pan to cover the bottom evenly. Lower the heat a little and fry the egg, making some holes when it starts to set to allow the uncooked egg to run through. Shake the pan to dislodge the omelette, then scatter the ham and cheese over the top. Roll it up gently, slide it out onto a plate and serve immediately.

Serves 1

----

1 VERY FRESH LARGE EGG, AT ROOM TEMPERATURE
1—2 TEASPOONS SOFT BUTTER
1 SLICE FRESH SOFT WHITE OR BROWN BREAD

Eggs with bread & butter

This is what my mum gave us so often   it is one of my earliest food memories. I have only to smell it and it takes me sailing back in time and fills me with wonderful memories. It is amazing how an egg and slice of bread can do that.

Put the egg in a pan of cold water and bring to the boil. Cook for 2½ minutes from when the water comes to the boil (the white should have just set and the yolk will still be soft and runny). Lift out with a slotted spoon. Meanwhile, butter the bread, break it into small bits and put in a little bowl. Hold the egg over the bowl, give it a sharp crack through the middle with a knife and scoop out the egg with a teaspoon. Add a little salt and mash together well with a fork. Serve immediately.

Serves 1

500 G (1 LB 2 OZ) POTATOES, PEELED AND CUT INTO
   CHUNKS
2 TABLESPOONS OLIVE OIL
20 G (³/4 OZ) BUTTER
2 GARLIC CLOVES, PEELED BUT LEFT WHOLE
3 SAGE SPRIGS
2 EGGS

Sautéed potatoes with egg

If you want just potatoes on their own, you can double this amount and add an extra spoonful of oil, but if you'll be adding the eggs to the pan you'll need this smallish amount of potatoes with a fairly large non-stick frying-pan. The one I use is about 30 cm (12 inches). I love making just this amount and taking the pan straight to the table to my two waiting children. You could also easily serve a chicken escalope on the side, or maybe another vegetable like sautéed broccoli or creamed spinach.

Boil the potato chunks in boiling salted water until they are cooked through but not breaking up.

Put the olive oil, butter, garlic and sage in a large non-stick frying pan and heat until the butter melts. Add the potatoes with a slotted spoon straight from their boiling pot, letting all the water drip off first. Sauté over fairly high heat at first, then, once they start to look golden, lower the heat slightly and leave them on the stovetop to get crusty, tossing them carefully from time to time. Take care not to mush them up, although just a bit is fine if it gives extra crusty bits. If the garlic looks like it may burn, sit it on top of the potatoes. Try to get the sage to the bottom of the pan so it crisps up nicely. Taste to see if there is enough salt.

When the potatoes are golden all over and crisp in parts, shuffle them to the side to make two big spaces for the eggs; like a pair of sunglasses in the pan. Break an egg into each space, sprinkle with a little salt and put the lid on. Cook over medium–low heat until the whites are just set. Serve at once, trying not to break the egg yolks because it's nice to mix them with the potatoes on your plate.

Serves 2

YELLOW

125 G (4½ OZ/1 CUP) PLAIN (ALL-PURPOSE) FLOUR
300 G (10½ OZ/1 CUP) FINE SALT
2 SACHETS SAFFRON OR A FEW DROPS OF FOOD
   COLOURING, IF YOU LIKE

Fun dough

Sometimes, when you have a lot of cooking to get through and you don't
need small helping hands, this can be fun. So, this is not to eat — but just
an easy pastry dough for children to work with while you get on with
things. If they want, you can bake the shapes or leave them to dry out
over the heaters in colder months. Make sure you put a good plastic
covering on the table so they can roll out the dough without giving you a
cleaning-up nightmare. This keeps for a day in a plastic bag in the fridge.

Put the flour and salt in a bowl and mix it through with your hands. If you're
using saffron or food colour, add it now and work in about 4 tablespoons of water
bit by bit. You may need a bit more or a bit less, so add it slowly until you get a soft
dough. Knead it well for a minute or two until smooth. Let the children make
shapes, either their own or using pastry cutters. If they want to bake them, put
them on a baking tray and bake at 70°C (150°F/Gas ¼) for about 30–40 minutes,
depending on the thickness, to dry them out.

---

310 ML (10¾ FL OZ/1¼ CUPS) MILK
310 ML (10¾ FL OZ/1¼ CUPS) POURING (SINGLE)
   CREAM
1½ TEASPOONS VANILLA EXTRACT
6 EGG YOLKS
55 G (2 OZ) CASTER (SUPERFINE) SUGAR
1 TABLESPOON CORNFLOUR (CORNSTARCH)

Custard

I like custard this way — a little thick — eaten on its own straight from
the fridge, or at room temperature with crumble or baked fruit. This is a
good way to use up the egg yolks after you've made pavlovas and is best
eaten on the day you make it. Use top-quality vanilla extract.

Put the milk and cream in a heavy-based saucepan and heat gently to just below
boiling point. Remove from the heat and stir in the vanilla extract.

Beat the egg yolks, sugar and cornflour in a heatproof bowl for a few minutes, until the sugar has dissolved and the mixture is pale and thick. Gradually add the warm milk, mixing constantly. When everything is mixed together, pour it back into the pan over low heat. Cook, stirring or whisking almost continuously, for about 4 minutes until the custard has thickened. Don't let it get too hot or it will scramble, so take the pan off the heat once or twice if necessary. Pour into a serving jug and either serve straightaway, or cover the surface with plastic wrap (this stops a skin forming) and put it in the fridge to chill.

Makes 750 ml (26 fl oz/3 cups)

750 ML (26 FL OZ/3 CUPS) MILK
1 LONG STRIP OF LEMON RIND
1 TEASPOON VANILLA EXTRACT
3 EGGS
60 G (2¼ OZ) SUGAR
150 G (5½ OZ) PLAIN (ALL-PUPOSE) FLOUR, SIFTED
PLAIN (ALL-PURPOSE) FLOUR, EXTRA, TO COAT
ABOUT 80 G (2¾ OZ) BUTTER
CASTER (SUPERFINE) SUGAR, TO SERVE

Fried custard squares

This is the sort of thing that would have appealed to my sweet tooth in childhood. It's what some Italians remember from theirs.

Put the milk in a heavy-based saucepan and add the lemon rind and vanilla. Bring just to the boil. Meanwhile, whip 2 eggs in a bowl until they are creamy, then whisk in the sugar. Add the flour and whisk to a smooth cream. Just as the milk comes to a rolling boil, whisk a ladleful into the eggs. Whisking constantly, add another ladleful or two of milk. Spoon it all back into the milk pan and put over the lowest heat, whisking all the time. It will thicken quickly so you may have to remove the pan for a minute and whisk vigorously until it's smooth. Put back on the heat for a few minutes to cook the flour, whisking until it's completely smooth and very thick.

Lightly grease a 17 x 27 cm (6½ x 11 inch) sandwich tin. Spoon the custard into the tin, smoothing the surface with a spatula. Let it cool and set completely, then turn out and cut into 5 cm (2 inches) squares. Break the last egg into a small flat bowl and scatter some flour on a plate. Melt 2-3 tablespoons of butter in a non-stick frying pan over medium-low heat. Working in batches, dip squares of custard first in the egg and then in the flour to coat lightly. Fry in the butter until golden on both sides, turning them gently. Add blobs of butter along the way to prevent burning. Lift the squares out onto kitchen paper to drain and then serve warm, sprinkled with some caster sugar.

Makes 15

250 G (9 OZ) BUTTER, SOFTENED
280 G (10 OZ/1¼ CUPS) CASTER (SUPERFINE) SUGAR
3 EGGS
310 G (11 OZ/2½ CUPS) PLAIN (ALL-PURPOSE) FLOUR
1½ TEASPOONS BAKING POWDER
FINELY GRATED ZEST AND JUICE OF 1 LEMON
185 ML (6 FL OZ/¾ CUP) POURING (SINGLE) CREAM
1 TEASPOON VANILLA EXTRACT

FILLING:
100 ML (3½ FL OZ) WHIPPING CREAM
2 TEASPOONS ICING (CONFECTIONERS') SUGAR
100 G (3½ OZ) GREEK-STYLE NATURAL YOGHURT
100 G (3½ OZ) RASPBERRIES, HALVED
ICING (CONFECTIONERS') SUGAR, FOR DUSTING

Lemon sandwiches with raspberries & cream

This basic lemon cake is very good on its own, fresh from the oven. But for something special, or to use the leftover cake, you can make these little sandwiches and serve them with coffee, or at an afternoon party. I use fresh raspberries and cream in these ones but you could use raspberry or strawberry jam and cream. The sandwiches are easier to cut when the cake is a day old.

Preheat the oven to 170°C (325°F/Gas 3) and butter and flour a 30 x 11 cm (12 x 4 inch) loaf tin.

Cream together the butter and sugar until light and fluffy. Beat in the eggs one by one. Sift in the flour and baking powder, then add the lemon rind, lemon juice, cream and vanilla. Whisk well to get a smooth batter.

Spoon into the loaf tin and bake for about 1 hour 10 minutes, or until a skewer poked into the centre comes out clean. If the top looks like it's getting too brown before the cooking time is up, cover it with foil. Remove and leave to cool completely in the tin.

For the filling, whip the cream and icing sugar together until the cream holds peaks, then fold the yoghurt through. Cut the cake like a loaf of bread into slices about 5 mm (about ¼ inch) thick. Spread half the slices with cream, and then top with the raspberries and the rest of the cake slices to make sandwiches. Dust with icing sugar to serve.

Makes about 20 sandwiches

4 EGG YOLKS
180 G (6½ OZ) CASTER (SUPERFINE) SUGAR
40 G (1½ OZ) BUTTER, CUT INTO BITS
FINELY GRATED ZEST OF 1 LEMON
JUICE OF 2 LEMONS
250 ML (9 FL OZ/1 CUP) MILK
375 ML (13 FL OZ/1½ CUPS) POURING (SINGLE) CREAM

Lemon curd
ice cream

This is for the lemon meringue cake, opposite, (because it gives you something perfect to make with your egg whites) but you can also just make this on its own and serve it with a bowl of cherries or raspberries. If you won't be making the meringue layers, then freeze your egg whites until you need them to make pavlova.

Bring a pan half-full of water to the boil and then lower the heat to the absolute minimum. Put the egg yolks and sugar in a wide glass or stainless steel bowl and whisk until they are thick and creamy. Sit the bowl on top of the pan of water, add the butter and let it melt. Whisk until it starts to get thicker and creamier, then add the lemon zest and juice and carry on whisking until it thickens. It doesn't have to be cooked out like a proper lemon curd, but just until it has thickened and the egg is cooked through from the warmth of the simmering water.

Meanwhile, warm up the milk a little. Whisk it into the lemony eggs and then remove the bowl from the heat. Whisk from time to time until it's cool before you whisk in the cream. Put the bowl in the fridge until it's completely cool and then, if your bowl doesn't have a lid, pour the mixture into one that does.

Cover the bowl and put in the freezer. After an hour give the mixture an energetic whisk with a hand whisk or electric mixer. Put it back in the freezer and whisk again after another couple of hours. When the ice cream is nearly firm, give one last whisk and put it back in the freezer to set.

Alternatively, pour the mixture into your ice cream machine and churn, following the manufacturer's instructions.

Makes 1.75 litres (61 fl oz/7 cups)

1 QUANTITY LEMON CURD ICE CREAM (OPPOSITE)

MERINGUE:
4 EGG WHITES
200 G (7 OZ) CASTER (SUPERFINE) SUGAR
1 TABLESPOON DESICCATED COCONUT
A FEW DROPS OF VANILLA EXTRACT
1 TEASPOON WHITE WINE VINEGAR

Lemon meringue ice cream cake

I like to throw some petals over the top of this, or some whole cherries or raspberries. It is really very lovely on a summer or spring day. When you come to putting the cake together, take out your ice cream beforehand so that it is manageable and you don't break up the meringue when you're trying to spread it. However, too soft and it may drip down the sides — you'll have to decide, according to the season.

Preheat the oven to 120°C (235°F/Gas ½). Get two sheets of baking paper and, on each one, draw around the base of a 24 cm (9½ inch) springform tin. Put each sheet of paper on a baking tray (with the drawn side down so that it doesn't mark the meringue).

For the meringue, put the egg whites into a comfortable wide bowl and whisk until they are firm and glossy. Add a third of the sugar and carry on whisking until they are even stiffer, then add another third of the sugar. Whisk again until the meringue is almost climbing up the beaters. Add the last of the sugar and the coconut, vanilla and vinegar, whisking them in quickly and well.

Mentally divide the meringue into two and spread half over each circle, flicking your wrists and using a spatula to smooth it out. Make a very slight indentation in the top of each.

Put both in the oven for 45 minutes, then swap them around and bake for another 45 minutes, or until they are firm and pale beige. Turn off the oven and leave them inside for 10 minutes with the door slightly ajar before removing them to cool completely. If you will not be putting the cake together immediately, wrap up the meringues in plastic wrap.

To assemble, take the ice cream out of the freezer 5 or 10 minutes in advance so that it softens a little and you can spread it more easily. Put a layer of meringue onto a lovely and freezer-friendly serving plate. Spoon the ice cream on top and spread it gently to cover the meringue, leaving just the edges showing. Top with the next layer of meringue. Cover with plastic wrap and put back into the freezer until you are ready to serve it.

Let the cake soften for 5 or 10 minutes before cutting it, using a clean swipe instead of sawing so that you don't destroy the meringue. It might crack a bit but that's fine, as long as it stays intact.

Serves 10-12

pink

Beetroot gnocchi
Baked ham & cheese bread pudding
Penne with prawns, cream & tomato
Prawn & spinach brown rice risotto
Poached fruit in vanilla syrup
Greek yoghurt with honey, cinnamon,
  pecans & pomegranate
Pomegranate sorbet
Pear & berry crumble
Fruit butters
Tiny cakes with pink icing

- memory -

We had huge sacks of marbles. The most important people had the most important and biggest sacks, others just carried theirs in an old sock or jam jar. At the end of break everyone would scurry along to stuff their bags into their lockers. The thought of them is what kept us going through the fraying edges of school. It looped it all together. This and those writing papers. I would lie in bed at night concentrating hard on the zillions of floral papers that other girls had and that we would swap at school. I would fall asleep watching papers in my mind. I dreamed of two in particular that I loved.

We all had our loops of elastic ready as we hopscotched our way two-by-two into the playground, past other pairs playing macrame with bright wools. The same partner that you sat with, and hung out with. It was not okay to not be a couple. We made cups and saucers with the wool and never ever got bored of swapping bits and pieces. But my mother's swaps collection still impressed me most of all. Writing paper and stickers kept my heart beating — I dreamed of having them. Oh, the careful trading that went on.

C A 22 5 A

40 G (1 ½ OZ) BUTTER
200 G (7 OZ) TINNED TOMATOES WITH JUICE, PUREED
250 G (9 OZ) PENNE
2 TEASPOONS OLIVE OIL
500 G (1 LB 2 OZ) RAW PRAWNS (SHRIMP), PEELED
   AND DEVEINED
2 GARLIC CLOVES, PEELED AND SQUASHED A BIT
2 TABLESPOONS CALVADOS
2½ TABLESPOONS SINGLE (POURING) CREAM
1 TABLESPOON CHOPPED PARSLEY

Penne with prawns, cream & tomato

This is simple and not too rich. I use calvados just because I like the way it turned out once when I didn't have brandy. The prawns here are not too many — so you can pick them out at the end and serve more to some, less to others. And there is just a little cream, to sweeten things up even more...

Melt half of the butter in a smallish pan and, when it is sizzling, add the tomatoes. Season with salt and a dash of pepper and then cook over medium heat for about 10 minutes, until it is thick.

Cook the pasta in a large pan of boiling salted water, following the packet instructions. Meanwhile, heat a large non-stick frying pan over high heat. Add the oil and the rest of the butter and, when it is sizzling, add the prawns and garlic. Over the highest heat possible, cook the prawns until they are quite bright and the undersides are golden and crusty in places. It is important that the heat is high and that you have a non-stick pan, so that the prawns fry quickly rather than boil in their own liquid. Turn them with tongs and, when they are cooked, scatter them with salt. Add the calvados and cook until it evaporates.

Drain the pasta, keeping a cupful of the cooking water. Add the tomato sauce to the prawns, along with the cream and parsley. Heat until just bubbling. Add the pasta and toss well. If it seems like you need it, add a little of the cooking water to help the sauce coat the pasta. Serve immediately with a grinding of pepper.

Serves 3

8 RAW PRAWNS (SHRIMP)
4 TABLESPOONS OLIVE OIL
2 GARLIC CLOVES, FINELY CHOPPED
250 ML (9 FL OZ/1 CUP) TOMATO PASSATA
    (PUREED TOMATOES)
4 PARSLEY STALKS, PLUS 1 TABLESPOON CHOPPED
    PARSLEY
2 SLICES LEMON
20 G (3/4 OZ) BUTTER
2 FRENCH SHALLOTS, FINELY CHOPPED
300 G (10½ OZ/1½ CUPS) BROWN RICE
100 G (3½ OZ) ENGLISH SPINACH LEAVES, CHOPPED
30 G (1 OZ) BUTTER, EXTRA

Prawn & spinach brown rice risotto

This is a very adaptable recipe with ingredients that can be easily swapped for others if you prefer. You can also make it with white rice: just add your broth as instructed and follow the same method, but the cooking time will be much shorter (about 20 minutes).

Peel and devein the prawns (keeping the shells), leaving the tails on four of them, if you like. Butterfly these four and chop up the rest. Put the butterflied prawns in one side of a bowl, the chopped prawns in the other side, then cover the bowl and keep it in the fridge.

Put the prawn shells and half the oil into a pan and cook on high for about a minute, stirring a few times, until the shells turn pink. Add the garlic and, when you can smell it, add the passata. Sauté for a few more minutes. Add 1.25 litres (44 fl oz/5 cups) of hot water, the parsley stalks and lemon slices. Season with salt and pepper and bring to the boil. Simmer for about 20 minutes, then strain into a clean pan and keep warm over very low heat.

Heat the butter and the remaining oil in a heavy-based pan suitable for making risotto. Add the shallots and sauté for a few minutes over medium heat until lightly golden and softened, then add the rice. Stir and turn it for a few minutes so that it is well coated. Add a ladleful of the broth and stir with a wooden spoon until the liquid has been absorbed. Reduce the heat to low, add another ladleful of broth and stir until it has been absorbed. Carry on like this for about 40 minutes, then add the chopped prawns, chopped parsley and spinach. Continue cooking in the same way for another 10 minutes or so, until the rice is tender but still a little bit firm in the centre. If you run out of broth before this time, just carry on with hot water. Add the extra butter, sit the whole prawns on top of the rice and cook for a few minutes more until the prawns are pink. Sprinkle a little salt over the prawns, put a cloth over the rice, remove from the heat and leave to stand for 10 minutes before serving.

Serves 3–4

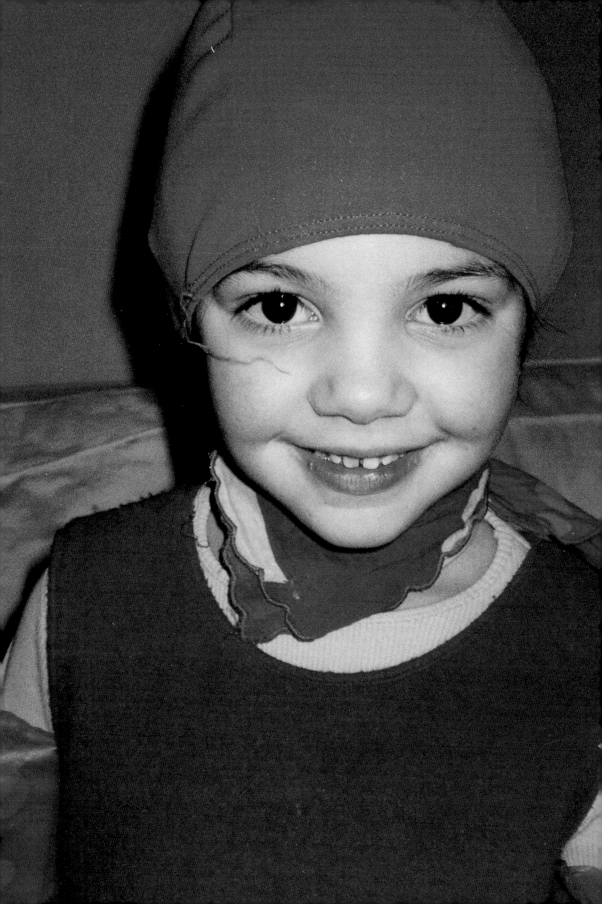

2 SMALL RIPE BUT FIRM PEARS
3 BRIGHT-RED RIPE BUT FIRM PLUMS
2 JUICY BUT FIRM PEACHES OR NECTARINES
A HANDFUL OF SEEDLESS GREEN AND BLACK GRAPES
200 G (7 OZ) CASTER (SUPERFINE) SUGAR
1 STRIP LEMON OR LIME RIND, PITH REMOVED
JUICE OF HALF A LEMON OR LIME
HALF A VANILLA BEAN, SPLIT LENGTHWAYS

Poached fruit in vanilla syrup

This is just fruit served in a bath of syrup. Use any fruit you like but I feel colour is important here, so a couple of berries or cherries can be splashed in at the last moment if you don't have very red plums. Choose fruit with a beautiful shape. I love serving something like this with a scoop of snow-white yoghurt or buttermilk ice cream. This is lovely for breakfast or dessert or just as a snack and you could also serve it with a fruit sorbet (mango or pomegranate, pages 110 and 162). Ladle any leftover syrup into cups for children to drink. You could also add different spices to your poaching syrup — a small cinnamon stick, cloves, a bay leaf, for instance.

Peel the pears, keeping their smooth shape. Halve lengthways and cut out the cores. Halve the unpeeled plums lengthways and remove their stones by gently twisting the halves. If the stones are stubborn, edge them out with a spoon or the point of a potato peeler. Cut each half in half again lengthways, if they are large. Do the same with the peaches or nectarines and halve the grapes too.

Put 1 litre (35 fl oz/4 cups) of cold water in a large saucepan and add the sugar, lemon or lime rind and the juice. Scrape the seeds from the vanilla bean into the pan and then throw in the bean as well. Bring to the boil and then simmer for about 5 minutes. Lower the heat and add the fruit you think will take the longest; probably the pears. Poach them gently for about 5 minutes, turning them with a slotted spoon so that they are totally immersed in syrup and don't darken in parts. Add the plums and peaches and carry on simmering for another 5 minutes or so, just until they surrender their firmness and have absorbed the syrup (not too long, or they will become soggy). Next add the grapes, which will only need a couple of minutes. In the meantime, if some of the fruit looks ready, remove it very carefully with the slotted spoon and put in a wide bowl, taking care not to mark the fruits with cuts or dents. If you have overdone it at any stage, pop the bowl into the freezer for a few minutes to cool the fruit down and stop it cooking further.

Cool the fruits at room temperature in a fly-free zone. If the skins of the peaches are wrinkled, slip them off. Otherwise leave them on, and leave the plum skins on, too. When the syrup has cooled, pour it over the fruit. Serve very slightly warm or at room temperature, and it is even good cold from the fridge in summer. This will keep well in the fridge, covered, for up to 5 days.

Serves 5-6

SEEDS FROM ¼ POMEGRANATE
ABOUT 25 G (1 OZ) SHELLED PECANS, BROKEN INTO
  BIG CHUNKS
300 G (10½ G) GREEK-STYLE NATURAL YOGHURT
4 TEASPOONS THICK RUNNY HONEY
GROUND CINNAMON

Greek yoghurt with honey, cinnamon, pecans & pomegranate

I would make my kids swallow pomegranate seeds whole if I could. Just for their sheer beauty and vitamins. This is a quick 'healthy' snack that you can literally produce in one minute if you have all the ingredients. The Greek yoghurt is important — its thick and creamy nature allows the honey, nuts and cinnamon to sit on it like a crown. The pomegranates dress it up well and the seeds from the rest of the pomegranate can be served up later to nibble on with a glass of prosecco or saved for filling little tartlets.

Pick all the seeds out of the pomegranate, making sure there is no white pith still attached. In a small dry frying pan, lightly toast the pecans just enough to bring out their flavour and crisp them up (take care not to overdo them or they'll be bitter and taste burnt). Leave them to cool.
  Spoon the yoghurt into bowls, scatter a child's fistful of nuts over the top, drizzle with honey and finish with a small scattering of pomegranate seeds and cinnamon. Best served immediately.

Serves 2

4 RIPE POMEGRANATES
JUICE OF 1 LEMON
120 G (4¼ OZ) CASTER (SUPERFINE) SUGAR

Pomegranate sorbet

My children are incredibly enthusiastic about this. I think it is probably the colour that delights them most: I make this when I have lovely rosy pomegranates. The colour of your sorbet will vary in intensity, depending on the colour of your pomegranate seeds. Sometimes I serve this on its own and sometimes with a scoop of vanilla ice cream. It looks beautifully colourful with a ball of bright mango sorbet next to it in the bowl, too (page 110).

Juice the pomegranates very thoroughly, using a levered juice extractor or a citrus juicer, and then strain. You should have about 435 ml (15 fl oz/1¾ cups) of juice. Put the lemon juice in a small saucepan with the sugar and 2–3 tablespoons of the pomegranate juice. Heat, stirring, over medium-low heat until the sugar has dissolved. Remove from the heat, leave to cool a little and then stir in the rest of the pomegranate juice.

Pour the mixture into a bowl or container that has a lid. Put the lid on and put it in the freezer. After an hour give the mixture an energetic whisk with a hand whisk or electric mixer. Put it back in the freezer and then whisk again after another couple of hours. When the sorbet is nearly firm, give one last whisk and put it back in the freezer to set.

Alternatively, pour into your ice cream machine and churn, following the manufacturer's instructions.

Serves 4

1 KG (2 LB 4 OZ) PEARS
1 CUP OF MIXED BERRIES (ABOUT 200 G/7 OZ
    DEPENDING ON THE BERRIES)
70 G (2½ OZ) CASTER (SUPERFINE) SUGAR
200 G (7 OZ) PLAIN (ALL-PURPOSE) FLOUR
50 G (1¾ OZ) LIGHT BROWN SUGAR
150 G (5½ OZ) BUTTER, SOFTENED
1 TEASPOON VANILLA EXTRACT

Pear & berry crumble

You can use any ripe sweet fruit you like for this, really — peaches, apples, apricots, nectarines, pineapples... This is best served warm, when it has cooled down a bit, with a jug of warm custard or just a blob of thick or clotted cream on the side, and a dusting of icing sugar. Sometimes I like the crumble topping to be soft soft, and then I use 60 g (2 oz) of icing sugar instead of the brown sugar and caster sugar. If you feel your fruit might not be sweet enough, sprinkle a dash more sugar over it before the crumble topping goes on. You can mix some chopped shelled walnuts (about 30 g/1 oz) through the topping for a nutty crunch.

Preheat your oven to 190°C (375°F/Gas 5). Generously butter a 36 x 22 x 6 cm (14 x 8½ x 2½ inch) ovenproof dish. Peel, core and slice the pears and put them in the dish. Mix in the berries and scatter half the caster sugar over the fruit.

Mix together the flour, brown sugar and the other half of the caster sugar in a bowl. Add the butter and vanilla and rub them in with your fingertips, working until the mixture isn't smooth but looks like damp clustery sand. Your fingers might be tired.

Scatter the topping over the fruit to cover it completely in a good thick layer. Bake for about 45 minutes, or until the top is nicely golden and some berry juice has oozed up a bit over the crust and darkened it here and there.

Let it cool down a touch and then serve warm with whipped thick or clotted cream, a jug of custard or vanilla ice cream.

Serves 8

120 G (4¼ OZ) UNSALTED BUTTER, SOFTENED
100 ML (3½ FL OZ/5 TABLESPOONS) FRUIT PUREE
  (BELOW)

PERSIMMON PUREE:
1 LARGE VERY RIPE PERSIMMON (ABOUT 250 G/9 OZ)
1 TEASPOON LEMON JUICE
ABOUT 1 TEASPOON ICING (CONFECTIONERS') SUGAR

PLUM PUREE:
175 G (6 OZ) DARK-FLESHED PLUMS
ABOUT 1 TABLESPOON CASTER (SUPERFINE) SUGAR

RASPBERRY PUREE:
120 G (4¼ OZ) FRESH RASPBERRIES (FROZEN
  RASPBERRIES WON'T WORK)
1 TABLESPOON ICING (CONFECTIONERS') SUGAR
½ TABLESPOON LEMON JUICE

BLUEBERRY BUTTER:
120 G (4¼ OZ) UNSALTED BUTTER, SOFTENED
1 TABLESPOON ICING (CONFECTIONERS') SUGAR
120 G (4¼ OZ) BLUEBERRIES

Fruit butters

These are wonderful for a special breakfast where everyone can choose what they want. Serve them with toast, rolls or brioche. I think mandarin, cranberry and strawberry butters would all be good, too. It's important to use unsalted butter here.

With a wooden spoon, beat the butter in a bowl until it is smooth. Add the purée a little at a time and, when it is all mixed through, beat the butter well until very smooth. Cover and keep in the fridge. It is spreadable even straight from the fridge.

Any fruit purée can be used, but here are some to try.

PERSIMMON: Pull the persimmon into pieces and put it in a food processor or blender, skin and all. Add the lemon juice and icing sugar and purée until very smooth. Taste for sweetness and add more icing sugar if it's needed.

PLUM: Halve the plums, throwing away the stones, and cut them into quarters. Put them in a frying pan, scatter with the sugar and stir them over medium-low heat for about 5 minutes, until they start to soften and caramelize slightly. Put into a food processor or blender and whiz until smooth. Taste for sweetness and add more sugar if it's needed.

RASPBERRY: Put the raspberries, icing sugar and lemon juice in a food processor or blender and whiz until smooth.

And this one doesn't even require you to make a purée first:

BLUEBERRY: With a wooden spoon, beat the butter and icing sugar together in a bowl until smooth. Add the blueberries and mix just until the butter turns slightly pinkish and the blueberries are still mostly whole.

250 G (9 OZ) BUTTER, SOFTENED
250 G (9 OZ) CASTER (SUPERFINE) SUGAR
3 EGGS
1 TEASPOON VANILLA EXTRACT
290 G (10¼ OZ/2⅓ CUPS) PLAIN (ALL-PURPOSE)
 FLOUR
1½ TEASPOONS BAKING POWDER
185 ML (6 FL OZ/¾ CUP) MILK OR CREAM

ICING:
250 G (9 OZ) ICING (CONFECTIONERS') SUGAR
RED FOOD COLOURING

Tiny cakes with pink icing

This makes about 60 small cakes in paper cases which are always successful at a party — perhaps for their exuberant colour once they are iced. I use tiny (3.5 x 2 cm/1½ x ¾ inch) paper cases. Make up half the quantity of icing at a time if you want to make two colours, a quarter quantity if you want four colours, rather than making the whole quantity and dividing it up to colour, and then having the icing harden as you work. Plain iced are good, but you could add extra decorations on top — jelly beans, hundreds and thousands, silver balls, smarties or other sweets. When I am in an all-natural mood I use beetroot juice to colour the icing.

Preheat your oven to 180°C (350°F/Gas 4). In a large bowl, thoroughly beat together the butter and sugar. Add the eggs one at a time, beating well after each one goes in. Add the vanilla and then sift in the flour and baking powder. Beat well, adding the milk a little at a time. You should have a thick and creamy batter.

Spoon heaped teaspoons of batter into small paper cupcake cases. Don't put in too much batter or the cakes will puff up too much, and these look lovely when the icing is flush with the top of the cases.

Put the filled paper cases on baking trays and bake in batches for 15 minutes or so, until they are golden on top. Cool completely before icing.

For the icing, put the icing sugar in a bowl, add a few drops of food colouring and gradually stir in 3 tablespoons of cold water until you have a smooth but thick icing that is stiff enough to cling to the cakes. Add more colouring if you think you'd like it brighter. Working a few at a time, drop about a teaspoon of icing on top of each cake and spread it gently with the back of the spoon so that it covers the top. If the icing gets too thick as you are working, add a few more drops of water. Sprinkle on any decorations before the icing dries.

Once the icing has dried, the cakes can be stored in a biscuit tin for 5-6 days.

Makes about 60

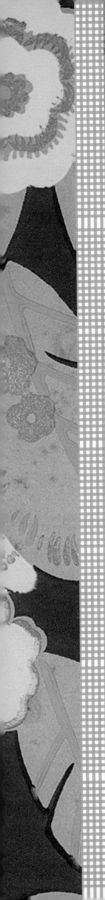

Green

Broccoli soup
Green vegetable soup with egg & lemon
Pasta with calamari & peas
Spinach & ricotta canneloni
Meat canneloni
Mince & rice dumplings with dill,
 egg & lemon sauce
Angel hair pasta with zucchini,
 mint & feta
Chicken escalopes with parsley & capers
Lamb & green bean casserole
Sole bundles with spinach
Zucchini omelette
Paillard
Pea & potato mash
Watercress omelette
Creamy spinach with feta
Sautéed broccoli with tomato
Squashed zucchini
Gratinéed broccoli
Gratinéed celery with tomato & parmesan
Green bean soufflé loaf
Peppermint crisp pie

– memory –

Our friends had a big monkey swing, right in the middle of their vegetable patch. I kept wondering if I would ever see a monkey as I swung up and down and dreamed of being in the circus with the other acrobatic and stylish swinging ladies. There were ducks following their mamma around everywhere while our mammas were inside rolling out trays of pizza for our lunch. We would roll down the steep and grassy hill and stare up, squinting, at the bright sun through the kaleidoscope of our minds to see dinosaur- and butterfly-shaped clouds. After a thick slice of pizza we might fiddle about making mud pies, or sit in a circle and play princesses for a while. The longest-haired girl would always be the princess. We had time to follow the trail of snails all the way to where it finished, and then examine the snails before we moved them to brighter green lawns, to better homes. We'd look for secret places filled with more and more secrets. At night then our mammas would pile us all into the same bath and there would be quite a bit of splashing about and water marks on the wall afterwards. We loved the soft pale fluffy towels that they would bundle us into and we would sit drying, smelling of soap and flicking through books.

ABOUT 500 G (1 LB 2 OZ) BROCCOLI, CUT INTO LARGE
  PIECES
2 POTATOES (ABOUT 350 G/12 OZ), PEELED AND CUT
  INTO BIG CHUNKS
1 RED ONION, PEELED AND QUARTERED
200 ML (7 FL OZ) POURING (SINGLE) CREAM

Broccoli soup

This is such a simple soup, consisting of a few ingredients, and is a perfect example of how good some straightforward things can be. You could really make it with your eyes closed. Adults should add a generous grinding of black pepper to this — which is what I believe makes the soup — and sometimes my kids ask for a tiny twist of pepper over theirs. I like to serve this as a first course for them, followed by a plate of cheese and their favourite buttered bread. Make sure your broccoli is deep chlorophyl-green in its headress and hasn't been sitting for days in your fridge getting paler and paler. My children like to see a deep green soup with cream swirls in it and are upset if I forget and stir in all the cream. So do it like this — just make sure you take the cream out of the fridge well beforehand so you don't ice the soup up with your swirl.

Save a handful of the florets and put the rest in a large saucepan with the potatoes and onion. Add 1.75 litres (61 fl oz/7 cups) of cold water, season with one or two teaspoons of salt and bring to the boil. Skim the surface if necessary. Lower the heat slightly and simmer uncovered for about 45 minutes. Add the other handful of florets 10 minutes before the end of this time. You should be able to squash the broccoli easily on the side of the pan with a wooden spoon.

Purée all this with a blender until it is completely smooth (and hope that you didn't get a woody broccoli to start with). It should be thick, but if you find it too thick then you can add some hot water. If it is too thin then carry on cooking it uncovered for a while to reduce the liquid. Add salt until you can really taste the depth of the broccoli. Swirl in half the cream and heat through. Serve immediately, with another swirl of cream through each portion and a good grinding of pepper for those who like it.

Serves 6

2 TABLESPOONS OLIVE OIL
3 OR 4 SPRING ONIONS (SCALLIONS), CHOPPED
A COUPLE OF LEAFY CELERY STALKS, CHOPPED
250 G (9 OZ) ZUCCHINI (COURGETTES),
  CUT INTO BLOCKS
400 G (14 OZ) POTATOES, PEELED AND CUT
  INTO BLOCKS
100 G (3½ OZ) SHELLED PEAS
100 G (3½ OZ) LETTUCE (ROMAINE/COS OR
  BUTTER), SHREDDED
50 G (1¾ OZ) WATERCRESS TIPS, CHOPPED
120 G (4¼ OZ) BABY ENGLISH SPINACH,
  SHREDDED
2 EGGS
JUICE OF 1 LARGE JUICY LEMON
GRATED PARMESAN CHEESE, TO SERVE

Green vegetable soup with egg & lemon

You can add any vegetables you like to this, preferably those that are in season. I like to use butter or romaine (cos) lettuce.

Heat the oil in a fairly large soup pot. Gently sauté the spring onions and celery until they have softened but not coloured, then add the zucchini, potatoes, peas and half of the lettuce and watercress.

Add 1.5 litres (52 fl oz/6 cups) of water, salt well and bring to the boil. Put the lid on, lower the heat and simmer for 30 minutes, or until the potatoes are soft. Add the remaining lettuce and watercress and the baby spinach and cook for 1 or 2 minutes more. Meanwhile, whip the eggs in a bowl and then whisk in the lemon juice and a pinch of salt. Take a ladleful of the hot broth from the soup and whisk it into the eggs to acclimatize them. Then add a couple more ladlefuls, whisking them in well.

Take the soup off the heat and tip all the egg mixture back into the pot, mixing all the time. Keep mixing, and put the pot back over the lowest possible heat for just a minute so the eggs cook through but don't scramble. Taste for salt, and serve warm with a generous scattering of parmesan, more lemon juice to taste and a good grinding of black pepper, if you like it.

Serves 6-8

3 TABLESPOONS OLIVE OIL
1 RED ONION, FINELY CHOPPED
600 G (1 LB 5 OZ) SMALL CALAMARI,
    CLEANED AND SLICED INTO RINGS
2 GARLIC CLOVES, FINELY CHOPPED
125 ML (4 FL OZ/½ CUP) WHITE WINE
200 G (7 OZ) TINNED DICED TOMATOES
150 G (5½ OZ) SHELLED PEAS
2 TABLESPOONS CHOPPED PARSLEY
350 G (12 OZ) PASTA

Pasta with
calamari & peas

This sauce could be served with some bread, boiled rice or potatoes. Here it is mixed through pasta, which I think works well for kids. You can make the sauce well in advance and just warm it up to serve at the last moment. If you prefer, ask your fishmonger to clean and slice the calamari for you (you'll end up with about 350 g /12 oz once it's cleaned).

Heat the oil in a frying pan and sauté the onion over medium heat until golden but not oversoft. Add the calamari, turn up the heat and stir with a wooden spoon until most of the liquid has evaporated. Stir in the garlic, cook for another minute and then add the wine. Cook until most of the wine has evaporated, and then add the tomato. Let that bubble up, squashing bits down with your wooden spoon, and then add 250 ml (9 fl oz/1 cup) of water and season with salt and pepper. Let it come back to the boil, lower the heat and simmer, covered, for about 45 minutes or until the calamari is very soft. Check it from time to time and add a few more drops of water if it is looking too dry.

Add the peas and parsley and cook for another 10 minutes or so until the peas are soft. Remove from the heat. There should be a good amount of sauce to serve with the pasta, so add water if necessary.

Leave the lid on and let it sit off the heat while you cook the pasta.

Cook the pasta in a large saucepan of boiling salted water, following the packet instructions. Drain well, keeping a few tablespoons of the cooking water.

Put the warm calamari and pea sauce in a serving bowl, add the pasta and toss together. If you think it needs it, add a bit of the cooking water to give a good coating. Serve immediately.

Serves 4

CREPES:
3 EGGS
150 G (5½ OZ) PLAIN (ALL-PURPOSE) FLOUR
50 G (1¾ OZ) BUTTER, MELTED, PLUS EXTRA
    BUTTER, FOR FRYING
250 ML (9 FL OZ/1 CUP) MILK

TOMATO SAUCE:
1 GARLIC CLOVE, PEELED AND SQUASHED A BIT
2 TABLESPOONS OLIVE OIL
400 G (14 OZ) TINNED DICED TOMATOES
ABOUT 4 BASIL LEAVES

FILLING:
300 G (10½ OZ) ENGLISH SPINACH LEAVES, ROUGHLY
    CHOPPED
500 G (1 LB 2 OZ) FRESH RICOTTA
1 EGG, LIGHTLY BEATEN
80 G (2¾ OZ) GRATED PARMESAN CHEESE
FRESHLY GRATED NUTMEG

BÉCHAMEL SAUCE:
60 G (2¼ OZ) BUTTER
40 G (1½ OZ) PLAIN (ALL-PURPOSE) FLOUR
550 ML (19 FL OZ) MILK, WARMED
FRESHLY GRATED NUTMEG

50 G (1¾ OZ) GRATED PARMESAN CHEESE

Spinach & ricotta canneloni

I learnt to make these with my brother and sister-in-law, Luca and Luisa. They really are amazing proper Italian cooks, who put this together effortlessly, as though they were just ironing a shirt. Sometimes they use fresh egg pasta squares instead of the crepes, boiling them first to soften and laying them out on clean kitchen towels to dry. Although this might seem a bit fiddly, it's worth it in the end because you can just take this one lovely dish to the table. If you want to break up the work load a bit, fry the crepes and make the tomato sauce and spinach mix in advance, keeping them covered until you are ready to use them. Then, at the last moment, you can heat up your oven, make the béchamel, fill and roll the crepes, dot the béchamel and tomatoes over the top, and bake. Your oven dish needs to be about 20 x 30 cm (8 x 12 inches) so that you can fit 12 rolled crepes in two rows. If the rolled crepes won't quite fit your dish, you can trim off their ends — it is a little fiddly, but they do look very smart that way.

For the crepes, whisk the eggs in a bowl and then whisk in the flour and a couple of pinches of salt. Add the butter, still whisking, and then slowly incorporate the milk to make a smooth batter. Leave it to stand for 20 minutes or so.

Heat a little butter in a 15 cm (6 inch) non-stick frying pan. Add half a ladleful of batter and quickly swirl the pan around so the batter covers it as evenly as possible. Cook until the underneath is golden, then flip the crepe over with a spatula and cook the other side. Move to a plate with the spatula and cook the rest of the batter. You will need 12 crepes and you should have enough mixture to allow for a couple of disasters.

For the tomato sauce, heat the garlic with the oil in a saucepan and, when you begin to smell the garlic, add the tomatoes. Season with salt, bring to the boil, then lower the heat and simmer for about 15 minutes until the tomatoes have melted. Add the basil and 125 ml (4 fl oz/½ cup) of water towards the end of this time. Purée to a smooth sauce.

For the filling, rinse the spinach under cold water, shake off the excess and then put in a saucepan with just the water clinging to the leaves. Cook over medium-low heat, turning with a wooden spoon, until the leaves have wilted. Cool a little and then squeeze out as much water as you can and chop the spinach. Put the spinach in a bowl with the ricotta, egg, parmesan, nutmeg and salt and pepper to taste. Mix well.

To make the béchamel, melt the butter in a small saucepan. Whisk in the flour and cook for a few minutes, stirring constantly, then begin adding the warm milk. It will be immediately absorbed, so work quickly, whisking with one hand while adding ladlefuls of milk with the other. When the sauce seems to be smooth and not too stiff, add salt, pepper and a grating of nutmeg and continue cooking, even after it comes to the boil, for 5 minutes or so, mixing all the time. It should be a very thick and smooth sauce.

Meanwhile, preheat the oven to 180°C (350°F/Gas 4) and grease a 20 x 30 cm (8 x 12 inch) baking dish.

To put together, dollop some béchamel in the bottom of the dish and rock it from side to side so that the béchamel thinly covers the bottom. Spoon a couple of tablespoons of filling along one side of a crepe and then roll it up tightly. Repeat with all the crepes and lay them on the béchamel like soldiers in two rows of six. Pour the rest of the béchamel over the top, then dot generously with the tomato sauce. Sprinkle with the parmesan and bake for about 40 minutes, until golden and bubbling nicely. Let it cool a dash before serving, then check carefully where each crepe begins and ends and lift them out with an egg flip.

Serves 6

APPLES FOR SAM

CREPES:
3 EGGS
150 G (5½ OZ) PLAIN (ALL-PURPOSE) FLOUR
50 G (1¾ OZ) BUTTER, MELTED, PLUS EXTRA
    BUTTER, FOR FRYING
250 ML (9 FL OZ/1 CUP) MILK

MINCE SAUCE:
3 TABLESPOONS OLIVE OIL
1 ONION, CHOPPED
1 GARLIC CLOVE, FINELY CHOPPED
400 G (14 OZ) MINCED (GROUND) BEEF
1 BAY LEAF
½ CINNAMON STICK
1 TABLESPOON WORCESTERSHIRE SAUCE
½ TEASPOON DRIED MINT
1 TEASPOON SWEET PAPRIKA
185 ML (6 FL OZ/¾ CUP) WHITE WINE
400 G (14 OZ) TINNED DICED TOMATOES
1 HANDFUL PARSLEY, CHOPPED

TOMATO SAUCE:
1 GARLIC CLOVE, PEELED AND SQUASHED
    A BIT
2 TABLESPOONS OLIVE OIL
400 G (14 OZ) TINNED DICED TOMATOES
ABOUT 4 BASIL LEAVES

BÉCHAMEL SAUCE:
60 G (2¼ OZ) BUTTER
40 G (1½ OZ) PLAIN (ALL-PURPOSE) FLOUR
550 ML (19 FL OZ) MILK, WARMED
FRESHLY GRATED NUTMEG

50 G (1¾ OZ) GRATED PARMESAN CHEESE

Meat canneloni

This is a bit of a job — but great. You can do it all in one go, or cook the mince the day before and make the crepes in the morning with the tomato sauce. Then all you have do is make up a béchamel, assemble it all together and bake. If not, I find it quite satisfying to put the whole thing together in a morning. Your baking dish needs to be about 30 x 20 cm (12 x 8 inches) and about 6 cm (2½ inches) deep so that two lines of filled crepes will fit together. Otherwise, it starts to get quite fiddly if you have to trim the crepes to fit your dish (although they do look very smart that way).

For the crepes, whisk the eggs in a bowl and then whisk in the flour and a couple of pinches of salt. Add the butter, still whisking, and then slowly incorporate the milk to make a smooth batter. Leave it to stand for 20 minutes or so.

Heat a little butter in a 15 cm (6 inch) non-stick frying pan. Add half a ladleful of batter and quickly swirl the pan around so the batter covers it as evenly as possible. Cook until the underneath is golden, then flip the crepe over with a spatula and cook the other side. Move to a plate with the spatula and cook the rest of the batter. You will need 12 crepes and you should have enough mixture to allow for a couple of disasters.

For the mince sauce, heat the olive oil in a large pan and sauté the onions over medium heat until quite golden. Stir in the garlic, then add the mince, bay leaf, cinnamon stick, worcestershire sauce, mint and paprika. Sauté over high heat for about 8 minutes until the meat starts to brown, stirring often to prevent sticking and to brown all the meat. Add the wine and cook for a few minutes until it has evaporated. Add the tomatoes, cook for a few minutes and then add 375 ml (13 fl oz/1 1/2 cups) of water. Season with salt. Bring to the boil, lower the heat and simmer uncovered for about 45 minutes. Add the parsley for the last 10 minutes of the cooking time.

For the tomato sauce, heat the garlic with the oil in a saucepan and, when you begin to smell the garlic, add the tomatoes. Season with salt, bring to the boil, then lower the heat and simmer for about 15 minutes until the tomatoes have melted. Add the basil and 125 ml (4 fl oz/1/2 cup) of water towards the end of this time. Purée to a smooth sauce.

To make the béchamel, melt the butter in a small saucepan. Whisk in the flour and cook for a few minutes, stirring constantly, then begin adding the warm milk. It will be immediately absorbed, so work quickly, whisking with one hand while adding ladlefuls of milk with the other. When the sauce seems to be smooth and not too stiff, add salt, pepper and a grating of nutmeg and continue cooking, even after it comes to the boil, for 5 minutes or so, mixing all the time. It should be a very thick and smooth sauce.

Meanwhile, preheat the oven to 180°C (350°F/Gas 4) and grease a 20 x 30 cm (8 x 12 inch) baking dish.

To put it all together, spread 2–3 tablespoons of tomato sauce over the bottom of the dish. Spoon 3 tablespoons of mince filling along one side of a crepe and then roll it up tightly. Repeat with all the crepes and lay them in two rows of six over the tomato sauce in the dish. Dollop the béchamel over the top, here, there and everywhere, and then spoon tomato sauce on top and inbetween, so that you can still see patches of béchamel. Scatter the parmesan over the top and bake for about 40 minutes, until it is bubbling nicely and is golden here and there. Let it cool a dash before serving.

Serves 6

DUMPLINGS:
1 KG (2 LB 4 OZ) MINCED (GROUND) PORK AND VEAL
1/2 TEASPOON OREGANO
3 TABLESPOONS CHOPPED DILL
3 TABLESPOONS CHOPPED PARSLEY
1 EGG
160 G (5 1/2 OZ) RICE
1 LARGE RED ONION, GRATED
150 ML (5 FL OZ) MILK
3-4 TABLESPOONS OLIVE OIL
2 GARLIC CLOVES, PEELED BUT LEFT WHOLE

SAUCE:
1 EGG
JUICE OF 2 LEMONS
2 TABLESPOONS CHOPPED DILL

Mince & rice dumplings with dill, egg & lemon sauce

These are wonderfully soft meat and rice dumplings that most Greek children eat on a regular basis. If you think that your children might not appreciate the green flecks of dill in the sauce then you can leave it out — they probably won't notice it in the dumplings and it does give a special and definite flavour.

For the dumplings, put the minced meat, oregano, dill, parsley, egg, rice and onion in a mixing bowl with the milk and season well with salt. Knead with your hands so it is all very well mixed. Shape the dumplings by breaking off chunks about the size of a large walnut and quickly patting them into balls or ovals.

Heat the oil and garlic in a non-stick frying pan and fry the dumplings in batches over medium–high heat, turning them carefully when they are lightly golden on the underside, and lifting the dumplings into a large flameproof casserole when they are golden all over.

When all the dumplings are in the casserole, gently pour in 1.25 litres (44 fl oz/5 cups) of hot water. Add a little extra salt and bring to a gentle boil. Lower the heat to a bare simmer, cover with a lid and cook for an hour. There should be a fair amount of liquid still at the end. Remove from the heat.

For the sauce, whip the egg in a bowl and then whisk in the lemon juice and a pinch of salt. Add a ladleful of the hot liquid from the pot (which you will have to tip to the side to get to). Quickly whisk the hot liquid into the egg mixture to acclimatize the eggs, then add another couple of ladlefuls along with the dill, mixing well.

With the pot off the heat, pour all the egg and lemon sauce back in, quickly hula-hooping the pot around to shift everything so that the eggs don't scramble. Cover the pot and let it sit for a few minutes — there should be enough heat left in the pot to just cook the eggs through. Taste that there is enough salt before serving, perhaps with a grinding of black pepper. Best served warm, but also good at room temperature.

Serves 5-6

---

3 TABLESPOONS OLIVE OIL
2 SMALL ZUCCHINI (COURGETTES), FINELY SLICED
2 GARLIC CLOVES, PEELED AND SQUASHED A BIT
½ TEASPOON DRIED MINT
100 G (3½ OZ) FETA CHEESE, CUT INTO SMALL BLOCKS
1 TABLESPOON LEMON JUICE
250 G (9 OZ) ANGEL HAIR PASTA
OLIVE OIL, TO SERVE
GRATED PARMESAN CHEESE, TO SERVE

Angel hair pasta with zucchini, mint & feta

This is light, elegant and very quick. You can get the preparation done and sauté the zucchini while the pasta is cooking and then just mix it all together.

Heat the olive oil in a large non-stick frying pan and add the zucchini and garlic. Sauté over quite high heat until the zucchini are cooked through and golden in places. If the garlic starts to burn, sit it on top of the zucchini. Season very lightly with salt and remove from the heat. Toss in the mint, crushing it between your fingers, and add the feta and lemon juice to the pan.

Meanwhile, cook the pasta in boiling salted water, following the packet instructions. Drain the pasta, not too thoroughly, and save a little cooking water. Toss the pasta directly into the zucchini pan, if it fits. If not, return it to its own pan and add the zucchini sauce. Add a tablespoon or two of olive oil and toss quickly and thoroughly to mix it all through (add a little cooking water if it seems at all dry). Serve immediately, with parmesan and an extra drizzle of olive oil, if you like.

Serves 3

3 CHICKEN ESCALOPES
ABOUT 3 TABLESPOONS PLAIN (ALL-PURPOSE) FLOUR
3 TABLESPOONS OLIVE OIL
1 GARLIC CLOVE, PEELED AND SQUASHED A BIT
JUICE OF HALF A LEMON
1 TABLESPOON CAPERS IN VINEGAR, DRAINED
  AND CHOPPED
2 TABLESPOONS CHOPPED PARSLEY

Chicken escalopes with parsley & capers

This is another very simple way to prepare a chicken breast. You can buy escalopes from your butcher or simply slice a chicken breast horizontally into three or four thin flat slices. You could even pound them out a bit thinner with a meat mallet, if you like. This is nice with mash, boiled potatoes, or chips and a simple vegetable like sautéed cauliflower.

Lightly pat both sides of the chicken in flour. Heat the oil with the garlic in a large frying pan over medium-high heat and add the chicken. Fry until lightly golden on the underside, then turn over and season the done sides with salt and pepper. When the new undersides are golden, turn them again, season and squeeze in the lemon juice. Add the capers, half the parsley and a couple of tablespoons of hot water. Let it bubble up, then put a lid on the pan and cook for an extra minute or two to make sure that the chicken is cooked through but still soft and moist and there is some liquid in the pan. Turn off the heat and leave the pan with the lid on for a few minutes. Mix in the remaining parsley and serve immediately.

Serves 3

Walking barefoot through fields,
knowing to zig zag if you see a snake.
The medicine chest is full — I have covered
mosquitoes, bees and bums.

GREEN

2 TABLESPOONS OLIVE OIL
500 G (1 LB 2 OZ) DEBONED TRIMMED LEG
    OR SHOULDER OF LAMB, CUT INTO 4 CM
    (1½ INCH) CHUNKS
1 RED ONION, FINELY CHOPPED
20 G (¾ OZ) BUTTER
2 GARLIC CLOVES, CHOPPED
300 G (10½ OZ) TINNED DICED TOMATOES
1 SMALL PIECE CASSIA BARK (OR CINNAMON)
400 G (14 OZ) GREEN BEANS, TOPPED (LEAVE
    THE TAILS ON)
200 G (7 OZ) FETA CHEESE, CUT INTO SMALL CHUNKS

Lamb & green bean casserole

I like to make this in advance and then leave it in the oven to cool down completely. This seems to make the meat even softer, and then I just warm it up a bit on the stovetop to serve. This is a great one-pot meal that needs just the time to prepare and chop up the ingredients, and not much more attention from then on. You can use chunks of lamb or beef here, and throw in a couple of potatoes, cut up into chunks, with the beans, if you like. The green beans alone are also delicious cooked like this; still served with crumblings of feta that melt a little into the tomato sauce.

Preheat the oven to 180°C (350°F/Gas 4). Heat the oil in a heavy-based casserole over high heat. When it is very hot, add the meat and brown on all sides. Add the onion and cook, stirring, for a few minutes to soften it. When the onion starts to brown, add the butter and garlic. When you can smell the garlic, add the tomatoes. Season with salt and add the cassia or cinnamon. Add 500 ml (17 fl oz/2 cups) of water and bring to the boil. Put on the lid and put the casserole in the oven.

Cook for 45 minutes or so until the meat is soft, and then add the beans, a little more salt and another 250 ml (9 fl oz/1 cup) of water if it needs it. Mix through well, cover and put the casserole back into the oven for another hour. Remove the lid and cook for another 15 minutes until it turns a little golden on the top. Turn off the oven, put the lid back on and leave the casserole in there for about an hour so that the meat is soft and melting. You can warm it up on the stovetop to serve.

Sprinkle the feta over the hot servings, so that it melts slightly, and serve with chunks of bread.

Serves 3

4 TABLESPOONS OLIVE OIL
2 GARLIC CLOVES, PEELED AND SQUASHED A BIT
200 G (7 OZ) TINNED DICED TOMATOES
2 BASIL LEAVES, TORN
150 G (5½ OZ) ENGLISH SPINACH LEAVES, CHOPPED
30 G (1 OZ) GRATED PARMESAN CHEESE
8 SOLE FILLETS WITHOUT SKIN
PLAIN (ALL-PURPOSE) FLOUR, FOR DUSTING
LEMON WEDGES, TO SERVE

Sole bundles with spinach

This is nice with mash or thin chips, or just on its own with some bread. If you can't get sole, use fillets from another white-fleshed fish such as whiting, silver dory or flounder. They need to be long fillets — fine-flaked, narrow and about 5 mm (1/4 inch) thick so that they can be rolled easily.

Heat 3 tablespoons of the oil and a garlic clove in a non-stick deep-sided frying pan that will hold all the sole bundles later on. Add the tomato and basil, season lightly with salt and simmer over low heat for about 10 minutes, or until everything has melted together into a sauce.

Heat the remainder of the oil with the other garlic clove in a saucepan and add the spinach. Sauté for a few minutes to wilt the leaves. Remove from the heat, season with salt and stir in the parmesan. Fish out the garlic clove.

Lay the fish fillets on a flat surface, former-skin-side down. Put about a teaspoon of the spinach mixture onto the tapered end of each fillet and roll up the fish compactly around the spinach. Secure with toothpicks. Roll the fish bundles in flour to coat lightly. Arrange them in a single layer over the tomato sauce in the pan and sprinkle with a little extra salt.

Put the lid on the pan and simmer for 5 minutes or so, until the undersides of the fish bundles become lightly golden. Very gently turn them over, sprinkle with salt and put the lid back on. Simmer for another 5 minutes, or until the inside of the fish is cooked. If the sauce seems at all dry, add a few drops of hot water and heat through. Serve with lemon wedges.

Serves 4

ABOUT 1 TABLESPOON OLIVE OIL
1 GARLIC CLOVE, PEELED AND SQUASHED A BIT
120 G (4¼ OZ) SMALL GREEN ZUCCHINI
  (COURGETTES), FINELY SLICED
3 OR 4 BASIL LEAVES, TORN UP
4 EGGS
4 TABLESPOONS GRATED PARMESAN CHEESE
A LITTLE LEMON JUICE

Zucchini omelette

The amount of zucchini here is enough to make four individual omelettes.
Just reduce the zucchini and eggs accordingly if you only want one or two.

Heat 2 teaspoons of oil in a non-stick pan. Add the garlic and zucchini and sauté
over medium-high heat until lightly golden, shuffling them with a wooden spoon
so that they cook evenly. Season with salt and mix in the basil. Remove from the
heat and remove the garlic.
  Whisk one egg in a bowl. Heat 1 teaspoon of oil in a 14 cm (6 inch) non-stick
frying pan over medium-low heat. Add the egg, swirling it evenly around the pan.
Scatter about a quarter of the zucchini over the omelette and about 1 tablespoon
of parmesan. Cook until the omelette is set and the underside is lightly golden.
Slip out onto a warm plate while you make the rest, adding more oil to the pan as
needed. Serve with a few drops of lemon juice and a grinding of pepper if you like.

Serves 4

----

2 TABLESPOONS OLIVE OIL
1 GARLIC CLOVE, PEELED AND SQUASHED A BIT
1 SMALL ROSEMARY SPRIG
2 LARGE SLICES OF VEAL RUMP, CUT 3-4 MM
  (⅛ INCH) THICK
2 LEMON WEDGES, TO SERVE

Paillard

This is a wonderful piece of meat to give children — very tender and soft.
Ask your butcher for long pieces of veal rump, cut about 3-4 mm (⅛ inch)
thick. It is essential here that the meat is just seared on the pan and
doesn't simmer and harden. It needs just a couple of minutes cooking in
total and your griddle pan has to be incredibly hot before you put the meat
on it. You need to think ahead a little and put your herbs and oil in a bowl
a while before you want to cook. This is nice with potato and pea mash
(opposite) or pan-fried chips.

APPLES FOR SAM

Put the olive oil, garlic and rosemary sprig in a small bowl and leave for about 45 minutes to flavour the oil.

If it's necessary, pound the veal slices (first covered with a sheet of plastic wrap) with a meat mallet to make them an even thickness.

Put your griddle pan over a high flame and let it stay there until it is very hot. Put the veal slices on the pan, one at a time if they won't both fit. They should sear immediately. As soon as the undersides come away easily with a pair of tongs and there are obvious grill marks, turn them over and do the other side. Both sides should take less than 30 seconds.

Remove to a plate, drizzle some of the oil over each one and add a small scattering of salt. Serve immediately, with a lemon wedge on the side.

Serves 2

---

400 G (14 OZ) POTATOES, PEELED AND CUT INTO LARGE CHUNKS
3 TABLESPOONS OLIVE OIL
1 FRENCH SHALLOT, PEELED BUT LEFT WHOLE
2 GARLIC CLOVES, PEELED BUT LEFT WHOLE
200 G (7 OZ) SHELLED PEAS, FRESH OR FROZEN
125 ML (4 FL OZ/½ CUP) MILK
ABOUT 30 G (1 OZ) BUTTER

Pea & potato mash

Sometimes I like this with variegated ripples of colour and sometimes I mix it in to make it all green. This is also delicious made with chickpeas (page 346). It is good next to any grilled (broiled) meat or fish and is best served immediately. If that's not feasible, you can heat it up over a double boiler, or directly in the pan with a little milk so that it doesn't stick.

Boil the potatoes in salted water until they are soft enough to mash.

Meanwhile, heat the olive oil, shallot and garlic in a saucepan over medium heat. Once you can smell the garlic, add the peas (straight from the freezer, if you're using frozen) and season with salt. Sauté for about 15 minutes, until they are soft and cooked through but still bright green. When the liquid has evaporated, add 125 ml (4 fl oz/½ cup) or so of hot water and carry on cooking until most of it has evaporated. Remove the shallot and garlic and purée the peas so that they are rather smooth. Drain the potatoes and put them through a potato mill back into the pan, or use a potato masher to make a light mash.

Meanwhile, heat the milk and butter in a small saucepan over low heat until the butter melts. Pour into the potatoes and mix through. Add the peas and either mix them in completely or just fold them through to get a rippled effect. Serve hot.

Serves 5

1 TABLESPOON OLIVE OIL
1 GARLIC CLOVE, PEELED AND SQUASHED A BIT
150 G (5½ OZ) WATERCRESS LEAVES WITH JUST THE
  TIPS OF THE STALKS
4 EGGS
30 G (1 OZ) PARMESAN CHEESE, GRATED
4 MINT LEAVES, TORN
20 G (¾ OZ) BUTTER
A COUPLE OF LEMON WEDGES, TO SERVE

Watercress omelette

You can use any soft green leafy vegetable here: spinach is good, or even lettuce.

Heat the oil and garlic in a large saucepan and add the watercress. Cook over medium-high heat for about half a minute, turning the watercress over with a wooden spoon until it has just wilted. Fish out the garlic clove.

Whip the eggs with a little salt and pepper in a bowl. Add the watercress, parmesan and mint and mix together.

Melt the butter in a large non-stick frying pan. Pour in the eggs and swirl them around. Cook for a few minutes over medium heat, swirling the pan around again to spread out any uncooked egg. Using a straight-bottomed wooden spatula, make a few holes on the bottom of the omelette and shake the pan so that the uncooked egg leaks through and sets. Loosen the side and bottom to make sure the omelette doesn't stick. The top will still be slightly soft and the bottom lightly golden. Remove from the heat and cut into wedges with the spatula. Serve hot from the pan, with a few drops of lemon juice squeezed over the top.

Serves 2-3

500 G (1 LB 2 OZ) ENGLISH SPINACH LEAVES,
  ROUGHLY CHOPPED
3 TABLESPOONS OLIVE OIL
2 GARLIC CLOVES, PEELED BUT LEFT WHOLE
150 G (5½ OZ) FETA CHEESE, CRUMBLED
40 G (1½ OZ) PARMESAN CHEESE, GRATED

Creamy
spinach with feta

I remember eating this as a child and I still like it this way now. Don't throw the spinach cooking water away — save it to make risotto in spinach broth (page 267).

Put about 1 litre (35 fl oz/4 cups) of water in a large pan, add a little salt and bring to the boil. Add the spinach, return to the boil and simmer for just about a minute, until the spinach has wilted. Drain, reserving the water.

Put the olive oil and garlic cloves in a large frying pan over medium heat. When you can smell the garlic, add the spinach, turning it over with a wooden spoon to collect the oil. Add the feta and 125 ml (4 fl oz/½ cup) of the spinach water. Mix the feta through, mashing it in with the spoon so it dissolves. Still at medium heat, sauté for a couple of minutes until everything has blended together and there is only a bit of liquid left in the pan. Remove from the heat, stir in the parmesan and taste for salt. Serve immediately, with some black pepper for adults only.

Serves 5

400 G (14 OZ) BROCCOLI FLORETS
4 TABLESPOONS OLIVE OIL
125 ML (4 FL OZ/½ CUP) TINNED DICED TOMATOES
2 GARLIC CLOVES, PEELED AND SQUASHED A BIT
CHILLI OIL, TO SERVE

Sautéed broccoli with tomato

This is a similar idea to the sautéed cauliflower (page 241), but with tomato, and to me it transforms something like plain boiled broccoli into an actual dish — comfortably dressed to show up at any type of meal. The leftover cooking water can be kept and used to cook rice or pasta.

Drop the broccoli into boiling salted water for a couple of minutes. Drain well, keeping about 3 tablespoons of the cooking water. Heat a tablespoon of the oil in a small saucepan and add the tomato and a dash of salt. Simmer over low heat for about 10 minutes, until it melts into a smoothish sauce. Heat the rest of the oil in a large non-stick frying pan over medium heat and add the garlic. When you can smell the garlic, add the broccoli. Sauté for a few minutes until it is a little crusty and then add the saved broccoli water. Dot the tomato here and there, put a lid on and cook for a few minutes so that everything mingles together. Serve warm or at room temperature, definitely with a drizzle of chilli oil for the adults.

Serves 4

We blew away our fallen eyelashes and the ladybirds that landed on us, together with our wishes to the nearest star.

1 GARLIC CLOVE, PEELED AND SQUASHED A BIT
3 TABLESPOONS OLIVE OIL
8 ZUCCHINI (COURGETTES)
4 BASIL LEAVES, TORN
SEA SALT FLAKES, TO SERVE
OLIVE OIL, TO SERVE

Squashed zucchini

This is hardly a recipe, but Giovanni's mother does them like this and so did his grandmother. Although as a young boy he didn't enjoy them, he grew into these. The zucchini tastes more concentrated somehow — more like a gem squash this way. I love this sort of thing that has been passed down through a family.

Put the garlic and oil in small bowl. Bring a large pan of salted water to the boil, add the zucchini and boil them for 20 minutes or so until they are nice and soft. Remove them with a slotted spoon and line them up on a plate. Put another plate on top and press down a little to squash the water out of the zucchini. Pour off the water and do the same thing again, so all the liquid is removed. Drizzle the garlic oil over the top, scatter with the basil leaves and sprinkle with salt flakes. Serve warm, whole or in thick slices, drizzled with more olive oil if you like it.

Serves 8

BÉCHAMEL SAUCE:
45 G (1$\frac{3}{4}$ OZ) BUTTER
30 G (1 OZ) PLAIN (ALL-PURPOSE) FLOUR
375 ML (13 FL OZ/1$\frac{1}{2}$ CUPS) MILK, WARMED
A LITTLE FRESHLY GRATED NUTMEG

400 G (14 OZ) BROCCOLI FLORETS
50 G (1$\frac{3}{4}$ OZ) PARMESAN CHEESE, GRATED

Gratinéed broccoli

As well as boiled broccoli dressed with olive oil and lemon, my children also like this gratinéed classic. Remove the harder broccoli stems and use only the florets. Don't throw out the hard stems; they can be added to a vegetable soup, or boiled and then sautéed with garlic and olive oil.

Preheat the oven to 180°C (350°F/Gas 4) and grease a 1 litre (35 fl oz/4 cup) shallow ovenproof dish that is suitable to take directly to the table. To make the béchamel, melt the butter in a small saucepan. Whisk in the flour and cook for a few minutes, stirring constantly, then begin adding the warm milk. It will be immediately absorbed, so work quickly, whisking with one hand while adding ladlefuls of milk with the other. When the sauce seems to be smooth and not too stiff, add salt, pepper and a grating of nutmeg and continue cooking, even after it comes to the boil, for 5 minutes or so, mixing all the time. It should be a very thick and smooth sauce.

Meanwhile, bring a saucepan of salted water to the boil and cook the broccoli for a few minutes until it has softened a little but is still bright green. Lift out with a slotted spoon, letting the water drain off, and put it in the oven dish. (Save the broccoli water for cooking rice or pasta, or adding to a roast instead of water.)

Stir the parmesan into the béchamel sauce and pour over the broccoli, leaving some florets still showing. Bake for about 30 minutes and then serve hot.

Serves 4

310 G (11 OZ) INNER CELERY STALKS, TRIMMED
2 TABLESPOONS OLIVE OIL
1 GARLIC CLOVE, PEELED AND SQUASHED A BIT
185 ML (6 FL OZ/³/4 CUP) TOMATO PASSATA
3 BASIL LEAVES, TORN
ABOUT 4 TABLESPOONS PLAIN (ALL-PURPOSE) FLOUR
4 TABLESPOONS GRATED PARMESAN CHEESE

Gratinéed celery with tomato & parmesan

This is aunt Julietta's recipe. I love having these types of things at her home — she always serves them alongside a beautiful roast. This also works very well with cauliflower broken up into smaller bits, zucchini (courgettes), cardoons or the thicker stems of silverbeet, and is especially good with pumpkin slices. It is very good fried first and then arranged on the tomato, but that's a bit more of a job.

With a sharp knife, trim the strings from the celery stalks and cut into short lengths (about 4 cm/1 ½ inches). Bring a pan of salted water to the boil and cook the celery for about 20 minutes until it is soft but not collapsing. Preheat the oven to 200°C (400°F/Gas 6) and lightly oil an 18 cm (7 inch) square shallow ovenproof dish.

Heat the olive oil and garlic in a small pan over medium heat. When you can smell the garlic, add the passata and 3 tablespoons of water. Season with salt and pepper and add the basil. Simmer over low heat for about 10 minutes for the flavours to mingle and the sauce to thicken a little. Fish out the garlic clove and throw it away.

Drain the celery. Spread the flour on a plate and pat the celery pieces lightly into it to coat both sides. Spread about a third of the tomato sauce over the bottom of the dish. Arrange the celery on top, in a single layer or slightly overlapping. Dollop the rest of the tomato sauce on top. Bake for 20 minutes, or until the top is golden in places. Sprinkle with the parmesan and bake for another 10 minutes or so until it is golden and crusty. Leave to cool for a few minutes before serving.

Serves 5

APPLES FOR SAM

1 KG (2 LB 4 OZ) GREEN BEANS, TRIMMED
ABOUT 50 G (1 3/4 OZ/1/2 CUP) DRY BREADCRUMBS
4 EGGS
80 G (2 3/4 OZ) GRATED PARMESAN CHEESE
1/2 TABLESPOON CHOPPED DILL

BÉCHAMEL SAUCE:
50 G (1 3/4 OZ) BUTTER
70 G (2 1/2 OZ) PLAIN (ALL-PURPOSE) FLOUR
400 ML (14 FL OZ) MILK, WARMED
FRESHLY GRATED NUTMEG

Green bean soufflé loaf

I like the idea of wrapping this up and taking it along on an autumn picnic, perhaps with a pile of schnitzels and the pear butter cake (page 248). Cooked beans are puréed and folded into a dense béchamel in a loaf tin, baked and served in thick slices... a little like a cross between a soufflé and a loaf. You can use another herb in place of dill, if you'd prefer. This makes two loaves but you could easily halve the quantity and you can use any shape tin you prefer.

Steam the beans over a pan of boiling water for about 20 minutes until tender. Put them in a blender or processor and pulse so that most are smooth, but there are some small bits, too. Pour into a bowl, season well with salt and leave to cool a bit.

Preheat the oven to 180°C (350°F/Gas 4). Grease two 20 x 10 cm (8 x 4 inch) loaf tins and sprinkle the bases and sides with breadcrumbs. Shake out the excess.

To make the béchamel, melt the butter in a small saucepan. Whisk in the flour and cook for a few minutes, stirring constantly, then begin adding the warm milk. It will be immediately absorbed, so work quickly, whisking with one hand while adding ladlefuls of milk with the other. When the sauce seems to be smooth and not too stiff, add salt, pepper and a grating of nutmeg and continue cooking, even after it comes to the boil, for 5 minutes or so, mixing all the time. It should be a very thick and smooth sauce.

Whisk the eggs, parmesan and dill together, then fold through the puréed beans. Whisk in the béchamel and add some salt, nutmeg or pepper if needed. Ladle into the tins and sprinkle the tops with a teaspoon or so of breadcrumbs. Put side by side in the oven and bake for about 45 minutes, or until they are set and the tops are nicely golden and crusty. Cool for a while before slicing to serve.

Serves 10

250 G (9 OZ) DIGESTIVE BISCUITS
   (GRAHAM CRACKERS)
100 G (3½ OZ) BUTTER, MELTED
600 G (1 LB 5 OZ/1½ TINS)
   CARAMEL CONDENSED MILK
400 ML (14 FL OZ) WHIPPING
   CREAM
100 G (3½ OZ) PEPPERMINT CRISP
   BARS, CRUMBLED OR COARSELY
   GRATED

Peppermint crisp pie

This outrageous pie is a base of crushed biscuits, a layer of caramel, a layer of whipped cream and then a scattering of crisp peppermint milk chocolate. It is incredibly rich and should probably be served in small spoonfuls, depending, of course, on your personal tastes. It makes me think of boarding school midnight feasts in books from the 1950s. You need to use chocolate bars with an apple-green crunchy filling, not a soft creamy centre. In South Africa we made this with 'tennis' biscuits, but digestives work just as well. It is possible to buy the condensed milk already boiled into caramel. If you can't get it, you will have to simmer the tins in a large pot of water for about 3½ hours so the condensed milk turns nutty golden brown. Let the tins cool in the pot before removing and opening them — your condensed milk should be caramelized.

Crush the biscuits and put them in a bowl with the butter. Mix together well and then press firmly onto the base and a little way up the sides of a 26 cm (10½ inch) pie dish. Put in the fridge to set.

Beat the caramel in a bowl with a wooden spoon until smooth. Carefully spread over the biscuit base, trying not to lift any of the biscuits crumbs.

Whip the cream until it holds its shape well, but take care not to overwhip it. Spoon it over the caramel to cover the whole surface and then scatter the peppermint chocolate over the top. Keep in the fridge before serving in slices if you can manage it, or dollops if you can't. This is also good the next day.

Serves 10-12

gold

Olive oil focaccia
Wholemeal focaccia
Half-moon rolls
Cheese pies
Steak pie
Fried mozzarella sandwiches
Macaroni cheese
Fried calamari
Pan-fried sole with lemon garlic butter
Mince & potato croquettes
Escalopes with ham & cheese
Fried buttermilk marinated chicken
Chicken escalopes with lemon & butter
Boiled potatoes with parsley
Sautéed chicken with bay leaves & juniper berries
Roast chicken & potatoes with thyme, lemon & garlic
Fish cakes
Very thin chips
Mayonnaise
Sautéed cauliflower
Fried potato halves with oregano
Pan-fried chips with rosemary & sage
White loaf with honey, butter & pecans
Toffee sauce
Pear butter cake
Semolina puddings with caramel
Crumpets
Waffles
Pancakes

- memory -

I could hardly wait to spring out of bed in the mornings, onto my two-wheeler down the drive. We played circus over Dixie's kennel and brushed Sumpi till she shone. Later were water-drinking competitions and just about anything else that came into our lush minds. Sometimes it was just such a drag to come in for a meal... we far preferred to take our plates to the shelter that the tree had made into a cave for us — or under the weeping willow. We didn't really mind if it was real parmesan — it was the shapes and the flavours that could carry us away and link arms with our fairies. I watch that same energy in my children, their days just tinged with trust and newness and full of spontaneous wonder, miracle and flowing along with whatever is happening. Sitting on hill-tops and dreaming of being kings in other places.

435 ML (15¼ FL OZ/1¾ CUPS) WARM (COMFORTABLE
TO YOUR FINGERS) WATER
20 G (¾ OZ) FRESH YEAST, CRUMBLED, OR 10 G
(¼ OZ) ACTIVE DRY YEAST
1 TEASPOON HONEY
2 TABLESPOONS OLIVE OIL
600 G (1 LB 5 OZ) PLAIN (ALL-PURPOSE) FLOUR

Olive oil focaccia

This is nice left to rise up high so that it is soft and can be split for filling sandwiches. A couple of squares of this filled with thinly sliced ham or salami, bresaola, chopped egg and cress, tomato and ricotta or robiola, mozzarella or roasted tomato and pesto makes a good lunch or emergency snack. The bread can also be frozen in bags in small portions and pulled out to thaw quickly. This is lovely also with some fresh herbs such as rosemary strewn across the top before baking. If you use rosemary, strip the leaves off a couple of stalks and chop them up very finely (as I think the long needles might not be appreciated by the kids). The amount of water and flour you need may vary slightly but the dough should be sticky and difficult to knead.

Put the water, yeast, honey, half the olive oil and 3 fistfuls of the flour in a bowl. Mix with electric beaters until smooth. Cover and leave for 20–30 minutes until it all froths up and looks foamy on the top. Mix in the rest of the flour and 1½ teaspoons of salt. Now, using a dough hook, mix for 4–5 minutes so that it is well incorporated. If you don't have a dough hook, then mix it with your hands in the bowl, just slapping it from one side to the other, as it will be too soft to knead. Cover the bowl with a couple of cloths and leave it in a warm and draught-free place for about 1½ hours, or until it has puffed up well.

Lightly oil a 28 x 38 x 4 cm (11 x 15 x 1½ inch) baking tray. Punch down the dough to flatten it. Spread the dough out gently into the tray, right out to the edges. If it won't stretch easily, leave it to relax for another 5 minutes and then gently stretch it out, starting from the centre. Make sure the dough doesn't break anywhere and that it is spread more or less evenly. Put in a warm draught-free place. So the dough doesn't stick to the cloth, arrange four glasses around the tray and drape a couple of tea towels or a towel over them like a tent to completely cover the tray. Leave for about 45 minutes until the dough puffs up.

Meanwhile, turn your oven to its highest temperature. In a small bowl, mix the remaining oil with 125 ml (4 fl oz/½ cup) of hot water and 1 teaspoon of salt and stir until the salt dissolves. Make some dimples on the top of the bread with your fingertips and then brush well with the saltwater mixture.

Put in the oven and bake for around 20–30 minutes (depending on the heat of your oven) until the bread is golden, a bit crusty here and there and sounds hollow when tapped. Remove from the oven and cool for a bit before cutting into pieces. This is best warm but can also be served at room temperature, or reheated.

Cuts up into 10-12 pieces

375 ML (13 FL OZ/1 1/2 CUPS) WARM (COMFORTABLE
  TO YOUR FINGERS) WATER
20 G (3/4 OZ) FRESH YEAST, CRUMBLED, OR 10 G
  (1/4 OZ) ACTIVE DRY YEAST
1 TABLESPOON CASTER (SUPERFINE) SUGAR
250 G (9 OZ) WHITE BREAD FLOUR
350 G (12 OZ) WHOLEMEAL (WHOLEWHEAT) FLOUR
4 TABLESPOONS OLIVE OIL

Wholemeal focaccia

Here is a wholemeal version of the focaccia overleaf. You can use any
proportion of wholemeal flour to white, or you could use another type, too,
such as farro (spelt) flour instead of the wholemeal. You could also
incorporate this into the pizza rossa on page 51, swapping some of the
white flour for wholewheat and carrying on with the tomato topping.

Put the water, yeast and sugar in a large bowl with 2 fistfuls of the white flour. Mix
with electric beaters until smooth. Cover and leave for about 30 minutes, until it all
froths up and looks foamy on the top. Add the rest of the plain flour, the wholemeal
flour, half the oil and 1 teaspoon of salt. Mix well with your hands: it will be very
soft, but try to work it without adding more flour. If it's too soft to knead, just slap
it around in the bowl for 4-5 minutes until it starts to feel elastic. Cover the bowl
with a couple of cloths and leave it in a warm and draught-free place for about
1 1/2 hours, or until it has puffed up well.

Lightly oil a 28 x 38 x 4 cm (11 x 15 x 1 1/2 inch) baking tray. Punch down the
dough to flatten it. Spread the dough out gently into the tray, right out to the
edges. If it won't stretch easily, leave it to relax for another 5 minutes and then
gently stretch it out, starting from the centre. Make sure the dough doesn't
break anywhere and that it is spread more or less evenly. Put in a warm
draught-free place. So the dough doesn't stick to the cloth, arrange four glasses
around the tray and drape a couple of tea towels or a towel over them like a tent
to completely cover the tray. Leave for about 45 minutes to 1 hour, until the
dough puffs up.

Meanwhile, turn your oven to its highest temperature. In a small bowl, mix the
remaining oil with 125 ml (4 fl oz/1/2 cup) of hot water and 1 teaspoon of salt and
stir until the salt dissolves. Make some dimples on the top of the bread with your
fingertips and then brush well with the saltwater mixture.

Put in the oven and bake for around 20-30 minutes (depending on the heat of
your oven) until the bread is golden, a bit crusty here and there and sounds hollow
when tapped. Remove from the oven and cool for a bit before cutting into pieces.
This is best warm but can also be served at room temperature, or reheated.

Cuts up into 10-12 pieces

100 ML (3½ FL OZ) WARM (COMFORTABLE TO YOUR
    FINGERS) MILK
100 ML (3½ FL OZ) WARM (COMFORTABLE TO YOUR
    FINGERS) WATER
15 G (½ OZ) FRESH YEAST, CRUMBLED, OR 7 G (¼ OZ)
    ACTIVE DRY YEAST
1 TEASPOON HONEY
400 G (14 OZ) CAKE FLOUR
40 G (1½ OZ) BUTTER, MELTED

TO GLAZE:
1 EGG, LIGHTLY BEATEN WITH A LITTLE MILK
POPPY SEEDS
SESAME SEEDS

Half-moon rolls

My kids love these for breakfast with butter and jam. You can freeze them
easily and take out a couple as you need them. For people who have never
made their own bread and think it sounds daunting, these are so much
easier to make than you would think. You can even freeze the dough once
it's been shaped... that way it has its second rising as it thaws.

Put the milk, water, yeast and honey in a small bowl and stir until the honey melts.
Leave it for about 10 minutes, or until it begins to froth a bit. Put the flour and
½ teaspoon of salt into a larger bowl. Add the yeast mixture and melted butter
and mix through well. Knead for 10 minutes or so until you have a soft elastic ball.
Only add extra flour if the dough is so sticky that it is unkneadable. Cover the bowl
with a cloth and leave it to rise in a warm draught-free place for 1½–2 hours, or
until it has puffed up well. Punch down the dough to flatten it, and roughly divide
it in half.
   On a lightly floured work surface, roll or stretch each piece of dough into a
circle like a pizza base, about 35 cm (14 inches) in diameter and 3 mm (1/8 inch)
thick. If the dough is hard to stretch, leave it for 5 minutes to relax before rolling it
out. Cut each circle into eight wedges like you would cut a pizza. Working with one
wedge at a time, stretch out the two outside corners a little, then roll up the dough
tightly from the outside and finishing at the point of the triangle. With this point to
the top, curve the roll slightly into a crescent shape.
   Line two baking trays with baking paper and arrange 8 rolls on each. Cover
with a cloth and leave to rise in the warm place for 30–45 minutes. Brush with the
egg and scatter seeds over the top.
   Preheat the oven to 180°C (350°F/Gas 4). Bake one tray at a time for about
15 minutes, or until the rolls are lightly golden and the bottoms sound hollow
when tapped. Serve warm or at room temperature with your favourite filling.

Makes 16

PASTRY:
300 G (10½ OZ) PLAIN (ALL-PURPOSE) FLOUR
200 G (7 OZ) BUTTER, CUT INTO BLOCKS
1 SMALL EGG, LIGHTLY BEATEN
50 ML (1¾ FL OZ) MILK
2 TEASPOONS WHITE VINEGAR

FILLING:
120 G (4¼ OZ) FETA
120 G (4¼ OZ) SMOOTH RICOTTA
2 TEASPOONS FINELY GRATED PARMESAN CHEESE
½ TEASPOON DRIED MINT, CRUSHED BETWEEN YOUR
    FINGERS
2 SMALL EGGS
½ TEASPOON SWEET PAPRIKA
ABOUT 1 TEASPOON MILK

Cheese pies

One of these works well as a snack and two or three could be a meal, perhaps served alongside a vegetable soup. You could even add some sautéed chopped leeks or spinach to the cheese filling. Sometimes I sprinkle the pies with sesame seeds after I have brushed them with the egg wash and then I dab at the tops a little more with the egg (I always feel that a few extra vitamins is a good idea wherever possible).

For the pastry, put the flour and butter in a bowl and add ½ teaspoon of salt. Rub the butter into the flour with your fingertips until it is crumbly, like sand. Add the egg and milk and continue working it until it comes together in a loose dough. Then add the vinegar and mix it in well so that the dough forms a loose ball. Flatten it slightly, cover with plastic wrap and refrigerate for an hour or so.

Preheat the oven to 180°C (350°F/Gas 4) and line two baking trays with baking paper (unless you have a very large oven and can fit everything on one big tray).

For the filling, mash the feta with a fork until smooth. Work in the ricotta, parmesan and the mint. Add 1 egg and the paprika and mix well.

Whip the remaining egg and milk together in a small bowl for a glaze. Roll out the pastry on a lightly floured surface to about 3 mm (⅛ inch) thick. Cut 10 cm (4 inch) rounds with a pastry cutter or a glass, cutting them as close to each other as you can. Re-roll the scraps if you need to. Brush around the edges of the pastry circles with the glaze. Dollop a fairly heaped teaspoon of filling in the centre of each one, spreading it out very slightly into an oval (you want enough filling to make your pies tasty — but not so much that it bursts out during cooking).

Flip the pastry over your thumb and forefinger to make half-moons. Stretch out the ends to lengthen and thin them a bit. Press the edges together firmly to seal, then roll them over to make a lip so that no filling can escape.

Put the pies on the trays and brush the tops with glaze. Bake one tray at a time for 20 minutes or so, until the pies have golden tops and bottoms and look ready to eat. Leave to cool for a while — they are best eaten just warm, not piping hot.

Makes about 20 small pies

APPLES FOR SAM

PASTRY:
300 G (10½ OZ/2½ CUPS) PLAIN (ALL-PURPOSE)
  FLOUR
200 G (7 OZ) BUTTER, CUT INTO SMALL BLOCKS
1 EGG, LIGHTLY BEATEN
50 ML (1¾ FL OZ) MILK
2 TEASPOONS WHITE WINE VINEGAR

FILLING:
4 TABLESPOONS OLIVE OIL
1 RED ONION, CHOPPED
3 FRENCH SHALLOTS, CHOPPED
2 GARLIC CLOVES, FINELY CHOPPED
850 G (1 LB 14 OZ) SIRLOIN OR RUMP STEAK IN THICK
  SLICES, TRIMMED AND CUT INTO 3 CM (1¼ INCHES)
  CHUNKS
4 TABLESPOONS PLAIN (ALL-PURPOSE) FLOUR
20 G (¾ OZ) BUTTER
1 TABLESPOON COGNAC
2 TABLESPOONS WORCESTERSHIRE SAUCE
ABOUT 7 ALLSPICE BERRIES
1 EGG YOLK
1 TEASPOON MILK

Steak pie

This is also lovely made into individual pies and you could even add
a few lentils, carrots, potatoes or other vegetables to the filling. I serve
this with some boiled broccoli, potatoes in their skins and zucchini
(courgettes) — all dressed with good olive oil and a small squeeze of
lemon to make an honest square meal. It's also stunning with mash
and peas.

For the pastry, put the flour and butter in a large bowl with ½ teaspoon of salt.
Work the butter into the flour with your fingertips until it is crumbly and looks
like sand. Add the egg and milk and continue working it until it comes together
in a loose dough. Then add the vinegar and mix it in well so that the dough
forms a loose ball. Flatten it slightly, cover with plastic wrap and refrigerate for
an hour or so.
    For the filling, heat half the oil in a large heavy-based pan and sauté the onion
and shallots over medium-low heat until they are nicely golden and sticky, stirring
often so they don't stick. Add the garlic and cook until you can smell it.
    In the meantime, heat the remaining oil in a non-stick frying pan. Toss the
meat pieces in the flour and fry in the oil, in two or three batches, until browned.
Add each batch to the onions as it is done.
    When all the meat is in the pan, add the butter and cook until it melts, then add
the Cognac. When that has evaporated, add the worcestershire sauce. Cook for a
minute or two and then add 500 ml (17 fl oz/2 cups) of hot water. Bring to the
boil, season with salt and pepper and add the allspice berries. Remember how
many you have added so that you can take them all out later. Simmer uncovered
for 30 minutes, stirring now and then.

Add 250 ml (9 fl oz/1 cup) of hot water, put on the lid and simmer slowly for another hour, stirring very often so nothing gets stuck on the bottom of the pan, until you have soft meat and a thick gravy. If you have a simmer mat, this is a good time to use it. Add a little more water if it seems necessary, or cook for longer with the lid off if there is too much liquid. Leave to cool slightly and fish out all the allspice berries.

Preheat your oven to 180°C (350°F/Gas 4). Divide the dough into two, one part slightly larger than the other. Roll out the bigger portion on a lightly floured surface to a thickness of about 3 mm (1/8 inch). Lower it into a 24 cm (91/2 inch) pie dish or springform cake tin, patting it flat against the side of the tin. Spoon in the filling and then trim the dough so that you have a 2-3 cm (1 inch) edge. Roll out the second piece of dough to about 3 mm (1/8 inch) thick, then cut out a neat circle to match the diameter of the tin. Fit this over the meat and then fold the edge of the lower piece of dough over it, pressing the edge gently to seal it.

Mix the egg with the milk and brush generously over the top. If you have any leftover pastry you can make shapes or letters to decorate the top and brush those, too, with the egg wash. Bake for about 45 minutes, until the pastry is crisp and deep golden. Take out of the oven and leave to cool slightly before serving.

Serves 4

I am ironing a shirt, keeping an eye on the cake and the chicken, and an ear outside as the kids are on their bikes. I am praying it will rain so I won't have to water the flowers today and it will cool everyone down a bit.

It is almost time for us to leave for tennis lessons. I notice Yasmine has a hole in her stocking. I call them in 5 minutes early — so that we will only be 5 minutes late — and I hope my petrol is above half. I love it when it is; such freedom. Why didn't I fill it up yesterday when I had those spare two hours?

2 EGGS
3-4 TABLESPOONS PLAIN (ALL-PURPOSE) FLOUR
ABOUT 4 TABLESPOONS DRY BREADCRUMBS
2 THIN HAM SLICES, ROUGHLY THE SAME SIZE AS
  THE BREAD
ABOUT 75 G (2¾ OZ) THINLY SLICED MOZZARELLA
  CHEESE
4 SLICES WHITE BREAD, CRUSTS REMOVED
OLIVE OIL, FOR FRYING

Fried mozzarella sandwiches

This can be a meal in itself. I like to serve it with a tomato salad dressed with olive oil, a drop of balsamic and a couple of torn basil leaves. You can just double up the bread and mozzarella, making as much as you need. Use good white bread and cut it about 1.5 cm (about ⅝ inch) thick. Make these with or without the ham — they are good either way.

Whip the eggs with a little salt in a flattish bowl. Sprinkle the flour over one plate and the breadcrumbs over another.

Make two ham and mozzarella sandwiches, using two slices of bread for each, and using up all the ham and cheese (if you have any mozzarella left over you can nibble at it while you work). Cut each sandwich in half.

Heat enough oil to come about 1 cm (½ inch) up the side of your frying pan. Holding each sandwich together firmly, dip them first in the flour on all sides, then in the egg and then in the breadcrumbs so that they are well coated. Fry them over medium heat until they are golden on both sides. Lift them out onto a plate lined with kitchen paper to soak up the excess oil. Serve immediately.

Serves 2-4, depending on whether it's a meal or a snack

MINI

1 TABLESPOON FINE DRY BREADCRUMBS
250 G (9 OZ) SHORT PASTA SUCH AS PENNE
30 G (1 OZ) THICKLY SLICED HAM, CUT INTO CHUNKS
   OR STRIPS
50 G (1¾ OZ) PARMESAN CHEESE, GRATED

BÉCHAMEL SAUCE:
70 G (2½ OZ) BUTTER
40 G (1½ OZ) PLAIN (ALL-PURPOSE) FLOUR
600 ML (21 FL OZ) MILK, WARMED
FRESHLY GRATED NUTMEG

Macaroni cheese

I have to say that pasta in bianco in some form or another is definitely my children's first choice favourite for dinner. When I make them plain pasta with parmesan and olive oil or butter they smile and behave well. So this is another serveable version of macaroni cheese with parmesan — but you might want to use another cheese, if you prefer. This version also has some chopped up ham added to it and some sautéed peas might be good, too, depending on what you think your family will like. If not, just totally white is also good. You can just put this onto the table and not worry about anything. We also make a plain cheese version often. Here I use short penne, because you can get them into your mouth easily, but you can use any: ordinary penne, rigatoni, macaroni etc... I make it in this fairly small dish as it's not fantastic the next day.

Preheat the oven to 160°C (315°F/Gas 2-3). Grease a 25 x 15 cm (10 x 6 inch) shallow ovenproof dish and scatter the breadcrumbs over it. To make the béchamel, melt 50 g (1¾ oz) of the butter in a small saucepan. Whisk in the flour and cook for a few minutes, stirring constantly, then begin adding the warm milk. It will be immediately absorbed, so work quickly, whisking with one hand while adding ladlefuls of milk with the other. When the sauce seems to be smooth and not too stiff, add salt, pepper and a grating of nutmeg and continue cooking, even after it comes to the boil, for 5 minutes or so, mixing all the time. It should be a very thick and smooth sauce.

Meanwhile, cook the pasta in a large pan of boiling salted water for a little less time than it says on the packet so that it is still a bit firm. Drain well and then tip into a bowl. Add the rest of the butter and half of the béchamel and mix until the butter melts. Scrape half the pasta into the ovenproof dish and level it out. Scatter the ham over the top, then a couple of tablespoons of the parmesan. Top with the rest of the pasta, then spread the remaining béchamel over this. Scatter the rest of the parmesan over the top. Bake for 20-30 minutes, until the top is getting a little bit crusty, then put it under a hot grill (broiler) until it is golden and crisp in places. Serve hot, scooped out in rough squares.

Serves 6

APPLES FOR SAM

500 G (1 LB 2 OZ) CALAMARI, ABOUT 10-12 CM
  (4 INCHES) LONG
ABOUT 500 ML (17 FL OZ/2 CUPS) MILK
100 G (3½ OZ) PLAIN (ALL-PURPOSE) FLOUR
LIGHT OLIVE OIL OR SUNFLOWER OIL, FOR FRYING
LEMON WEDGES, TO SERVE

Fried calamari

I love eating fried food out in a restaurant, but sometimes I make it at home, too. My children like these quite plain — and if you find making chips at the same time is just too much of a job with all that frying, then serve some broken up bits of tender crunchy lettuce hearts with feta and a light drizzling of pink sauce. The important thing here really is the quality of the calamari, which must be tender to start with (although soaking them in the milk first helps make them beautifully tender). You could also add a few shelled prawns here with the calamari. I use a deep wok-type pan for this — you have to take care as the calamari are quite unpredictable and often spit and splutter just as they are ready. If you have a fry cover, use it here.

Clean out the calamari and peel off their skin and wings. Halve the tentacles, if they are large, and cut the bodies into 2-3 cm (1 inch) rings. Rinse them well, put them in a bowl and pour in enough milk to cover them. Cover the bowl and leave it in the fridge for at least a couple of hours, or overnight.

Drain the calamari well and pat them dry. Sprinkle the flour over a plate and season with salt and pepper. Pour enough oil into a wok or pan to comfortably fry the calamari and put it over medium heat. Pat the calamari in the flour so that they are well but lightly covered.

When the oil is hot, fry the calamari in batches, turning them as the undersides become golden and crispy. Take care with the hot oil and jumping calamari — you might need to stand back and reach out with long tongs to turn and lift them out when they are ready. Put them on a plate lined with a couple of layers of kitchen paper to soak up the oil, then transfer them to a clean plate and serve straightaway with lemon wedges and salt.

Serves 4

SAUCE:
40 G (1 ½ OZ) BUTTER
2 GARLIC CLOVES, PEELED AND SQUASHED A BIT
¼ TEASPOON SWEET PAPRIKA
JUICE OF 1 LEMON

ABOUT 4 TABLESPOONS PLAIN (ALL-PURPOSE) FLOUR
2 WHOLE SOLE, ABOUT 200 G (7 OZ) EACH, SKINNED
   AND GUTTED
30 G (1 OZ) BUTTER
1 TABLESPOON CHOPPED PARSLEY

Pan-fried sole with lemon garlic butter

This sauce is also very good over a grilled (broiled) chicken breast or steak. You can make as much or as little of it as you need, but I try to have at least two generous tablespoons per serving. Your fishmonger should be able to skin the fish when he guts them (and you can use different fish, if you prefer). It's best to decide beforehand how you are going to serve the sole — you can cook them ready-filleted, or cook them whole and serve with sauce spooned over and let everyone fillet their own on their plate. They come away from the bone easily, but it's still always worth double-checking for tiny missed bones. They do look impressive served whole — so often I serve them like that, then move the fish to a clean empty plate, quickly fillet it and return the fillets to the plate of sauce. You will need to work quickly, so have everything ready before you start.

For the sauce, put the butter and garlic in a small pan and cook over medium heat until sizzling. Add the paprika, season well with salt, and sizzle a bit more so that the flavours mingle. When it starts looking a bit golden brown, add the lemon juice and cook for a minute longer. Keep warm.
   Sprinkle the flour over a plate and lightly pat both sides of the fish in it. Heat the butter in a large non-stick frying pan and add the fish. Cook over medium-high heat until their undersides are nicely golden. Sprinkle with salt and then gently flip them over. Salt the cooked side and fry until the new underside is golden. Cover the pan with a lid now and cook for a few minutes to make sure the fish are cooked through. If you think there is not enough butter or it is browning too much, then add another blob of butter to the pan. Remove the fish to plates.
   Add about 2 tablespoons of your sauce to the frying pan and heat through to collect the pan flavours. Spoon over the fish and sprinkle with parsley. Serve immediately, with the remaining warm sauce spooned over.

Serves 2

600 G (1 LB 5 OZ/ABOUT 4) POTATOES, SCRUBBED
360 G (12¾ OZ) GOOD-QUALITY MINCED
    (GROUND) BEEF
50 G (1¾ OZ) PARMESAN CHEESE, GRATED
1 EGG
1 TEASPOON SALT
ABOUT 100 G (3½ OZ/1 CUP) DRY BREADCRUMBS
ABOUT 4 TABLESPOONS OLIVE OIL

Mince & potato croquettes

These are very popular and seem to just disappear when there are kids around. You could also add some freshly chopped parsley to the mix.

Put a pan of salted water on to boil. Add the unpeeled potatoes and boil, covered, for about 20 minutes, or until they are soft and completely cooked through. Preheat the oven to 180°C (350°F/Gas 4).

Drain the potatoes and, when they are cool enough, peel them. Mash them well in a wide bowl. Add the mince, parmesan, egg and salt and mix thoroughly with your hands.

Roll into balls about the size of small walnuts and then flatten them a bit into little ovals. Put the breadcrumbs on a plate and pat the croquettes in them to coat both sides. Drizzle about 2 tablespoons of oil over the bottom of a large baking tray, spreading it around with the back of a spoon. Pack the croquettes like tight soldiers on the tray and drizzle lightly with another couple of tablespoons of oil.

Put the tray in the oven and bake the croquettes for about 30 minutes, or until the undersides are nicely golden and a bit crisp. Turn them over gently and bake for another 10 minutes, or longer if necessary, until the new undersides become nicely golden (even a little crisp here and there — but not dried out).

Serve warm or at room temperature with a small scattering of salt, if you think they need it.

Makes about 40 small croquettes

BECHAMEL SAUCE
20 G (³/4 OZ) BUTTER
1 TABLESPOON PLAIN (ALL-PURPOSE) FLOUR
125 ML (4 FL OZ/¹/2 CUP) MILK, WARMED
FRESHLY GRATED NUTMEG

4 LARGE THIN SLICES BEEF, ABOUT 50 G (1³/4 OZ)
   EACH AND 2 MM (¹/16 INCH) THICK
4 THIN SMALL SLICES FONTINA CHEESE OR SIMILAR
4 THIN SMALL SLICES HAM
ABOUT 4 TABLESPOONS PLAIN (ALL-PURPOSE) FLOUR
1 EGG
ABOUT 65 G (2¹/2 OZ/²/3 CUP) DRY BREADCRUMBS
20 G (³/4 OZ) BUTTER
2 TABLESPOONS OLIVE OIL

Escalopes with ham & cheese

This is a definite favourite for most of the kids I hang around with. I serve it with the potato and chickpea mash (page 346) and it's greatly appreciated. The important thing is to have quite large flat slices of meat as you need to fold them over double.

To make the béchamel, melt the butter in a small saucepan. Whisk in the flour and cook for a few minutes, stirring constantly, then begin adding the warm milk. It will be immediately absorbed, so work quickly, whisking with one hand while adding ladlefuls of milk with the other. When the sauce seems to be smooth and not too stiff, add salt, pepper and a grating of nutmeg. Continue cooking, even after it comes to the boil, for 5 minutes or so, mixing all the time. It should be a very thick and smooth sauce. Remove from the heat to cool a little.

Lay a slice of beef flat on a board. Lay a slice of cheese over one half of it and put a slice of ham on top of that. Add a dollop of béchamel and spread it gently to almost cover the ham, but leaving a border all around the edge. Fold the other half of the meat over the béchamel, pressing it down well to seal the edges.

Put the flour on a large plate and season with a twist or two of pepper, if you like. Break the egg into a flat bowl and whisk with a little salt, and put the breadcrumbs on a large plate. Pat the meat parcels gently in the flour, coating both sides, and then dip in the egg, turning them to coat well. Now pat them in the breadcrumbs so that they are well covered.

Heat the butter and oil in a non-stick frying pan over medium-high heat until sizzling. Add the parcels and fry until they start to become firm and are deep golden on the underside. Adjust the heat so they don't burn. Turn over carefully, taking care not to pierce them, and cook the other side. Don't worry if some of the filling starts to ooze out. Lift out onto a plate lined with kitchen paper to soak up the excess oil. Serve warm with a small sprinkling of salt, if necessary.

Serves 4

1 CHICKEN, CUT INTO 10 PIECES, WITH SKIN
2 GARLIC CLOVES, PEELED BUT LEFT WHOLE
2 ROSEMARY STALKS
450 ML (16 FL OZ) BUTTERMILK
ABOUT 125 G (4½ OZ/1 CUP) PLAIN (ALL-PURPOSE)
    FLOUR
2 TEASPOONS SWEET PAPRIKA
LIGHT OLIVE OIL, FOR FRYING
LEMON WEDGES, FOR SERVING

Fried buttermilk marinated chicken

My friend Anabelle told me about this — that the buttermilk makes the chicken really soft and this is the way a lot of proper fried chicken is cooked in the American deep south. You will need to marinate the chicken for 12-24 hours (the longer the better). This dish has a very honest and simple flavour at the end so you might like to add some extras — adults might appreciate some chilli and extra herbs mixed into the paprika flour. You can also do this with skinless chicken breasts — just flatten them out a bit, fry them in the same way and serve them in hamburger buns with lettuce and mayonnaise. Or you could cut the breast into strips, then you might like to make a dip with a bit of mustard, honey, some lemon and salt if your family like to dip into sauces. I like to serve this with the potato and yoghurt salad (page 271) and also the cabbage salad with oranges and lemons (page 89).

Put the chicken pieces in a large bowl. Add the garlic and rosemary, sprinkle with a teaspoon of fine salt and pour in the buttermilk. Turn the chicken over to coat well — it needs to be covered by the buttermilk. Cover with plastic wrap and put into the fridge for at least 12 hours, even for over 24 hours. Turn the chicken once or twice to distribute the flavours.

Pour into a colander to drain (you don't need to keep the buttermilk marinade). Put the flour on a plate and add the paprika and about 1 teaspoon of fine salt. Add pepper, if you like, and mix everything together.

Pour at least 5 cm (2 inches) of oil into a large frying pan over medium heat. Heat until the oil is hot. Pat the chicken in the flour to coat it on all sides, making sure that all the nooks and crannies are covered. Add the chicken to the hot oil and fry until it is crispy and golden. If the chicken seems to be browning too quickly, turn down the heat a little. It is important that the chicken is cooked right through to the bone — use tongs to turn the pieces over a couple of times until you are satisfied that they are deep golden and cooked through. Lift out onto a plate lined with kitchen paper to absorb the excess oil. Serve immediately, with a sprinkling of salt and some lemon wedges to squeeze over the top.

Serves 4

ABOUT 4 TABLESPOONS PLAIN (ALL-PURPOSE) FLOUR
4 CHICKEN ESCALOPES
1 TABLESPOON OLIVE OIL
50 G (1¾ OZ) BUTTER
1 GARLIC CLOVE, PEELED AND SQUASHED A BIT
8 SAGE LEAVES
JUICE OF HALF A LEMON

Chicken escalopes with lemon & butter

Buy chicken escalopes from your butcher, or buy one chicken breast and thinly slice it horizontally into three or four escalopes. It is important not to overcook the chicken — you want to end up with a thin chicken breast with a little sauce to cover it. You will need to have all your ingredients organized before you start, and then this simple dish is ready to serve in a matter of minutes. You can serve them straight from the pan (once the escalopes have cooled a dash). You might also like to throw some finely chopped fresh herbs into the pan at the last moment — parsley, basil, thyme or mint — which will add a totally different flavour.

Put the flour on a plate and dust the chicken on both sides. Heat the oil with roughly a third of the butter in a large non-stick saucepan over medium-high heat. Add the chicken when the pan is sizzling and cook until the underside is lightly golden. Turn over and salt this side. Add the garlic, sage leaves and another third of butter to the pan (this helps to prevent the rest of the butter burning). Cook until the underside of the chicken is golden, turn again and sprinkle lightly with salt. If at any time the garlic or sage look like over-browning, sit them on top of the chicken. Add the last of the butter and, when it all sizzles up, add the lemon juice. Let it bubble up for a minute and then serve immediately with a good spoonful of sauce over each serving and maybe some bread to wipe up the rest of the pan juices. If you can't serve it immediately, put a lid on the pan, then reheat with just a few drops of water to loosen the sauce.

Serves 4

A THIN BUNCH OF PARSLEY, STALKS AS WELL
  AS LEAVES
800 G (1 LB 12 OZ) POTATOES, PEELED
7 PEPPERCORNS
4 TABLESPOONS OLIVE OIL

Boiled potatoes with parsley

These are simple boiled potatoes cooked with parsley stems and dressed later with olive oil. You can use any other herbs you like to just take the edge off plain boiled potatoes. Furthermore, these are good at room temperature, so you can prepare them beforehand for an outdoor occasion. They are lovely with barbecued meats, fish dishes and stews and casseroles.

Bring a large pan of salted water to the boil and add the parsley, potatoes and peppercorns (remembering exactly how many you put in so you can take them all out again and no-one has to bite into one). Boil for about 20 minutes, or until the potatoes are soft and a little crumbly but not totally collapsing. Lift out with a slotted spoon to a serving dish. You can leave behind all the parsley, if you prefer, but I like it when some leaves cling to the potatoes.

Check you've left all the peppercorns in the water. Pour the olive oil over the potatoes, toss gently and taste for salt. Serve warm, but even at room temperature they're good.

Serves 6-8

Remember how many peppercorns you put in a dish, so that you can remember to take them all out again before you serve.
You might do seven — one for every day of the week; three — for the number of children in your family; four — how many times you've been to France...

3 TABLESPOONS OLIVE OIL
8 FRESH BAY LEAVES
25 JUNIPER BERRIES
1 CHICKEN, CUT INTO 10 PIECES, SKIN REMOVED
125 ML (4 FL OZ/½ CUP) WHITE WINE

Sautéed chicken with bay leaves & juniper berries

My friend Francesca, a great and creative cook, taught me this. The fresh bay leaves give a wonderful flavour and smell. With a simple pan of boiled potatoes with parsley (previous page) and green vegetables sautéed in olive oil and garlic, this is the kind of thing I would present to my family on a cool autumn night.

Put the oil, bay leaves and juniper berries in a large non-stick frying pan or flameproof casserole. Put the chicken on the bay leaves, turn the heat to medium and put the lid on the casserole. Cook until the underside of the chicken is lightly golden and the top is white. Turn over and salt and pepper the done side. Add 1 or 2 tablespoons of hot water if the chicken looks like sticking, then cover and cook until the juices have all evaporated. Turn again and salt and pepper lightly.

Squash the juniper berries with a fork to release the flavour, but still keep them fairly intact. Pour in the wine and cook uncovered until the wine has evaporated and the chicken is deep golden on all sides. When there is very little liquid in the pan, and even the bay leaves seem covered by some crusty sauce, turn off the heat, cover and leave to stand for 10 minutes or so before serving.

Serves 4

1 CHICKEN (ABOUT 1.6 KG/3 LB 8 OZ)
4 GARLIC CLOVES, PEELED BUT LEFT WHOLE
ABOUT 10 THYME SPRIGS
3 BAY LEAVES (FRESH, IF POSSIBLE)
1 KG (2 LB 4 OZ) POTATOES, PEELED AND CUT
    INTO CHUNKS
JUICE OF 2 LEMONS
60 G (2¼ OZ) BUTTER, SOFTENED
3 TABLESPOONS POURING (SINGLE) CREAM

Roast chicken & potatoes with thyme, lemon & garlic

This is a lovely roast chicken... with just a dash of cream to bring everything and everyone together. You will need to use a roasting tin that can also be put on the stovetop to heat up the sauce. If you don't have anything suitable, you can transfer all the chicken juices to a small saucepan.

Preheat the oven to 200°C (400°F/Gas 6). Wipe the chicken with paper towels and put breast-side-down in a large roasting tin. Put a little salt, a garlic clove, 3 of the thyme sprigs and 1 of the bay leaves in the cavity of the chicken. Scatter the potatoes and remaining garlic around and pour the lemon juice over the top. Rub the skin of the chicken with some of the butter and dot the rest over the potatoes. Bury the rest of the thyme sprigs under the potatoes, then sprinkle salt over the potatoes and the chicken. Pour 250 ml (9 fl oz/1 cup) of water around the edge of the dish.

Roast for about 1 hour or until the chicken is nicely golden, then turn it over and shuffle the potatoes around. Spoon the pan juices over the top of the chicken and potatoes and scatter some salt over the new top of the chicken. Roast for about 30 minutes, shuffling the potatoes around again halfway through without breaking them up too much, or until the chicken is deep golden and crispy and its juices run clear. Transfer the chicken to a generous serving platter with a bit of a raised edge and arrange the potatoes around the chicken. Keep warm.

Put the roasting tin of cooking juices over medium heat on the stovetop. Using a wooden spoon, scrape up all the golden bits from the sides and bottom of the tin. If there isn't much liquid, add 3-4 tablespoons of water. Bring to the boil and cook until slightly thickened. Stir the cream through and let it all bubble up, whisking so it all comes together as one. Pour over the chicken on the platter and serve immediately.

Serves 4

900 G (2 LB) POTATOES
OLIVE OIL
1 GARLIC CLOVE, PEELED AND SQUASHED A BIT
1 ROSEMARY SPRIG
1 SAGE SPRIG

Pan-fried chips with rosemary & sage

This is a nice and simple version of chips for kids. They are a little more elegant than ordinary chips and you don't have to use much oil and have a smell of frying hanging around your house for a couple of days, which is sometimes a good option.

Peel the potatoes and cut them into fat slices, then into chunks of 3–4 cm (about 1 1/2 inches). If you do this in advance, keep them in a bowl of cold water with a splash of milk so that they don't darken. Drain and dry them well with kitchen paper.

Heat enough oil in a large wide frying pan to generously cover the bottom. Add the potatoes in a single layer and fry them over medium heat, shuffling them after a while when they are golden, and shaking the pan to turn them around so that they cook evenly. You might need to adjust the heat so that they don't brown before cooking through. When they are lightly golden all over, add the garlic clove, rosemary and sage sprigs, making sure they are in the oil. Continue cooking and shuffling the potatoes until they are golden brown, sitting the herbs and garlic on top of the potatoes if they look like they're burning. Lift out the chips with a slotted spoon to a wide serving bowl, scatter with salt and shake them around again so it distributes. Serve now!

Serves 4

1 LOAF WHITE BREAD, UNSLICED
80 G (2¾ OZ) BUTTER, MELTED
100 G (3½ OZ/⅓ CUP) RUNNY HONEY
20 G (¾ OZ) LIGHT BROWN SUGAR
50 G (1¾ OZ) PECANS, CHOPPED

White loaf with honey, butter & pecans

I use a home-made white loaf (page 263) to make this. If you prefer, you can use an unsliced bought one — white sourdough is good. My friend Sue taught me how to make this. I think it's fantastic — especially for a picnic.

Preheat the oven to 180°C (350°F/Gas 4) and line a baking tray with baking paper. Remove the crusts from the bread and cut it in half horizontally to give two layers (if your loaf is extra high, you can make three layers). Put the pieces on the tray.

Mix the butter, honey, sugar and pecans to get a gooey mixture. Pour and spread over the tops of the two bread halves. Bake for about 30 minutes, until the bread is crusty and golden on top (don't burn it or the nuts will be bitter). Let it cool a dash, then cut into thick fingers. It will crisp up and become crunchier.

Makes about 16 fingers

---

50 G (1¾ OZ) BROWN SUGAR
20 G (¾ OZ) BUTTER
1 TABLESPOON MAPLE SYRUP
4 OR 5 DROPS OF VANILLA EXTRACT
125 ML (4 FL OZ/½ CUP) POURING (SINGLE) CREAM

Toffee sauce

This is good warm, drizzled over an ice cream sundae or a bowl of Greek yoghurt with some chunks of apple. You can leave it to cool in the pot and warm it up just slightly to serve.

Put the sugar, butter, syrup and vanilla in a small pan and cook over very low heat for a few minutes until it all turns a good, deep toffee colour. Add the cream, drop by drop at first, mixing it in with a wooden spoon. Cook until the sauce is bubbling up and has a lovely colour. Be careful not to burn yourself while you're tasting it.

Makes 125 ml (4 fl oz/½ cup)

180 G (6½ OZ) BUTTER, SOFTENED
150 G (5½ OZ/⅔ CUP) CASTER (SUPERFINE)
  SUGAR, PLUS 1½ TABLESPOONS FOR THE TOP
1 TEASPOON VANILLA EXTRACT
1 TEASPOON FINELY GRATED LEMON RIND
A GOOD PINCH OF GROUND CARDAMOM
A LARGE PINCH OF NUTMEG
3 EGGS
220 G (7¾ OZ/1¾ CUPS) PLAIN (ALL-PURPOSE)
  FLOUR
1½ TEASPOONS BAKING POWDER
125 ML (4 FL OZ/½ CUP) POURING (SINGLE)
  CREAM
4 SMALL RIPE PEARS, ABOUT 700 G (1 LB 9 OZ)

Pear
butter cake

This is rich and delicious and you can use just about any fruit you like.
Serve it in a bowl with a bit of warm custard or a dollop of thick cream
— or the way I like it, which is completely on its own. You can use
buttermilk instead of the cream or just milk. Leave out the spices if you
like something plainer, or add a little more if you prefer your cake spicier.

Preheat the oven to 180°C (350°F/Gas 4) and grease a 24 cm (9½ inch) springform cake tin.
    Beat the butter and sugar together until creamy. Add the vanilla, lemon rind,
cardamom and nutmeg and then add the eggs one by one, beating well after each
one. Add the sifted flour and baking powder alternately with the cream and mix
until you have a smooth batter.
    Scrape out every drop into the cake tin. You don't need to be particular about
levelling the surface because it will spread evenly during the baking. Bake for
about 20 minutes.
    Meanwhile, peel, quarter and core the pears. Take the cake from the oven and
quickly scatter the pears over the top. Sprinkle with the 1½ tablespoons of sugar.
Return to the oven and bake for another 45 minutes or so more, until the pears
are lovely and golden in places, the cake is crusty and a skewer poked into the
middle comes out clean.
    Cool slightly before cutting and serving warm or at room temperature. Keep
the cake covered tightly with foil, so that it doesn't harden and you can then warm
it through to serve.

Serves 10-12

CARAMEL:
120 G (4¼ OZ) CASTER (SUPERFINE) SUGAR

700 ML (24 FL OZ) MILK
1 CINNAMON STICK
100 G (3½ OZ) FINE SEMOLINA
55 G (2 OZ) CASTER (SUPERFINE) SUGAR
½ TEASPOON VANILLA EXTRACT
1 EGG

Semolina puddings with caramel

Make these in little individual pudding pots — they look like tiny cream caramels. If you are up in time, they make a wonderful breakfast.

Preheat the oven to 170°C (325°F/Gas 3) and butter six 125 ml (4 fl oz/½ cup) ovenproof pots.

For the caramel, put the sugar and 2–3 teaspoons of water in a heavy-based non-stick pan over medium heat. Heat it up until the sugar starts to melt, then tilt the pan to swirl it around — don't stir or the sugar will crystallize. Carry on heating and swirling a few times until all the sugar has melted and turned golden caramel brown. Pour about 1 tablespoon into the bottom of each pot, swirling the pot at the same time so that the caramel covers the bottom evenly.

Put the milk and cinnamon stick in a large heavy-based saucepan over medium heat. Just before it comes to the boil, whisk in the semolina in a thin steady stream so that no lumps form. Lower the heat and simmer, whisking all the time, for around 8 minutes, or until the milk has absorbed all the semolina. Stir in the sugar and vanilla and remove from the heat. Sit the saucepan in a sink of cold water for 15 minutes to cool it down a little.

Whip the egg lightly in a bowl and then whisk it into the semolina. Spoon over the caramel in the pots, smoothing the top with the back of your spoon. Put all the pots in a baking dish and then pour enough hot water into the dish to come halfway up the side of the pots. Carefully move to the oven and bake for about 45 minutes, until the puddings look set, golden and slightly puffed up. Take the pots out of the dish and leave them to cool for a bit.

Upturn the pots and turn the puddings out onto individual plates. If you sit the bottoms of the empty pots in boiling water for a few minutes you'll be able to get more caramel out of them. The puddings are best served warm, with as much caramel as possible drizzled over them.

Serves 6

1 TABLESPOON CASTER (SUPERFINE) SUGAR
1 EGG
A FEW DROPS OF VANILLA EXTRACT
20 G (³/4 OZ) BUTTER, MELTED
125 G (4¹/2 OZ/1 CUP) PLAIN (ALL-PURPOSE) FLOUR
1 TEASPOON BAKING POWDER
125 ML (4 FL OZ/¹/2 CUP) MILK
BUTTER, FOR FRYING

Crumpets

These are good and quick for breakfast or an afternoon snack. I remember
them fondly from when I was young. This small amount is just sufficient, I
find, for my family, as they need to be served immediately. It's easy enough
to double the quantities if you're serving a crowd, just make sure everyone
is waiting at their plate to drizzle their crumpet with honey or spread with
jam and cream. Actually, I remember crumpets as ESPECIALLY good with
a little drizzle of honey or syrup and a small dollop of vanilla ice cream.

Whisk together the sugar, egg and vanilla until foamy. Whisk in the melted butter
and then add the flour and baking powder. Pour in the milk, whisking it all
together to make a smooth, thick batter.
    Melt a little butter in a non-stick frying pan — just enough to coat the bottom.
When it is sizzling, drop in tablespoons of batter, allowing enough room between
them so that you can turn them over easily. Fry over medium heat until air
bubbles appear on the surface and the bottoms are golden and set. Flip them over
with a spatula and fry the other side. When the new undersides are golden brown,
lift them onto a plate with your spatula and cook the rest of the batter, adding
more butter to the pan as it is needed. Make sure that the pan keeps a steady heat
and doesn't get too hot. Serve immediately.

Makes 20

2 EGGS, SEPARATED
80 G (2³/4 OZ/¹/3 CUP) CASTER (SUPERFINE) SUGAR
¹/2 TEASPOON VANILLA EXTRACT
60 G (2¹/4 OZ) BUTTER, MELTED
180 G (6¹/2 OZ/1¹/2 CUPS) PLAIN (ALL-PURPOSE)
   FLOUR
¹/2 TEASPOON BAKING POWDER
185 ML (6 FL OZ/³/4 CUP) MILK

Waffles

Ideally, you need a waffle-iron to make these. If you are lucky enough to
have one — great. If not, you can make them in a frying pan as below, or
you could even just fry little spoonfuls, flick your wrist a bit here and
there and serve up crisp little make-believe waffles. And, if you're really
pushed for time, you can just mix all the ingredients together without
even whisking the egg whites, although your waffles won't be quite so
light and cloud-like. I like to serve these with cranberry syrup (page 15),
filling up all the holes of the waffles. Otherwise, butter and jam or honey,
golden syrup and a blob of whipped cream, or chocolate sauce are all
fantastic… you decide.

Whisk the egg whites until they are fluffy and just holding soft peaks. In a larger
bowl, whisk the egg yolks with the sugar and vanilla until creamy. Whisk in the
butter, then the flour and baking powder. Add the milk, then fold in the egg whites.
   Heat a waffle-iron or a non-stick frying pan and brush with a little butter. If
you're using a waffle-iron, add about 4 tablespoons of batter into each space and
close the machine. Cook, following the manufacturer's instructions, until the
waffles are golden brown.
   If you're using a frying pan, ladle about 4 tablespoons of mixture into the
middle of the pan. Cook over medium heat until the underside is golden and the
top has formed air holes. Flip over and cook the other side. When the waffle is deep
golden and crispy in places, lift it out onto a plate and keep warm while you make
the rest. Serve hot.

Makes 10-12

2 EGGS
1/2 TEASPOON VANILLA EXTRACT
1 TABLESPOON CASTER (SUPERFINE) SUGAR
100 G (3½ OZ) PLAIN (ALL-PURPOSE) FLOUR
1 TEASPOON BAKING POWDER
250 ML (9 FL OZ/1 CUP) MILK
BUTTER, FOR FRYING

TO SERVE:
FRESHLY WHIPPED CREAM
CASTER (SUPERFINE) SUGAR
LEMON WEDGES
MAPLE SYRUP
GROUND CINNAMON

Pancakes

I use a small non-stick frying pan about 20 cm (8 inches) in diameter for these. The batter makes about 10–12 pancakes, which are not huge, and if your frying pan is bigger you'll get less. This makes just enough for our family of four (allowing for one or two leftovers), with two each being just about perfect for the children. We often have our first one with lemon juice and a scattering of cinnamon sugar and our second with maple syrup and whipped cream. If we make it to the third one, then that's nice with a dollop of home-made jam. Often, if I make the pancakes for dinner, I put a little leftover batter in the fridge for the next morning, when I make a couple for the kids with jam. If the batter looks a bit thick after a night in the fridge, just thin it down with a little milk. A pinch or two of ground aniseed in the batter is a nice addition that even children seem to like.

Whip together the eggs, vanilla and sugar. Add the flour and baking powder alternately with the milk, whisking well until it's smooth. Cover and leave to stand at room temperature for at least half an hour.

Melt a little butter in a non-stick frying pan — just enough to coat the bottom. When it's sizzling, add a small ladleful of batter. Tilt the pan so that the batter swirls out and around to thinly cover the bottom, mingling with some of the butter. Fry over medium heat until the underside is nicely golden, using a spatula to lift up the edge to check. Loosen the side with the spatula and flip the pancake over. Fry until the new underside is lightly golden, then slide out of the pan onto a plate and keep warm while you cook the rest of the batter, adding more butter when you need it. The first pancake is often not so great, but once you've got the hang of it and have got the pan temperature perfect, they'll work well.

Put out bowls of whipped cream, caster sugar, lemon wedges, maple syrup and enough cinnamon for everyone to help themself to their own favourite topping. Make cinnamon sugar by mixing 3 teaspoons of sugar with 1 teaspoon of cinnamon, and that's lovely with a squeeze of lemon juice over the top.

Makes 12 pancakes

white

Granola
Leek & potato soup
Semolina soup with butter & sage
White milk bread or rolls
Thin pizza with stracchino cheese
Ricotta gnocchi with tomato pesto
White risotto in spinach broth
Pasta with cheese
Potato and yoghurt salad
Baked fish parcels
Vanilla cake
Honey cake
Vanilla yoghurt ice cream
Lemon rice pudding with roasted peaches
Baked cinnamon apples with buttermilk
  ice cream

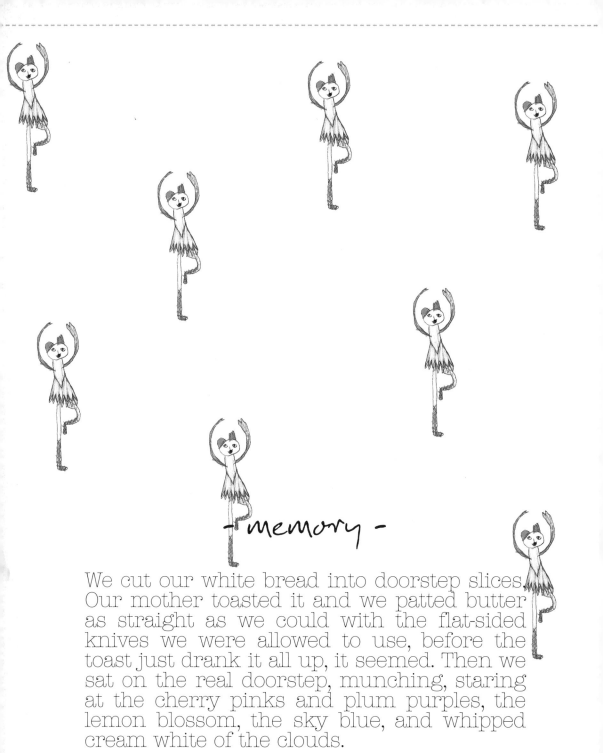

– memory –

We cut our white bread into doorstep slices.
Our mother toasted it and we patted butter
as straight as we could with the flat-sided
knives we were allowed to use, before the
toast just drank it all up, it seemed. Then we
sat on the real doorstep, munching, staring
at the cherry pinks and plum purples, the
lemon blossom, the sky blue, and whipped
cream white of the clouds.

200 G (7 OZ) QUICK-COOKING OATS
4 TABLESPOONS SUNFLOWER SEEDS
2 TABLESPOONS SESAME SEEDS
50 G (1¾ OZ) SHELLED WALNUTS, CHOPPED
½ TEASPOON CINNAMON OR GROUND ALLSPICE
80 G (2¾ OZ) LIGHT BROWN SUGAR
125 ML (4 FL OZ/½ CUP) RUNNY HONEY
40 G (1½ OZ) BUTTER

Granola

This is a healthy breakfast topped with some thick natural yoghurt and fresh sliced fruit, and is always good splashed with cold milk. It is great to have at home and even serves as an emergency snack. You can use any nuts in place of the walnuts here, and add other ingredients or vary these to your liking. You can make more than the amounts given here and keep it in an airtight container or glass jar — but remember before baking it that it needs to be spread out in a flat, fairly thin layer on your trays.

Preheat the oven to 160°C (315°F/Gas 2–3) and grease two large baking trays. Put the oats, sunflower seeds, sesame seeds, walnuts and cinnamon in a bowl. Put the sugar, honey and butter in a pan and heat, stirring, until the butter has melted. Pour over the oat mixture in the bowl and mix well. (I like to do this with my hands and then get the children to take over, but you can mash it around with a wooden spoon, if you like, until it feels like wet sticky sand.)
    Put half the mixture on each baking tray, spreading it out and then pressing it into a thin layer. Put both trays in the oven and bake for about 20 minutes. Turn the mixture over with a spoon and return the trays to the oven, the bottom one now on the top. Bake for another 15–20 minutes, or just until the granola is deep golden, turning it again during this time to give it an even colour and break it up slightly (although it's nice if a few clustery bits remain). Take care not to overcook it, as just a bit past perfect can make it taste bitter. Turn off the oven and leave it in for another 10 minutes or so, then get it out of the oven and leave it to cool completely on the trays. Once cool, this keeps very well in a biscuit tin or something else airtight.

Makes 600 g (1 lb 5 oz/4 cups)

6 LEEKS
40 G (1 1/2 OZ) BUTTER
2 GARLIC CLOVES, PEELED BUT LEFT WHOLE
2 TEASPOONS BRANDY
600 G (1 LB 5 OZ) POTATOES, PEELED AND CUT
   INTO CHUNKS
FRESHLY GRATED NUTMEG
100 ML (3 1/2 FL OZ) SINGLE (POURING) CREAM
GRATED PARMESAN, TO SERVE

Leek & potato soup

This lovely warm soup is a simple classic combination, but one might not imagine that children could eat leeks so readily. You can add depth here by using chicken stock instead of water, or adding a few basic vegetables to the pot, but I like the purity of this recipe. Follow with a sautéed chicken breast with a couple of drops of white wine, or a simple fish fillet in herbs.

Trim the leeks and cut off the harder ends — you'll need about 400 g (14 oz) of trimmed leek. Slice the leeks quite finely and put them in the sink with cold water. Swish them around with your hands to get rid of any dirt. Scoop them up into a colander to drain and wash them again if they are still sandy.

Melt the butter in a fairly large pan. Add the leeks and garlic and sauté over medium-low heat until all the water has evaporated and the leeks are soft and faintly golden. Add the brandy and carry on cooking until it has evaporated. Add the potatoes and season well with salt. Add 1.5 litres (52 fl oz/6 cups) of hot water and bring to the boil. Turn down the heat slightly, cover with a lid and simmer for about 45 minutes, or until the leeks and potatoes are very soft. Grate in a little nutmeg. Purée the soup until it is totally smooth. If it is too thick for your taste, add a little hot water. If it seems too thin, return it to the pan and cook uncovered until it has thickened a bit. Taste for seasoning and add salt if necessary. Add the cream, heat through and serve immediately, with a good tablespoon of parmesan sprinkled over each serve.

Adults should grind pepper over theirs and, ideally, top with a few very fine slices of truffle!

Serves 6

1.25 LITRES (44 FL OZ/5 CUPS) MEAT, CHICKEN OR
  VEGETABLE BROTH
150 G (5½ OZ) FINE SEMOLINA
100 G (3½ OZ) BUTTER
6 OR 7 SAGE LEAVES
2 TABLESPOONS GRATED PARMESAN CHEESE
GRATED PARMESAN CHEESE, TO SERVE

Semolina soup with butter & sage

This is a great emergency meal — ready in a few moments. If you use broth (meat, vegetable or chicken) you will have a more profound tasting bowl of semolina, but if you don't have any to hand you can use a cube, as I sometimes do, from a health food shop, with no additives. Like this, it is simple, quite delicious and just easy to eat. The semolina can be made to any consistency you like: thicker or thinner and more soupy than this version. This is a simple Italian standard that I have seen served to children, elderly folk and even invalids — whenever easy eating is required — and just with lashings of olive oil and parmesan instead of the golden butter and sage. The pot will clean easily if you fill it with hot soapy water and leave it to soak for a while.

Put the broth in a large saucepan and bring to the boil (if you are using water, add 1½ teaspoons of salt). Pour in the semolina in a thin and steady stream, mixing with a wooden spoon and continuing to stir while it thickens. Lower the heat slightly so that it doesn't splutter up, and then cook for a few minutes, stirring all the time.

Take half the butter and melt a little knob of it in a small frying pan and then fry the sage leaves over medium heat until they crisp up. As the butter starts to turn golden, keep adding more, bit by bit, to slow down the cooking and burning process. Remove from the heat when the leaves are crisp and you have used up half of the butter. Keep the pan to one side.

Keep stirring the semolina so that there are no lumps and nothing gets stuck. Simmer gently for about 10 minutes until there are air bubbles glooping on the surface. Stir in the 2 tablespoons of parmesan and the other half of the butter. If it is too thick for your taste, stir in hot water as needed. Taste for salt.

Ladle into bowls, drizzle a little sage butter into each and add a sage leaf or two and another scattering of grated parmesan. Adults can add a good grind of pepper. Eat immediately.

Serves 4

250 ML (9 FL OZ/1 CUP) WARM (COMFORTABLE TO
   YOUR FINGERS) MILK
15 G (½ OZ) FRESH YEAST, CRUMBLED, OR 7 G (¼ OZ)
   ACTIVE DRY YEAST
1 TEASPOON HONEY
450 G (1 LB) BREAD FLOUR
1 EGG, LIGHTLY BEATEN
40 G (1½ OZ) BUTTER, MELTED

White milk
bread or rolls

You can make this as one loaf or shape into smaller rolls. Children love
small soft white rolls, it seems. Naturally, you can make different sizes, or
a different shape — long are nice for hot dogs. You can easily make a
batch and freeze them in small bags, a few together, to whip out at almost
the last moment of need. My kids like these with butter spread so thickly
that they can see their teeth marks.

Put the milk, yeast and honey in a small bowl and stir until the honey melts.
Leave it for about 10 minutes, or until it begins to froth a bit. Put the flour and
½ teaspoon of salt into a larger bowl. Add the yeast mixture, the egg and butter
and mix through well. Knead for 10 minutes or so and, if it seems sticky, just hold
the bowl firmly and move the dough around with your hand, rather than add more
flour. Cover the bowl with a cloth and leave in a warm draught-free place to rise for
1½-2 hours, or until it has puffed up well.
   Lightly grease a 30 x 11 cm (12 x 4 inch) loaf tin and dust it with flour. Punch
down the dough to flatten it and shape it into a rough loaf of a size to fit the tin.
Cover with a cloth and leave in the warm place for another 45-60 minutes, or until
it puffs right up in the tin. Meanwhile, preheat the oven to 190°C (375°F/Gas 5).
   Put the tin in the oven and bake for about 25 minutes, or until the top is firm
and crusty and the loaf sounds hollow when tapped. Remove from the oven, knock
the loaf out of the tin and cool on a rack in a fly-free zone.
   This is best sliced warm and spread with butter, but you can keep the loaf for a
few days in an airtight container (not a plastic bag) for excellent toast.

Makes 1 loaf or about 18 small rolls

DOUGH:
185 ML (6 FL OZ/³/4 CUP) WARM (COMFORTABLE TO
   YOUR FINGERS) WATER
12 G (½ OZ) FRESH YEAST, CRUMBLED, OR 7 G (¼ OZ)
   ACTIVE DRY YEAST
½ TEASPOON HONEY
½ TABLESPOON OLIVE OIL
300 G (10½ OZ) BREAD FLOUR

TOPPING:
250 G (9 OZ) FRESH STRACCHINO CHEESE
170 ML (5½ FL OZ/²/3 CUP) MILK
1 TABLESPOON OLIVE OIL

Thin pizza with stracchino cheese

My friend Julia showed me this. This amount of dough will make you two pizza bases — you can freeze the unused half of dough once it has been punched down. Stracchino is a sour creamy cheese.

For the dough, put the water, yeast, honey and oil in a large bowl with a fistful of the flour. Mix with electric beaters until smooth. Cover and leave for 30 minutes or so until it all froths up and looks foamy on the top. Add the rest of the flour and ½ teaspoon of salt. Mix well with your hands — it will be very soft, but try to work it without adding more flour. If it's too soft to knead, just slap it around in the bowl for a few minutes until it starts to feel elastic. Cover the bowl with a couple of cloths and leave it in a warm and draught-free place for about 1½ hours, or until the dough has puffed up well.

Preheat the oven to its highest temperature. Lightly brush a 30 cm (12 inch) round, square or rectangular baking tray with olive oil. Punch down the dough to flatten it and divide it in half to make two bases, or freeze half.

Spread the dough out gently on the tray to give a thin even base. If it won't stretch easily, leave it to relax for 5 minutes and then gently stretch it out with the palms of your hands, starting from the centre.

For the topping, put the cheese, milk and oil in a blender or processor and pulse until smooth. Gently spread over the top of the dough, almost to the edge but leaving a small border. Turn this border in and over the cheese topping. Bake for 20–25 minutes (depending on the heat of your oven) until the top is quite deep golden in various places. Remove and cool for a few minutes before cutting into squares. Eat warm.

Serves 8–10

500 G (1 LB 2 OZ) GOOD-QUALITY RICOTTA CHEESE
2 TABLESPOONS GRATED PARMESAN CHEESE
100 G (3½ OZ) PLAIN (ALL-PURPOSE) FLOUR
1 QUANTITY TOMATO PESTO (BELOW), TO SERVE
BUTTER AND GRATED PARMESAN CHEESE, TO SERVE

Ricotta gnocchi

I learnt these from Giacomo, one of my brother-in-laws. They are palest white, cloud-soft and delicate and need to be served the minute they are cooked. We normally have these with the tomato pesto, below, but they are also great with just butter, sage and parmesan.

If you are serving these with tomato pesto, make sure it is ready before you cook the gnocchi.

Bring a large pan of salted water to the boil. Mix together the ricotta, parmesan, flour and a pinch of salt in a large bowl. With lightly floured hands, roll out the dough into thin sausages (about 1.5 cm/⁵⁄8 inch thick). Try to avoid adding extra flour or your gnocchi will be tough. Cut with a sharp knife into little dumplings about 2 cm (³⁄4 inch) long.

Drop the gnocchi into the boiling water and cook for about 45 seconds until they float to the surface. As they bob up, lift them out with a slotted spoon and put them into warmed serving bowls. If you need to, stir a couple of tablespoons of the cooking water through the pesto to give a good coating consistency, and spoon a dollop over each serve. Add a little butter and grated parmesan and serve at once.

Serves 4

---

100 ML (3½ FL OZ) OLIVE OIL
2 GARLIC CLOVES, PEELED
400 G (14 OZ) TINNED DICED TOMATOES
25 G (1 OZ/½ CUP) BASIL LEAVES, TORN
3 TABLESPOONS PINE NUTS
30 G (1 OZ) PARMESAN CHEESE, GRATED

Tomato pesto

Heat 2 tablespoons of the olive oil in a saucepan with one of the garlic cloves. When it sizzles, add the tomato and season with salt. Simmer over medium heat for about 15 minutes until the tomato thickens and becomes smooth, crushing it up with a wooden spoon from time to time.

Finely chop the other garlic clove and put it in a small processor or blender with the basil leaves and pine nuts. Pulse until finely chopped. Add the remaining olive oil and the parmesan and pulse just long enough to combine. Stir into the tomato sauce and heat for about 20-30 seconds. Fish out the whole garlic clove before serving.

Note: if you are making the tomato pesto in advance, keep the pesto separate and add to the heated tomato sauce just before serving.

Serves 4

1 LITRE (35 FL OZ/4 CUPS) SPINACH COOKING WATER
3 TABLESPOONS OLIVE OIL
1 SMALL RED ONION, PEELED BUT LEFT WHOLE
300 G (10½ OZ) RISOTTO RICE
50 G (1¾ OZ) PARMESAN CHEESE, GRATED
30 G (1 OZ) BUTTER
A LITTLE FRESHLY GRATED NUTMEG
GRATED PARMESAN CHEESE, TO SERVE

White risotto in spinach broth

Just a suggestion for what to do with your spinach cooking water. My children's favourite food is white rice or pasta with parmesan and olive oil or butter. Boiling the pasta with a spinach or other vegetable broth, I feel, makes it more tasty and healthy. So, next time you boil broccoli or spinach, save the cooking water. I often boil the spinach quickly to fill an omelette as a second course, then cook rice in the water for a first-course risotto.

Put the spinach broth in a large pan and bring to the boil, then reduce the heat to keep it at a slow simmer. Heat the oil in another large saucepan. Add the onion and rice and cook over medium–high heat for about 30 seconds, stirring to coat the rice with oil. Reduce the heat to low and stir in a ladleful of hot broth. Season with salt (depending on whether your broth is already seasoned) and, when the broth has been absorbed, stir in another ladleful.

Continue in this way for about 20 minutes until the broth has been used up and the rice is soft but still a little bit firm in the centre. If you run out of spinach broth before the rice is tender just carry on with boiling water. This risotto is best when it's left a little liquidy, like a thick soup. Check for salt, fish out the onion and stir in the parmesan, butter and nutmeg. When the butter has melted, ladle the risotto into serving bowls and serve immediately with extra parmesan and black pepper for whoever wants it.

Serves 4

350 G (12 OZ) PASTA (I LIKE PENNE OR RIGATONI)
400 G (14 OZ) SMOOTH SHEEPS' MILK RICOTTA
ABOUT 150 ML (5 FL OZ) MILK
70 G (2½ OZ) GRATED PARMESAN OR PECORINO
   CHEESE
FRESHLY GRATED NUTMEG
GRATED PARMESAN CHEESE, TO SERVE

Pasta
with cheese

My kids just love anything that looks quite white and simple, so this is a
very basic recipe that you can build on, even adding some cooked peas or
zucchini (courgettes). You can add any cheese you like to the basic ricotta
mixture: mascarpone, mozzarella, pecorino, parmesan... Adults might like
some gorgonzola or similar added to theirs. My friend Caterina used a
mature pecorino, which was stunning.

Bring a large pot of salted water to the boil and cook the pasta, following the
instructions on the packet.
   Put the ricotta in a large serving bowl, add the milk and whisk the two together
with a fork. Add the parmesan or pecorino, a good grind of nutmeg and about
½ teaspoon of salt, tasting to see if it needs more. Whisk well.
   Drain the pasta, saving a few tablespoons of the water, and put with the ricotta
mixture in the serving bowl. Toss through well, adding a little of the cooking water
if it seems very dry. Serve immediately, with some extra parmesan and a few
twists of black pepper for the adults.

Serves 4

700 G (1 LB 9 OZ) POTATOES
500 G (1 LB 2 OZ/2 CUPS) NATURAL YOGHURT
½ TEASPOON GROUND CUMIN
½ TEASPOON DRIED MINT
½ RED OR YELLOW PEPPER (CAPSICUM), CHOPPED
1 SMALL FRENCH SHALLOT, FINELY CHOPPED

Potato &
yoghurt salad

I love this with schnitzelly things but it's also good for barbecues and picnics. This is the kind of salad I ate so many times when I was young, only with mayonnaise. I make it often with yoghurt now, as it's lighter. You can add anything else that you feel may be appreciated — some boiled carrots or peas, green beans, parsley or chopped boiled egg.

Bring a pan of salted water to the boil and cook the potatoes until they are tender. Drain, leave them to cool a bit and then peel. When they have completely cooled, cut them into small blocks.
  Mix the yoghurt, cumin and mint in a large serving bowl and season to taste with salt and pepper. Add the potatoes, pepper and shallot and mix through well, taking care not to mash up the potatoes.

Serves 6

The girl across the road from us had a TV when they had just come out. We sat on the open veranda with the TV moved out almost into the garden, eating a boiled potato salad that had many — too many, now that I think about it — spoonfuls of mayonnaise. We sat there for ages watching everything and anything in black and white.

ABOUT 55 G (2 OZ/½ CUP) DRY BREADCRUMBS
4 THICK FIRM WHITE FISH FILLETS (ABOUT
    120 G/4¼ OZ EACH), BONES REMOVED
4 THICK SLICES OF LEMON, RIND REMOVED
125 ML (4 FL OZ/½ CUP) OLIVE OIL
2 LARGE GARLIC CLOVES, PEELED AND HALVED
8 SMALL THYME SPRIGS
4 TABLESPOONS RED WINE

Baked fish parcels

This is really an example rather than a recipe, because once you have made these a couple of times you'll find it easy to go off and add your own choice of the herbs and spices that you know will be loved in your own household. I like this with plain boiled potatoes with parsley (page 233). Try it with salmon instead of white fish.

Preheat the oven to 200°C (400°F/Gas 6). Cut four pieces of foil or baking paper, quite a bit larger than your fish fillets. Put the breadcrumbs on a plate and pat the fish in them to coat both sides. Sprinkle the fish lightly with salt and put each fillet on a separate piece of foil. Put a lemon slice on top, drizzle with a scant tablespoon of oil and put a garlic half and 2 thyme sprigs on each.

Close up the parcels so that you will be able to open them easily: hold the top sides of the foil up and then fold or roll them down. Fold in the ends to seal them. Drizzle the rest of the oil over the bottom of your oven dish. Put the fish parcels in the dish and bake for about 20 minutes. You should be able to smell the cooked fish, but I usually gently open one parcel with a fork and spoon, just to check that it is cooked, and then seal it up again. Wait for 3-4 minutes (so that the oil doesn't spit) then drizzle the wine into the dish and put it back into the oven. When you start to hear activity from the oil, in about 3 or 4 minutes, remove the dish from the oven again. The wine will have reduced to almost nothing, but adds a lovely perfume to the fish. Serve the parcels immediately, unopened, helping children to open their packages and not get too close to the steam.

Serves 4

WHITE

250 G (9 OZ) BUTTER, SOFTENED
250 G (9 OZ) CASTER (SUPERFINE) SUGAR
3 EGGS
1 TEASPOON VANILLA EXTRACT
290 G (10¼ OZ) PLAIN (ALL-PURPOSE) FLOUR
1½ TEASPOONS BAKING POWDER
185 ML (6 FL OZ/¾ CUP) POURING (SINGLE) CREAM,
    MILK OR BUTTERMILK

ICING:
100 G (3½ OZ) BUTTER, SOFTENED
200 G (7 OZ) ICING (CONFECTIONERS') SUGAR
1 TEASPOON VANILLA EXTRACT
ABOUT 3 TABLESPOONS MILK

Vanilla cake

I love this mattressy and soft cake. Here it is plain with a beautiful white icing, but on occasion you could slice it in half through its equator and fill it with some whipped cream and a layer of not-too-sweet jam. The kids appreciate it when I stick sweets all over the icing. Or you could make a chocolate icing and stick raspberries into that.

Preheat the oven to 180°C (350°F/Gas 4) and grease a 24 cm (9½ inch) spring-form cake tin.

Beat the butter and sugar together very well in a large bowl. Add the eggs one at a time, beating well after each one goes in. Add the vanilla and then sift in the flour and baking powder. Beat well, adding the cream or milk a little at a time. You will have a thick and creamy batter. Scrape it out into the cake tin and bake for about 45 minutes, or until a skewer poked into the centre comes out clean. Leave to cool completely before filling and icing.

For the icing, put the butter into a bowl and gradually beat in the icing sugar. Add the vanilla and 2 tablespoons of milk and beat well, then slowly beat in the rest of the milk, stopping when you have a smooth but fairly stiff icing. Gently spread it all over the cake — it doesn't have to be perfect.

Cuts into 10–12 slices

150 G (5½ OZ) BUTTER
115 G (4 OZ/½ CUP) DARK BROWN SUGAR
175 G (6 OZ/½ CUP) HONEY
200 G (7 OZ/1⅔ CUPS) PLAIN (ALL-PURPOSE) FLOUR
1½ TEASPOONS BAKING POWDER
½ TEASPOON GROUND CINNAMON
1 TABLESPOON FINELY CHOPPED ROSEMARY LEAVES
2 EGGS, BEATEN

LEMON ICING:
250 G (9 OZ/2 CUPS) ICING (CONFECTIONERS') SUGAR
100 G (3½ OZ) BUTTER, SOFTENED
1 TEASPOON GRATED LEMON ZEST
2 TABLESPOONS LEMON JUICE

Honey cake

I love the idea of children having honey cakes — like Winnie the Pooh. I hope you are lucky enough to have tiny purple flowers on your rosemary when you make this, so you can scatter them over the finished cake.

Grease and line the base of a 22 cm (8½ inch) springform tin. Put the butter, brown sugar and honey in a small saucepan and add 1 tablespoon of water. Heat gently, stirring once or twice, until the butter melts and the sugar dissolves. Leave to cool for 15 minutes. Preheat the oven to 180°C (350°F/Gas 4).

Sift the flour, baking powder and cinnamon into a bowl and add the rosemary. Add the honey mixture and eggs and beat until smooth.

Pour into the tin and bake for 35–40 minutes, or until a skewer comes out clean when you poke it into the centre. Leave in the tin to cool completely.

To make the lemon icing, sift the icing sugar into a bowl. Add the butter, lemon zest and juice and 1 tablespoon of water and beat until smooth. You might like to add a few more drops of lemon juice after tasting it. Spread over the top and side of the cake. The cake softens as it sits and will keep well for up to a week in a cake tin.

Cuts into 8–10 slices

250 ML (9 FL OZ/1 CUP) POURING (SINGLE) CREAM
200 G (7 OZ) CASTER (SUPERFINE) SUGAR
1 TEASPOON VANILLA EXTRACT
500 G (9 OZ/2 CUPS) GREEK-STYLE NATURAL YOGHURT

Vanilla yoghurt ice cream

This is lovely — not too sweet — as it just really tastes like frozen yoghurt. It's beautiful served with poached fruit or with a fresh fruit sauce, like apricot or raspberry (pages 107 and 54), dribbled over the top. You could even add a couple of biscuits to the side of the plate, or sprinkle a fistful of granola over the top.

Whisk the cream with the sugar and vanilla until all the sugar has dissolved and the cream starts to thicken. Add the yoghurt, whisking it in to incorporate and then pour into a bowl or container that has a lid. Put the lid on and put in the freezer. After an hour give the mixture an energetic whisk with a hand whisk or electric mixer. Put it back in the freezer and then whisk again after another couple of hours. When the ice cream is nearly firm, give one last whisk and put it back in the freezer to set.

Alternatively, pour into your ice cream machine and churn, following the manufacturer's instructions.

Makes 1.5 litres (52 fl oz/6 cups)

Sometimes I watch them and see that they are counting between each bite to make their ice cream or chips last as long as possible. And they separate the food up into groups on their plates and save, just like I did, the best for last.

APPLES FOR SAM

2 TABLESPOONS OLIVE OIL
200 G (7 OZ) SHORT-GRAIN RICE
1.25 LITRES (44 FL OZ/5 CUPS) MILK
250 ML (9 FL OZ/1 CUP) SINGLE (POURING) CREAM
1 TEASPOON FINELY GRATED LEMON ZEST
1/2 VANILLA BEAN, SPLIT IN HALF
FRESHLY GRATED NUTMEG
50 G (1³/4 OZ) CASTER (SUPERFINE) SUGAR,
   PLUS A LITTLE EXTRA FOR THE PISTACHIOS
60 G (2¹/4 OZ) PISTACHIOS, SKINS REMOVED
SOFT DARK BROWN SUGAR, FOR SPRINKLING
3 PEACHES, PITTED AND HALVED
6 SMALL BLOBS OF BUTTER

Lemon rice pudding with roasted peaches

My friend Jo — a wonderful cook — gave me this. You can use nectarines, if you prefer them to peaches, and it is also nice with plums. If you have any rice pudding leftover, whisk an egg white into it, shape it into little balls and pan-fry them in butter. Sprinkle them with a little sugar and serve warm.

Preheat the oven to its highest temperature. Heat the olive oil in a heavy-based pan, add the rice and stir gently to warm it. Add the milk, cream, lemon zest, vanilla bean and nutmeg and bring to the boil. Lower the heat and simmer steadily for about 10 minutes, stirring quite often to make sure it doesn't stick. Add the caster sugar and simmer for another 10 minutes, stirring as before. Meanwhile, toss the pistachios with a dash of the brown sugar in a small tray and roast in the oven until they are just crisp in places.

Put the peaches in a baking dish, cut side up. Scatter about 1/2 tablespoon of brown sugar over each peach half and top with a small blob of butter. Roast without turning until the tops are golden brown and the peaches are still in shape but with some juices bubbling.

Just as the rice is tender and creamy, but with quite a bit of milky liquid left, remove it from the heat and dish up into flat bowls. Serve with one or two peach halves with a little juice drizzled here and there and a small pile of sugared pistachios. This is good warm or cold.

Serves 6

BUTTERMILK ICE CREAM:
250 ML (9 FL OZ/1 CUP) POURING (SINGLE) CREAM
200 G (7 OZ) CASTER (SUPERFINE) SUGAR
1 TEASPOON VANILLA EXTRACT
500 ML (17 FL OZ/2 CUPS) BUTTERMILK

50 G (1¾ OZ) BUTTER
4 LOVELY APPLES, CORED AND HALVED
80 G (2¾ OZ) LIGHT BROWN SUGAR
1 TEASPOON GROUND CINNAMON
2 TABLESPOONS MARSALA OR PORT

Baked cinnamon apples with buttermilk ice cream

This is the sort of thing I like to eat on Christmas Eve — quite healthy and homely and just delicious. We eat it with teaspoons, scraping the soft apple out of the skins and eating it with the juice and ice cream. You could also fold a slightly sweetened fruit purée into the ice cream before churning it. You'll need an ovenproof dish that's about 26 x 20 cm (10 x 8 inches) and just large enough to take the eight apple halves compactly. You could bake the apples in advance, cover them with foil and then just heat them up a bit before serving.

For the ice ceam, whisk the cream with the sugar and vanilla until all the sugar has dissolved and the cream starts to thicken. Add the buttermilk, whisking it in to incorporate and then pour into a bowl or container that has a lid. Put the lid on and put in the freezer. After an hour give the mixture an energetic whisk with a hand whisk or electric mixer. Put it back in the freezer and then whisk again after another couple of hours. When the ice cream is nearly firm, give one last whisk and put it back in the freezer to set.

Alternatively, pour into your ice cream machine and churn, following the manufacturer's instructions.

Preheat the oven to 180°C (350°F/Gas 4) and use some of the butter to grease a shallow ovenproof dish, just large enough to fit all 8 apple halves quite compactly. Halve the apples and neatly core them, making sure you don't pierce the skin. Arrange them in the baking dish, cut side up. Mix the sugar and cinnamon and sprinkle over the apples. Put a blob of butter on each apple, sprinkle the marsala over the top and dribble 125 ml (4 fl oz/½ cup) of water around the dish.

Bake for about 30 minutes, then dribble the pan juices over the apples and add another 125 ml (4 fl oz/½ cup) of hot water to the dish. Bake for another 30 minutes or so, or until the apples are soft inside and golden on top but still have their shape. Serve warm or at room temperature, with some sauce spooned over the apples and a scoop or two of the ice cream.

Serves 4 (although there will be ice cream leftover for another time)

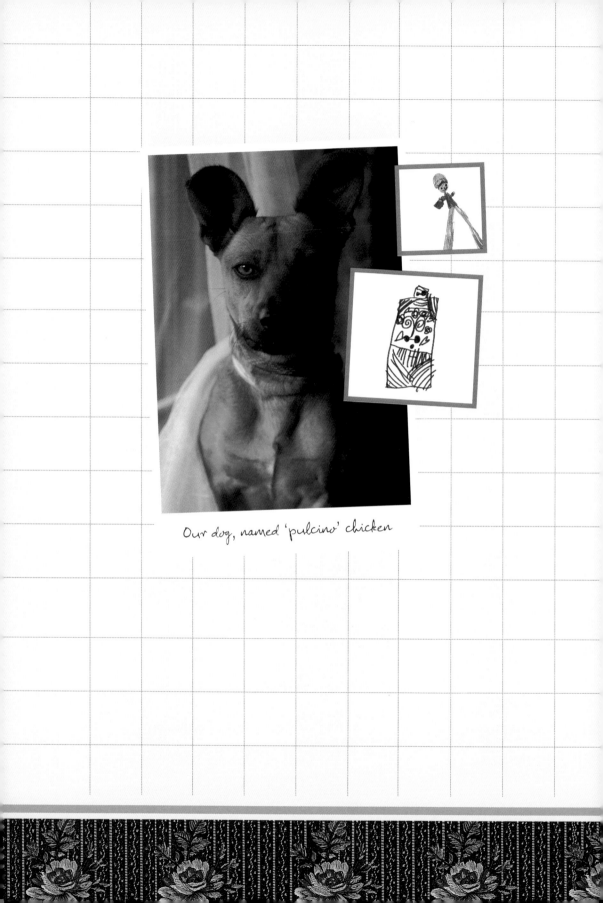

Our dog, named 'pulcino' chicken

Brown

Chocolate loaf
Mixed brown bread
Spaghetti with mince
Farro & borlotti bean soup
Lentil soup
Lentil rice
Lentils & sausages
Brown rice risotto with butter & parmesan
Pot-roasted veal with sage & garlic
Barbecued fillet & bread spiedini
Hamburgers
Brown bread & butter ice cream
Chocolate pannacotta
Chocolate cake with icing
Brownies
Hot chocolate
Hazelnut chocolate balls
Chocolate bread pudding
Mars Bar sauce
Chocolate fudge sauce

- memory -

On April Fools' Day once we went to the local shop and asked for 2 rands' worth of 1 cent chappies. When poor old George had counted out the 200 we flew out of the shop, chorusing 'April Fool'. This is the same café where we bought our ice creams. Our mother would sometimes let us take an ice cream as we walked to school with our plaits and braids and other girly hairstyles, and I loved that. Past the other silky pinks, colourful floral and checked ribbons, class dunces, older gangs and fears accumulated on the pavement, waiting for the bell.

We loved the secret meetings in sweetshops, and looking for small spaces outside to sit and eat, hiccupping our way home afterwards.

I wanted to toast marshmallows on fires but didn't really enjoy children's camping where the porridge looked like home-sickness in the smallest portion I had requested. I wanted to find my way with a torch through a clearing and eat brownies with the brownies and girl scouts and drink bright berried drinks and roll chocolate through my hands, hopping with messy face to the beat of the birds.

15 G (½ OZ) FRESH YEAST
40 G (1½ OZ) CASTER (SUPERFINE) SUGAR
310 ML (10¾ FL OZ/1¼ CUPS) MILK
400 G (14 OZ/3⅓ CUPS) BREAD FLOUR, OR PLAIN
  (ALL-PURPOSE) FLOUR
40 G (1½ OZ) UNSWEETENED COCOA POWDER
40 G (1½ OZ) BUTTER, MELTED

Chocolate loaf

This is a wonderful addition to your breakfast table. Despite its looks, it is definitely a bread and is quite a surprise, so you might need to prepare people who are expecting it to be cake. It is beautiful plain or toasted with butter or home-made mandarin or strawberry jam (pages 106 and 68).

Crumble the yeast into a large bowl and add the sugar. Gently heat the milk in a small pan until it feels just a bit hotter than your finger, then add it to the yeast. Stir through and leave for 10 minutes or so, until the surface starts to turn spongy. Add the flour, cocoa powder, butter and a pinch of salt and mix in well. Knead with your hands for about 6 minutes until the dough is smooth and elastic with no lumps. If your dough is very soft, leave it in the bowl and just punch it around and squeeze it with one hand, holding the bowl with the other. Cover the bowl with a heavy tea towel and leave it in a warm, draught-free place for 1½–2 hours until it has puffed right up. Butter and flour a 30 x 11 cm (12 x 4 inch) loaf tin.

Knock the dough down to flatten it and shape it to the size of the tin. Drop it in, cover the tin with the tea towel and leave it again in a warm place for anywhere between 30 minutes and an hour, until the dough has puffed up over the rim of the tin. While the dough is rising, preheat the oven to 180°C (350°F/Gas 4).

Remove the tea towel and bake the loaf for about 25 minutes, or until the top is firm and the bread sounds hollow when tapped on the bottom. Tip out onto a rack to cool. Once it has cooled down completely, this loaf can be frozen (even just a chunk of it) in a plastic bag and saved for another moment in time.

Makes 1 loaf

ABOUT 375 ML (13 FL OZ/1 1/2 CUPS) WARM
(COMFORTABLE TO YOUR FINGERS) WATER
20 G (3/4 OZ) FRESH YEAST, CRUMBLED, OR 10 G (1/4 OZ)
ACTIVE DRY YEAST
2 TEASPOONS HONEY
1 TABLESPOON OLIVE OIL
120 G (4 1/4 OZ) FARRO (SPELT) FLOUR
100 G (3 1/2 OZ) BUCKWHEAT FLOUR
80 G (2 3/4 OZ) RYE FLOUR
100 G (3 1/2 OZ) WHOLEMEAL (WHOLEWHEAT) FLOUR
100 G (3 1/2 OZ) BREAD FLOUR
15 G (1/2 OZ) LINSEEDS
40 G (1 1/2 OZ) SESAME SEEDS
60 G (2 1/4 OZ) SUNFLOWER SEEDS

Mixed brown bread

I love going to the organic shop and coming out with the various brown paper bags with all the different goods in to make this bread. It really makes me feel like I'm doing well when my kids have this for their school sandwiches. Apart from its healthy aspect this is just simply lovely — nice for sandwiches or toasted with butter or jam. You might like to try other flours or combinations, too. This makes one large loaf or two smaller ones, and, if you like, you can easily freeze one and keep it for another moment.

Put the water in a smallish bowl and add the yeast, honey and oil. Stir until the honey melts and then leave it for 10 minutes or so, until it begins to froth up a bit.

Put the farro, buckwheat, rye, wholmeal and bread flours in a fairly large wide bowl and add the linseeds and 1 teaspoon of salt. Toast the sesame and sunflower seeds lightly in a dry frying pan and stir them into the flours.

Add the yeast mixture to the flours and mix through well, kneading it in the bowl for at least 5 minutes until it is elastic. It may still be a little sticky, but only add more bread flour if you can't knead it because it's sticking to your hands. Cover the bowl with a couple of cloths and leave it in a warm and draught-free place for about 1 1/2 hours, or until it has puffed up well. Punch down the dough to flatten it, divide it in half and dust a large baking tray with flour. Shape the dough into two longish loaves and sit them on the tray, leaving space between as they will rise. Make a few slashes on their tops and cover with a cloth, making sure it loops in the middle of the two loaves. Leave it in the same draught-free spot for another 45 minutes or so, until the dough has puffed right up again.

Meanwhile, preheat the oven to 200°C (400°F/Gas 6). Remove the cloth and bake for about 25 minutes, until the bread is golden and crusty all over and sounds hollow when you tap it. Remove from the oven and cool a bit before serving. Best warm or at room temperature.

Makes 2 loaves

125 ML (4 FL OZ/½ CUP) OLIVE OIL
3 ONIONS, CHOPPED
2 GARLIC CLOVES, FINELY CHOPPED
1 KG (2 LB 4 OZ) MINCED (GROUND) BEEF
2 BAY LEAVES
1 CINNAMON STICK
2 TABLESPOONS WORCESTERSHIRE SAUCE
1 TEASPOON DRIED MINT
2 TEASPOONS SWEET PAPRIKA
3 TABLESPOONS BUTTER
375 ML (13 FL OZ/1½ CUPS) WHITE WINE
800 G (1 LB 12 OZ) TINNED DICED TOMATOES
1 SMALL BUNCH PARSLEY, CHOPPED
500 G (1 LB 2 OZ) SPAGHETTI
GRATED PARMESAN, TO SERVE

Spaghetti with mince

This is exactly how my sister makes her mince. The pasta will serve five or six people but you should have about half the sauce leftover. I always make my mince sauce in double quantities... leftovers can be frozen in small portions for quick dinners. It's great on toast with some parmesan sprinkled over the top, dolloped into mashed potato or over gnocchi. And, of course, you can use it for making lasagne. If you are suspicious of your cooking pot (that the meat might burn while you're browning it) then sauté the meat and onions in a non-stick frying pan and tip everything into the larger pot for cooking.

Heat the olive oil in a large pan. Sauté the onions with a pinch of salt over medium heat, stirring often until they are quite golden, soft and sticky. Add the garlic, cook for a minute and then add the mince. Mix it in with the onions, breaking up any lumps with a wooden spoon. Add the bay leaves, cinnamon stick, worcestershire sauce, mint and paprika and sauté over high heat for 8-10 minutes until the meat loses its moisture and starts sizzling. Add 1 tablespoon of the butter and continue frying for about 10 minutes until the meat changes colour. Stir often, to prevent sticking and to brown all the meat.

Add the wine and cook for about 5 minutes until it has evaporated. Add the tomatoes, let them melt down for a bit and then add 750 ml (26 fl oz/3 cups) of water. Season with salt. Bring to the boil, lower the heat and simmer uncovered for about 50 minutes until it looks like a good, not-too-dry sauce. Add the parsley and simmer for another 10 minutes.

Cook the pasta in boiling salted water, following the packet instructions. Drain and serve with a good dollop of meat sauce, a sprinkling of parmesan and a small blob of the remaining butter on each serving.

Serves 5-6

200 G (7 OZ) DRIED BORLOTTI BEANS, SOAKED
   OVERNIGHT IN COLD WATER
3 TABLESPOONS OLIVE OIL
1 SMALL ONION, CHOPPED
1 GARLIC CLOVE, CHOPPED
1 CELERY STALK, CHOPPED
80 G (2¾ OZ) UNSMOKED PANCETTA
200 G (7 OZ) FARRO (SPELT) GRAIN, SOAKED
   OVERNIGHT IN COLD WATER
125 ML (4 FL OZ/½ CUP) TOMATO PASSATA
   (PUREED TOMATOES)
2 SAGE LEAVES
OLIVE OIL, TO SERVE

Farro & borlotti bean soup

This is a good soup to try on children in winter: rich in iron and vitamins. You will have to check the type of farro you have as to whether it requires soaking or not. It should be available in health food shops, if not at the supermarket. Pearl barley can be used instead, if you like.

Drain the beans, put them in a large saucepan and cover abundantly with cold water. Bring to the boil and then skim the surface. Lower the heat slightly and cook for 1-1½ hours, until the beans are soft but not mushy. Top up with a little hot water when necessary during the cooking time. Season with salt towards the end.

Heat the olive oil in a large pan and sauté the onion over medium heat until softened and very lightly golden. Add the garlic, celery and pancetta and sauté for a few minutes more. Drain the farro and add to the pan with the tomato passata, sage leaves and salt to taste. Stir through well and then add 1.5 litres (52 fl oz/ 6 cups) of water. Bring to the boil, lower the heat and cook uncovered for about an hour, or until the farro is soft. There should be enough liquid to be able to stir the farro loosely with a wooden spoon.

Drain the beans, keeping the cooking water. Purée the beans with just enough of their water to keep the purée moist. Add to the farro pan and stir in about 250 ml (9 fl oz/1 cup) of the bean cooking water, or enough to make a thick soup. Cook for a couple of minutes for the flavours to mingle, adjust the seasoning and serve with a good drizzle of olive oil. Adults might like to stir some freshly chopped chilli into theirs.

Serves 6

250 G (9 OZ/1⅓ CUPS) BROWN OR GREEN LENTILS
1 LEAFY CELERY STALK, CHOPPED
2 CARROTS, PEELED AND CHOPPED
¼ RED PEPPER (CAPSICUM), SEEDED AND CHOPPED
1 SMALL RED ONION, CHOPPED
125 ML (4 FL OZ/½ CUP) TOMATO PASSATA
  (PUREED TOMATOES)
100 G (3½ OZ) PEAS
100 G (3½ OZ) ENGLISH SPINACH LEAVES, ROUGHLY
  CHOPPED
100 G (3½ OZ) CABBAGE, CHOPPED
OLIVE OIL, TO SERVE

Lentil soup

Sometimes I just open the fridge and, having completely forgotten that I had bought some or other vegetable, I put together a soup like this. This makes a nice big pot, so you'll have leftovers for the next day. I like to serve this with toasted bread and a faint drizzle of balsamic vinegar with the olive oil on top — vinegar over lentil soup is quite Greek. Or I cook up some small pasta in a separate pan and add a little to each serving.

Rinse the lentils, getting rid of any hard stony bits. Put them in a large pan and add the celery, carrots, red pepper, onion and passata and season with salt.
    Cover with about 1.25 litres (44 fl oz/5 cups) of cold water and bring to the boil. Put the lid on the pan, lower the heat and simmer for about 1 hour. Add the peas, spinach and cabbage and cook for another 15-20 minutes. Taste for salt. Serve with a good drizzling of olive oil and a few grinds of black pepper for adults.

Serves 5

Sometimes, if you didn't make it to the bathroom on time, they would give you a long aprony dress to wear while your clothes dried. That way everyone knew that you'd wet yourself. So the next couple of hours were horrid — and you still had to go to the enormous ancient dining room that smelled of wood and old cherries.

4 TABLESPOONS OLIVE OIL
1 LARGE RED ONION, FINELY CHOPPED
2 GARLIC CLOVES, PEELED AND FINELY CHOPPED
1/4 TEASPOON GROUND CINNAMON
1/4 TEASPOON SWEET PAPRIKA
1/4 TEASPOON GROUND CORIANDER
250 G (9 OZ/1 1/3 CUPS) BROWN OR GREEN LENTILS,
    RINSED AND PICKED OVER
220 G (7 OZ) LONG-GRAIN RICE, RINSED WELL
30 G (1 OZ) BUTTER
4 TABLESPOONS CHOPPED PARSLEY

Lentil rice

My kids love a bowl of lentils with rice, so I make this in some form or another once or twice a week. Some nice bread and a ripe tomato salad makes it a complete, not-too-heavy meal. Although I think it would be nice, too, with a roast chicken or meat dish. I like this with some chilli oil and a few drops of lemon juice sprinkled over the top, and the children enjoy it with quite a few spoonfuls of thick natural yoghurt.

Heat the oil in a frying pan and fry the onion over medium–low heat, stirring often, until it is golden and sticky looking. Add the garlic, cinnamon, paprika and coriander and stir until you can smell the garlic. Remove from the heat.

Meanwhile, put the lentils in a large pot, cover with 1 litre (35 fl oz/4 cups) of water and bring to the boil. Skim the surface and then simmer for 30 minutes, adding some salt halfway through.

Scrape the onion mixture into the lentil pot and add the rice, butter, half the parsley, 250 ml (9 fl oz/1 cup) of water and a dash more salt. Stir well and bring back to the boil. Cover, turn the heat as low as possible and cook for 15 minutes or so, until all the water has been absorbed and the rice is cooked through.

Remove from the heat and fluff up. Cover the top of the pot with a clean tea towel, put the lid back on and leave it for about 10 minutes. Add the remaining parsley and fluff it up again before serving.

Serves 4

I can still picture those ladies, round as Mr Plod and bursting out of their chequered uniforms, dishing up soupy plates of lentils and dribbling some vinegar over the top so that it sat like a still pool. They would be swinging their way in and out of those slatted kitchen doors as though they were barn dancing.

520 G (1 LB 3 OZ) BEEF FILLET SLICES
2-3 THYME SPRIGS
2 ROSEMARY SPRIGS
2 GARLIC CLOVES, PEELED AND SQUASHED A BIT
125 ML (4 FL OZ/½ CUP) OLIVE OIL
ABOUT 4 SLICES (1 CM/½ INCH THICK) DAY-OLD
  WHITE BREAD
LEMON WEDGES, TO SERVE
OLIVE OIL, TO SERVE

Barbecued fillet & bread spiedini

These are very small and easy-to-eat skewers with soft cubes of beef fillet alternating with tiny blocks of bread. Rather like antipasto for adults, and a perfect size for kids. Keeping the meat and bread pieces small is important, as they must be cooked really quickly on all sides so that the bread toasts beautifully rather than burns. I like to make them into about 1 cm (½ inch) cubes but, if you like, you can make them a dash bigger. You will need to marinate the meat in the herbs and oil for a few hours before you barbecue them. Adults can add some ground dried chilli to their marinade. If you're using bamboo skewers, remember to soak them in water first so that they don't catch fire on the barbecue. I love to serve this with a handful of home-made salted potato crisps and a butter lettuce salad. If you don't have time to make your own crisps, even just a few bought crisps is nice.

Trim away any fat from the beef and cut it into 1 cm (½ inch) cubes. Put them in a bowl with the thyme, rosemary, garlic and olive oil and add a small scattering of salt. Turn everything over to coat the beef well, cover the bowl and leave it in the fridge or a cool place for a few hours. Turn the beef over a few times while it's marinating so that the flavours mingle. Take out of the fridge 30 minutes or so before cooking.

For the bread, blocks which have some crust attached are needed here, so cut the crusts off the bread by slicing 1 cm (½ inch) in. Keep the bread middles to make fresh breadcrumbs or to feed to the ducks. Cut along the crusts to make 1 cm (½ inch) blocks. Thread the skewers alternately with beef and bread, starting and finishing with a piece of beef.

Preheat the barbecue or chargrill. Cook the skewers about 5 cm (2 inches) away from the embers, using the rosemary and thyme sprigs to brush on the marinade and turning the skewers over quite quickly so that the bread doesn't burn. They must be seared golden on all sides and dark with flavour in some parts. Sprinkle with a little salt and serve immediately, drizzled with a squeeze of lemon juice and some olive oil.

Makes 10 skewers

PINK SAUCE:
125 ML (4 FL OZ/½ CUP) BEST-QUALITY TOMATO
   KETCHUP
2 TABLESPOONS MAYONNAISE
1 ½ TABLESPOONS LEMON JUICE
1 ½ TEASPOONS WORCESTERSHIRE SAUCE
1 TEASPOON SWEET PAPRIKA

ABOUT 4 TABLESPOONS OLIVE OIL
2 LARGE RED ONIONS, THINLY SLICED
3 THYME SPRIGS
780 G (1 LB 11 OZ) MINCED (GROUND) BEEF
2½ TABLESPOONS CHOPPED PARSLEY
1 EGG, LIGHTLY BEATEN
6 SLICES GOUDA CHEESE (SOME MAY LIKE
   GORGONZOLA)
2 JUICY TOMATOES, SLICED
ABOUT 50 G (ABOUT 2 OZ) TENDER BUT CRISP INNER
   BUTTER LETTUCE LEAVES
ABOUT 4 GHERKINS (PICKLED CUCUMBERS), THINLY
   SLICED DIAGONALLY
6 SESAME BUNS, HALVED

Hamburgers

We all love these, especially all the fiddling around with so many small and different bowls in the middle of the table, and being able to choose our own fillings. Kids might even like the onions and gherkins, when they're choosing for themselves. You can decide if you want to make the meat patties bigger or smaller, depending on who you will be serving. Your mince will need some fat in it so that it stays moist and quite juicy after cooking. Make sure not to overcook the patties and dry them out — they should be just nicely charred here and there for flavour. This might seem like a lot of fuss but it is all work done beforehand and, hopefully, there might even be someone who will take over the fire and cooking part for you. I usually serve these with pan-fried chips (page 245) or just a handful of potato chips.

For the pink sauce, put the tomato sauce, mayonnaise, lemon juice, worcestershire sauce and paprika in a serving bowl and season with some salt and pepper. Mix with a fork until smooth.

Heat 3 tablespoons of the oil in a non-stick frying pan and add the onions. Fry over low heat until they are golden and sticky, but take care that they don't burn. Add the thyme sprigs and a pinch of salt and continue frying the onions, stirring with a wooden spoon, for about 15 minutes until they get a little crisp.

Meanwhile, put the beef, parsley and egg in a bowl and season with some salt and black pepper. Mix well with your hands and then shape into six large flat patties. They should be about 10 cm (4 inches) in diameter and not more than 2 cm ($3/4$ inch) thick, so squeeze them between your palms and shape them with your fingers. Preheat a barbecue or chargrill plate and brush it lightly with oil.

Barbecue the patties over a medium–high flame until they are nicely browned and charred in a couple of places. Make sure they don't get smoked and don't fry them slowly or they will just become hard. They should be cooked through but moist and juicy inside, and should ooze a little cooked meat juice onto your bun. Cover the patties with a slice of cheese and let it just melt (if it seems necessary, cover it loosely with a square of foil).

Put the tomatoes, lettuce, gherkins and warm onions out on the table in separate bowls. Heat the bun halves on the barbecue for a couple of seconds and then put the patties inside and serve immediately, letting everyone make their own by adding sauce, tomatoes, lettuce, gherkins and onions as they like. Serve with chips, baked potatoes or just a green salad.

Makes 6

We saved our chip packets and then we'd sit them on a baking tray and slow-roast them in the oven to shrink them down to miniatures, turning out their corners carefully while they were still hot to keep their shapes. We loved to glue pins on the back and wear them as brooches.

100 G (3½ OZ) BROWN BREAD, TORN INTO CHUNKS
100 G (3½ OZ) BROWN SUGAR
60 G (2¼ OZ) BUTTER
2 EGGS
1 TEASPOON VANILLA EXTRACT
125 ML (4 FL OZ/½ CUP) MILK
375 ML (13 FL OZ/1½ CUPS) POURING (SINGLE)
CREAM

Brown bread & butter ice cream

I was most excited when I first heard about this. I thought how great for kids but adults love it, too. I added the butter and I love it sometimes with a faint drizzling like English rain of not-too-rich toffee sauce. I make this when I have some leftovers from the mixed brown loaf (page 291) but, of course, you don't have to make your own bread especially for this ice cream. I love to serve this as an afternoon snack. The crumbs have to be caramelly and hardened so that they taste like praline in the ice cream.

Preheat the oven to 200°C (400°F/Gas 6). In a processor, pulse the bread into crumbs. Grease a large baking tray with a little butter and scatter the crumbs and the sugar over it, then mix together with your hands. Bake for about 12 minutes until the crumbs are golden and crisp, turning them over twice during this time. Watch that the crumbs don't burn and become bitter. Leave the crumbs to cool, then break up any clumps with your hands.

Melt the butter in a small pan until it starts to turn a little golden and smells good. Pour into a bowl to cool.

Meanwhile, whisk the eggs with the vanilla. Heat the milk with 125 ml (4 fl oz/½ cup) of the cream in a pan over medium–low heat until almost boiling. Whisk a ladleful into the eggs, mixing constantly to prevent them from scrambling. Gradually pour in the rest of the liquid, whisking all the time. Pour it all back into the saucepan, lower the heat to minimum and heat for a few minutes, whisking all the time, to cook the eggs and thicken the mixture a bit. Remove from the heat and cool for 10–15 minutes, whisking now and then. Stir in the remaining cream, the melted butter and the sugary crumbs and pour into a bowl or container that has a lid. Put the lid on and leave in the fridge until totally cool.

Put the bowl in the freezer. After an hour give the mixture an energetic whisk with a hand whisk. Put it back in the freezer and then whisk again after another couple of hours. When the ice cream is nearly firm, give one last whisk and put it back in the freezer to set.

Alternatively, pour into your ice cream machine and churn, following the manufacturer's instructions.

Makes 1 litre (35 fl oz/4 cups)

6 G (¹/₈ OZ) LEAF GELATINE, OR 2 TEASPOONS
  POWDERED GELATINE
250 ML (9 FL OZ/1 CUP) MILK
500 ML (17 FL OZ/2 CUPS) POURING (SINGLE) CREAM
60 G (2¹/₄ OZ) CASTER (SUPERFINE) SUGAR
80 G (2³/₄ OZ) DARK (SEMI-SWEET) CHOCOLATE,
  BROKEN UP
20 G (³/₄ OZ) UNSWEETENED COCOA POWDER, SIFTED

Chocolate pannacotta

These are light and creamy, soft and chocolatey. They are lovely just on their own, eaten straight out of their pots but, if you want to be a bit dressy, you could serve them with white chocolate sauce or surrounded by a bright ring of cranberries and a blob of cream. Or perhaps some sautéed quinces, nectarines or peaches.

Put the gelatine leaves in a bowl of cold water to soften them. If you're using powdered gelatine, put 3 tablespoons of the milk in a small bowl and stir in the gelatine. Leave for a minute or two until it dissolves and swells a bit.

Meanwhile, put the milk, cream, sugar, chocolate and cocoa in a saucepan over low heat. Stir it with a wooden spoon as it heats so that it becomes completely smooth and nothing sticks to the bottom. Turn off the heat just before it reaches boiling point.

Squeeze the water out of the softened gelatine leaves and stir them into the hot chocolate milk. If you're using powdered gelatine, stir some of the hot chocolate milk into it to soften, then stir it all back into the saucepan and carry on stirring until it's completely smooth. Leave it to cool, whisking now and then to make sure the gelatine has dissolved.

Pour the mixture into six 125 ml (4 fl oz/¹/₂ cup) pudding or pannacotta moulds and then cover them with plastic wrap. Put in the fridge overnight or until set.

To unmould, loosen the top edges gently with your fingers. Dip the bottom of the moulds into hot water for just a couple of seconds (any longer might turn your pannacotta to liquid again) and tip out onto serving plates.

Makes 6

APPLES FOR SAM

180 G (6½ OZ) BUTTER
50 G (1¾ OZ) DARK (SEMI-SWEET) CHOCOLATE,
    BROKEN UP
30 G (1 OZ) UNSWEETENED COCOA POWDER
3 EGGS, SEPARATED
180 G (6½ OZ) CASTER (SUPERFINE) SUGAR
125 G (4½ OZ/1 CUP) PLAIN (ALL-PURPOSE) FLOUR
1½ TEASPOONS BAKING POWDER
3 TABLESPOONS MILK

ICING:
80 G (2¾ OZ) BUTTER, SOFTENED
60 G (2¼ OZ) ICING (CONFECTIONERS') SUGAR
30 G (1 OZ) UNSWEETENED COCOA POWDER
2 TABLESPOONS MILK
2 GENEROUS TEASPOONS GOLDEN SYRUP

Chocolate cake with icing

This is exactly the kind of chocolate cake I loved as a child. Sometimes I make this just chocolate, sometimes halved and filled with not-too-sweet raspberry or strawberry jam or purée and a few dollops of cream (and then I don't ice it). If you like, you might also add some chopped nuts in with the flour or scatter some over the top.

Preheat the oven to 180°C (350°F/Gas 4). Butter and flour a 24 cm (9½ inch) springform tin. Melt the butter in a small saucepan over low heat, then add the chocolate and cocoa and stir until melted. Remove from the heat. Whisk the egg whites in a bowl until they are creamy and stiff. In another bowl, whisk the egg yolks until they are foamy, then beat in the sugar. Add the chocolate mixture, a bit at a time initially to acclimatize the eggs. Next, sift in the flour and baking powder and mix well. Add the milk and mix until smooth.

Carefully fold in the beaten whites, trying not to deflate them, and gently mix until they are completely incorporated into a fluffy but dense mixture. Scrape out into the tin and bake for about 30–35 minutes. Remove from the oven and cool completely in the tin before moving to a serving plate.

For the icing, whip the butter with the icing sugar until fluffy. Whisk in the cocoa a bit at a time so that it doesn't fly everywhere. When it is completely incorporated, add the milk and golden syrup and whisk until very smooth. Spread it over the top of the cake with a spatula, using swift smooth strokes. I like it not completely smooth but in chocolate waves.

Cuts into 10–12 slices

350 G (12 OZ) BUTTER
300 G (10½ OZ) DARK (SEMI-SWEET) CHOCOLATE, BROKEN UP
60 G (2¼ OZ) UNSWEETENED COCOA POWDER, SIFTED
6 EGGS, SEPARATED
350 G (12 OZ) CASTER (SUPERFINE) SUGAR
1 TEASPOON VANILLA EXTRACT
200 G (7 OZ) PLAIN (ALL-PURPOSE) FLOUR

FILLING:
360 ML (12½ FL OZ) WHIPPING CREAM
½ TABLESPOON ICING (CONFECTIONERS') SUGAR
FEW DROPS OF VANILLA EXTRACT
250 G (9 OZ) STRAWBERRIES, HULLED, AND HALVED IF LARGE

ICING:
150 G (5½ OZ) DARK (SEMI-SWEET) CHOCOLATE, CHOPPED
100 ML (3½ FL OZ) POURING (SINGLE) CREAM

Brownies

Towards the middle of the baking this has the most gorgeous smell, which runs like streamers through your home when you take the brownies out of the oven. This is my friend Artemis' recipe. She makes them so often that this is the most familiar smell from her kitchen. She likes them with whipped, unsweetened cream. You can add some toasted nuts, apple or pear chunks, or anything else you think might go well. Serve these on their own in squares to nibble on or slightly warm with a dribbling of chocolate sauce and a scoop of vanilla ice cream. They also freeze well so I like to make up this big batch and freeze a few for an emergency snack, but you could also make half the amount in a smaller tray (15 x 20 cm/ 6 x 8 inches). I sometimes make this large quantity (in my big rectangular tray) and then cut it in half into two squares once it's cooled. Layered with strawberries and whipped cream, it makes a beautiful cake. It's a bit messy maybe to cut and serve but I have noticed all the kids eyeing this at our parties. Use really good-quality chocolate.

Preheat the oven to 180°C (350°F/Gas 4). Butter and flour a 29 x 39 cm (11½ x 15½ inch) baking tray that is at least 3 cm (1¼ inches) deep. Put the butter in a medium-sized pan over low heat. When it begins to melt a little, add the chocolate. Stir frequently with a wooden spoon until all the chocolate has melted and the mixture is smooth. Don't overheat it or the chocolate might seize up. Remove from the heat and whisk in the cocoa powder, then leave it to cool a bit.

In a clean bowl, whisk the egg whites until soft peaks form. In another large bowl, whisk the egg yolks with the sugar and vanilla until creamy, then fold in the flour. Add the cooled chocolate and butter, mixing well, and then fold in the whites until everything is thoroughly mixed.

Scrape out every drop into your tray and put in the oven for about 25 minutes, or until a skewer poked into the centre comes out clean. Don't overcook it though; the brownie should be quite moist in the centre with a crusty top and edges. Leave it to cool completely.

If you are going to fill and ice the brownie, cut it in half across the long side. Whip the cream, icing sugar and vanilla together until firm peaks form and spread over the top of one piece. Scatter with the strawberries and then put the other piece of cake on top to make a sandwich.

For the icing, gently melt the chocolate and cream together in a small saucepan, stirring all the time. As soon as it is smooth, take from the heat. Add a few more drops of cream, if needed, so that it will drip onto the cake. Spread the icing all over the top of the cake, letting some dribble over the edges. Wait for the icing to set before cutting.

For brownies, cut the cake into 5 cm (2 inch) squares. If you are not going to eat them immediately, let them cool completely and then store in a biscuit tin, or well covered with plastic wrap so that they don't dry out. Leftover brownies can be broken up into bits and scattered into just-about-set vanilla ice cream.

Makes about 48 brownies or 1 cake

----

100 G (3½ OZ) BEST-QUALITY DARK (SEMI-SWEET)
   CHOCOLATE, CHOPPED
500 ML (17 FL OZ/2 CUPS) MILK
125 ML (4 FL OZ/½ CUP) WHIPPING CREAM
1 TEASPOON ICING (CONFECTIONERS') SUGAR
UNSWEETENED COCOA POWDER OR GROUND
   CINNAMON, TO SERVE

Hot chocolate

This is lovely and wintery and makes a nice start to a birthday, a special day, a Sunday, the New Year or just any old day. It also looks beautiful in small glasses and you can make mocha chocolate by replacing 125 ml (4 fl oz/½ cup) of the milk with freshly made, very strong espresso coffee.

Heat the chocolate and milk in a heavy-based saucepan over medium heat, stirring constantly with a wooden spoon so it doesn't catch. Bring it to just below boiling point and whisk with a wire whisk to make sure it is completely smooth.

Meanwhile, whisk together the cream and icing sugar until quite thick but not stiff — just dense enough to sit on top of the hot chocolate.

Pour the hot chocolate into cups and gently spoon the cream over the top, dropping it first onto the back of a spoon and letting it slide onto the top of the chocolate. Sieve a tiny amount of cocoa powder or cinnamon over the top and serve at once. This can be drunk as it is so the chocolate streams through the cream, or the cream can be stirred through first.

Serves 2

3 HAZELNUT WAFER BISCUITS
250 G (9 OZ) ROASTED PEELED HAZELNUTS, CHOPPED
  QUITE FINELY
ABOUT 185 G (6½ OZ) CHOCOLATE HAZELNUT
  SPREAD
250 G (9 OZ) DARK (SEMI-SWEET) CHOCOLATE

Hazelnut chocolate balls

My kids absolutely love to help me roll these in their small sweet palms — although it is difficult for them to try not to lick all the mixture off their hands. These are from a friend of Giovanni — he tasted them at work and spoke about them in such very descriptive terms that I made him hound her until she finally gave me the recipe.

Crumble the biscuits into a bowl and add the hazelnuts and about two-thirds of the hazelnut spread to start with. Mix together until it all looks a bit like mud cake. Try rolling a small portion into a ball — if it breaks up, mix in more chocolate hazelnut spread until it will hold a shape. If the weather is hot, put the mixture into the fridge for a while before rolling.

Line a tray or large flat plate with foil. Roll slightly heaped teaspoonfuls of mixture between your cool palms into compact little balls. Put them on the tray and into the fridge for an hour or so to firm up.

Melt the chocolate in the top of a double boiler, making sure that the water doesn't touch the top bowl. Remove from the heat and let the chocolate cool for a few minutes. Drop the balls in one by one, turning them around so that they are completely covered. Return them to the tray, where they will flatten a bit on the bottom. Let them set completely, even in the fridge for the first half hour or so if the weather's hot. Bring them out to room temperature and store in a tin in a cool dark place (or in the fridge in hot weather). They will keep for a couple of weeks.

Makes about 30

80 G (2¾ OZ) BUTTER
140 G (5 OZ) DARK (SEMI-SWEET) CHOCOLATE,
    CHOPPED
115 G (4 OZ/½ CUP) CASTER (SUPERFINE) SUGAR
60 ML (2 FL OZ/¼ CUP) POURING (SINGLE) CREAM
4 EGGS
14–15 SLICES SANDWICH BREAD, CRUSTS REMOVED

Chocolate bread pudding

This is quick, good and really easy and it produces a lovely soft chocolate pudding with a crusty top. You can use any bread you like here — I just use plain ready-sliced soya sandwich bread, which leaves just a whisper of salt on the tongue. You can use brown, white or any other bread. You could also use a home-made white loaf (page 263). I make this in a round dish that's about 20 cm (8 inches) wide and about 7 cm (3 inches) high and can be taken straight to the table.

Preheat the oven to 180°C (350°F/Gas 4) and butter a shallow 1 litre (35 fl oz/ 4 cup) ovenproof dish.

Melt the butter, chocolate and sugar together in the top of a double boiler, stirring towards the end with a wooden spoon so that it is all smooth. Remove from the heat, stir in the cream and leave to cool slightly.

Beat the eggs until they are creamy. Gradually add the chocolate mixture, starting with just a little and eventually mixing it all in to make a smooth custard.

Cut each slice of bread in half diagonally. Use half the slices to make an overlapping layer in the bottom of the dish. Pour over just less than half of the custard, making sure that all the bread is coated. Leave for 5 minutes for the bread to soak up some custard, then layer on the rest of the bread. Pour over the remaining custard and rock the dish so that all the bread is covered with chocolate custard. Leave for 5 minutes.

Put the dish in a larger baking dish and pour in enough hot water to come halfway up the side of the pudding dish. Put in the oven for about 30 minutes, until the custard is set and the top is crusty.

Serve warm, in wedges or spoonfuls, with thick cream or vanilla custard.

Serves 6

250 ML (9 FL OZ/1 CUP) SINGLE (POURING) CREAM
300 G (10½ OZ) MARS BARS, ROUGHLY CHOPPED

Mars Bar sauce

This is wonderfully rich and good — and really quick to make in an emergency. We like it dribbled down the side of a milkshake or slightly warm over ice cream, so that the cold makes the toffee set just slightly. When the pot is left covered on the stove or in the fridge, everyone goes with a teaspoon and takes out a healthy scoop and the marks of the diggers clearly remain.

Pour half the cream into a heavy-based pan and heat gently. Drop in the pieces of Mars Bar and heat, stirring all the time with a wooden spoon, until they are completely melted. Make sure that the cream is not too hot and that nothing gets stuck on the bottom of the pan, which would ruin your chocolate. When everything is nearly all melted together, add the rest of the cream and whisk to break up the soft lumps. Remove from the heat and carry on whisking until the sauce is completely smooth. Cover when it has cooled a bit. Serve warm or even at room temperature, but store in the fridge if you don't finish it all. Even a teaspoon of it cold or at room temperature is great for lifting the spirits.

Makes 500 ml (17 fl oz/2 cups)

---

60 G (2¼ OZ) BUTTER
80 G (2¾ OZ) CASTER (SUPERFINE) SUGAR
80 G (2¾ OZ) DARK BROWN SUGAR
125 ML (4 FL OZ/½ CUP) POURING (SINGLE) CREAM
60 G (2¼ OZ) UNSWEETENED COCOA POWDER, SIFTED

Chocolate fudge sauce

This is ideal for making ice cream sundaes, or just pouring over vanilla ice cream or warm brownies.

Put the butter, sugars and cream in a pan and heat gently, stirring a few times, until the butter has melted. Add the cocoa and cook, stirring all the time now until the sauce is smooth and glossy. Use hot, warm or at room temperature. You can keep this in a covered container in the fridge for a couple of weeks.

Makes 325 ml (11 fl oz/1⅓ cups)

Monochrome

Fish soup with poached fish to follow
Chicken broth
Pasta in chicken broth
Bread dumplings in chicken broth
Chicken croquettes
Chicken soup
Vegetable broth
Meat broth
Cottage pie
Fish pie
Pork schnitzels
Pan-fried breaded lamb cutlets
Fried fish fillets
Baked fish fillets
Potato & chickpea mash
Zucchini bread
Banana bread
Apple bread with sugar & cinnamon topping
Oat biscuits
Maple syrup & vanilla ice cream
Pecan butter biscuits
Gingerbread biscuits

- memory -

Christmas was my best time, probably. It seemed like I hardly ever slept a wink the night before, wondering how and where he would actually come into the house, and if we'd left the milk and biscuits in an obvious enough place. And there was all that anticipation of whether or not our lists would come true. So we would rise with the sun and faff around making as much softly deliberate noise as possible until our mother got up. She was normally the first up in the house. But we still had to wait for our father, so he could see the presents that had come in the night, and he had a habit of sleeping in on Sundays and days like these. That was solid torture. It seemed as if he would go on sleeping forever, through any amount of noise. And then, at last, we would get into the actual presents room — I will always remember the beautiful boxes everywhere, mountains of things from grandfathers and cousins, flowing almost out of the room like a wild, rushing and very alive river. We might have picked on the gingerbread biscuits and other goodies, cross-legged on the floor with cups of warm milk and still in our pyjamas. We could linger that day, much longer than usual, in our pyjamas.

1 CHICKEN (ABOUT 1.2 KG/2 LB 12 OZ)
1 LEAFY CELERY STALK, ROUGHLY CHOPPED
2 SMALL CARROTS, PEELED AND HALVED
1 SMALL LEEK, TRIMMED AND HALVED
ABOUT 12 BLACK PEPPERCORNS
50 G (1³/₄ OZ) BUTTER
30 G (1 OZ) PLAIN (ALL-PURPOSE) FLOUR
1 EGG
2 TABLESPOONS MARSALA OR PORT
FRESHLY GRATED PARMESAN OR PECORINO CHEESE,
    TO SERVE

Chicken soup

When I asked Giovanni about his childhood food memories, he said there was a chicken soup so velvety and creamy that he can never forget it. Here is my father-in-law Mario's chicken soup that all generations love. It has a very thick, almost porridgy, consistency — if you prefer, you can cut all the chicken into strips instead of puréeing it, and save the leftovers for sandwiches.

Put the chicken in a large pot with the celery, carrot, leek and peppercorns. Add about 3 litres (104 fl oz/12 cups) of water and some salt and bring to the boil. (If the water doesn't all fit in your pot, put in as much as you can and add the rest when it has reduced.) Skim the surface with a slotted spoon, lower the heat, and simmer for 1¹/₂ hours. Lift the chicken out onto a plate to cool and strain the broth into a clean pan.

Pick all the chicken meat from the bones. Chop about 150 g (5¹/₂ oz) of the chicken meat into longish strips and put the rest of it into a blender. Chop until it is almost a purée and keep on one side for now.

Melt the butter in a smallish pan, then add the flour and stir with a wooden spoon for a few minutes until it begins to turn golden. Add a ladleful of hot broth and mix in well and, when the flour has absorbed this, whisk in another ladleful of broth. Simmer for about 10 minutes, whisking every now and then so that it is very smooth. Add the Marsala and then pour it all back into the large broth pan together with all the chicken meat. Simmer for another 10 minutes.

Whip the egg in a small bowl. Add a ladleful of the hot broth to the egg, whisking to avoid scrambling it, and then mix this back into the broth. Return the pan to the lowest possible heat and stir with a wooden spoon for a minute or so to just cook the egg through.

Serve immediately, scattering a heaped tablespoon of parmesan or pecorino over each bowl.

Serves 8 or more

3 CARROTS, PEELED AND HALVED
2 ZUCCHINI (COURGETTES)
2 SPRING ONIONS (SCALLIONS), TRIMMED
2 LEAFY INNER CELERY STALKS
3 RIPE CHERRY TOMATOES, HALVED
2 GARLIC CLOVES, PEELED BUT LEFT WHOLE
A SMALL HANDFUL OF PARSLEY
7 PEPPERCORNS

Vegetable broth

This is so quick and easy and is, I feel, an essential dish when you're cooking for children. It can be used for cooking a white risotto, a ladleful will add depth to a casserole or stew, or it can just be drunk from a cup. You can add anything you fancy to flavour this broth in another way. Sometimes I put in a piece of red pepper, just for extra and new vitamins. And you could add some stronger herbs — a bay leaf or some basil. Make sure your vegetables are top quality though, not those that are leftover and exhausted in the bottom of the fridge.

Put all the ingredients in a very large pan with 1 teaspoon of salt and 2.5 litres (87 fl oz/10 cups) of cold water. Bring to the boil and then lower the heat to simmer. Put the lid on the pan and continue cooking for about 1 1/2 hours, until the vegetables have surrendered all their goodness and flavour into the broth. Taste for salt and add more if necessary.

Strain through muslin or a fine sieve. (Don't throw the vegetables away; someone might like to eat them with a little olive oil and a few slices of leftover roast.) The broth will keep in the fridge for a couple of days and can also be frozen.

Makes 2 litres (70 fl oz/8 cups)

700 G (1 LB 9 OZ) BEEF ON THE BONE SUITABLE
  FOR BOILING, FAT REMOVED
200 G (7 OZ) CARROTS, PEELED
2 LEAFY INNER CELERY STALKS
A SMALL HANDFUL OF PARSLEY
2 RIPE TOMATOES, QUARTERED
1 LARGE GARLIC CLOVE, PEELED BUT LEFT WHOLE
ABOUT 7 BLACK PEPPERCORNS
2 CHICKEN LEGS
1 RED ONION OR 2 FRENCH SHALLOTS, PEELED
  BUT LEFT WHOLE

Meat broth

I love to serve broth in a tazza (a large tea cup) just before a meal, like they do in the old-style Florentine restaurants. Or you could make this a full meal with tortellini or other pasta, dumplings or plain rice for a 'risotto in bianco' with grated parmesan or grana. I make this with two chicken legs (the whole legs with thighs, not just the drumsticks) and some meat suitable for boiling so that it isn't too strong and meaty for the kids, but you can do all meat if you prefer a heftier broth. You can leave a bit of fat on the meat but I prefer to remove that heavier layer. Try making meat and chicken croquettes from the meat if your family isn't wild about eating plain boiled meat.

Put the beef in a large stockpot with 2.5 litres (87 fl oz/10 cups) of water. Add the carrots, celery, parsley, tomatoes and garlic and bring to the boil. Skim the surface and then add the peppercorns and a teaspoon of salt. Lower the heat and simmer uncovered for about half an hour. Add the chicken and bring back to the boil. Lower the heat and simmer, covered, for 1 1/2 hours. Add 375–500 ml (13–17 fl oz/ 1 1/2–2 cups) of hot water after 45 minutes or so to maintain the level.
  Turn off the heat and leave with the lid on for 15 minutes to cool down a bit. Carefully remove the beef and any bits that you'd like to keep, then strain the liquid into a clean pot or a bowl, depending on what you are going to do with it.

Makes 2 litres (70 fl oz/8 cups)

4 TABLESPOONS OLIVE OIL
750 G (1 LB 10 OZ) MINCED (GROUND) BEEF
3 TABLESPOONS DRY WHITE WINE
1 LARGE ONION, CHOPPED
2 GARLIC CLOVES, FINELY CHOPPED
1 LARGE CARROT, CHOPPED
400 ML (14 FL OZ) TOMATO PASSATA (PUREED
  TOMATOES)
1 BAY LEAF
2 ALLSPICE BERRIES
4 BASIL LEAVES, TORN
2 TABLESPOONS CHOPPED PARSLEY
100 G (3½ OZ) SHELLED PEAS
1.1 KG (2 LB 7 OZ) POTATOES, SCRUBBED BUT
  NOT PEELED
40 G (1½ OZ) BUTTER
170 ML (5½ FL OZ/⅔ CUP) MILK
A LITTLE FRESHLY GRATED NUTMEG

Cottage pie

You can make one large pie here or use small dishes for individual servings. Just remember how many allspice berries you put in so you can count them out again once the mince is ready. If you prefer not to use wine in your cooking, you could always add some unsweetened grape juice (red or white) instead.

Heat half the oil in a non-stick frying pan and fry the mince over fairly high heat for about 10 minutes until it is golden brown, stirring often and breaking up any clusters with a wooden spoon. Pour in the wine and scrape up any bits that are stuck to the bottom of the pan. When the wine has evaporated, remove the pan from the heat.

Meanwhile, heat the remaining oil in a large saucepan. Sauté the onion for 5 minutes or so over low-medium heat until it is lightly golden and a bit sticky. Add the garlic and carrot and sauté for a few minutes more so that the carrot looks a bit caramelly. Add the passata and cook for a couple of minutes, then add the browned mince. Season well with salt and add the bay leaf, allspice berries, basil and parsley. Stir in 500 ml (17 fl oz/2 cups) of hot water. Bring to the boil and then turn the heat to low, cover the pan and cook for 30 minutes. Add the peas and 250 ml (9 fl oz/1 cup) of hot water and simmer uncovered for another 30 minutes. Add a little water if the meat sauce seems very dry; it should neither be runny nor too stiff. Check the seasoning and try to find all the allspice berries.

Preheat the oven to 180°C (350°F/Gas 4). Meanwhile, boil the potatoes in salted water for about 30 minutes (depending on their size) until they are soft enough to mash. Drain and, when they're cool enough to handle, peel and mash or pass through a potato mill. In a small saucepan, heat the butter and milk and, when the butter has melted, add to the potatoes. Add the nutmeg, taste for salt and mix to a soft and fluffy mash (add a dash more butter or milk if it seems too stiff).

Butter a 2.5 litre (87 fl oz/10 cup) ovenproof dish or 6-8 individual dishes. Spoon in the meat sauce, smoothing the surface, and then spoon mashed potato over the top, spreading it very gently to completely cover the mince. Roughen the mash with a fork here and there so you get some crispy bits. Bake for 30 minutes until the top is softly crusted and golden in places.

Serves 6-8

...and at night, once they are sound asleep, there are opened tubs of cream here and there, and not-even-half-eaten apples and strawberries. And still bits of chewed-up liver or other meat they tossed to their friend — the dog.

SAUCE:
30 G (1 OZ) BUTTER
30 G (1 OZ) PLAIN (ALL-PURPOSE) FLOUR
300 ML (10½ FL OZ) VEGETABLE BROTH (PAGE 334), WARMED
100 ML (3½ FL OZ) POURING (SINGLE) CREAM

60 G (2 OZ) BUTTER
1 GARLIC CLOVE, PEELED AND SQUASHED A BIT
200 G (7 OZ) BUTTON MUSHROOMS, SLICED
2 TABLESPOONS WHITE WINE
500 G (1 LB 2 OZ) SKINLESS HALIBUT, COD OR SNAPPER FILLETS
500 G (1 LB 2 OZ) RAW PRAWNS (SHRIMP), PEELED, DEVEINED
2 TABLESPOONS CHOPPED PARSLEY
1 KG (2 LB 4 OZ) POTATOES, PEELED AND CUT INTO CHUNKS
185 ML (6 FL OZ/¾ CUP) MILK, WARMED
LEMON WEDGES, TO SERVE

Fish pie

This is Harriet's — my mum's friend in Finland — a wonderful, stylish lady and cook. I tasted this many years ago and have always remembered it. Her original recipe uses pike-perch fillets, but you can use any fish fillets you like, just make sure they have no bones. In this pie the mash is only around the rim, not covering the whole thing, and it is important to use a dish that is no deeper than 6 cm (2½ inches). Maybe make a few smoked salmon crostini for a starter and serve a green salad and bread with your pie and that really is a complete family dinner, I feel.

For the sauce, melt the butter in a smallish saucepan and then stir in the flour. Cook for a minute or so over medium heat and then add the broth, whisking well to make a smooth sauce. Let it bubble up for a few minutes and then stir in the cream. Taste for salt and pepper (your broth will probably be seasoned already).
    Preheat the oven to 200°C (400°F/Gas 6) and butter a 32 x 22 x 6 cm (13 x 9 x 2½ inch) ovenproof dish. Heat 20 g (¾ oz) of the butter and the garlic in a frying pan and, when it is sizzling, add the mushrooms and a little salt. Sauté over high heat, shifting the mushrooms around with a wooden spoon until all the juices have evaporated and they turn golden. Add the wine and some pepper and cook until the wine has evaporated. Remove from the heat.
    Cut the fish into large chunks of about 5-6 cm (2 inches) and put in the bottom of your dish. Scrape the mushrooms out over the fish, then add the prawns. Scatter with the parsley and a few grinds of pepper. Pour the sauce over the top. Bake for about 20 minutes or until the sauce is bubbling and a bit golden here and there.
    Meanwhile, boil the potatoes in salted water until soft. Heat the remaining butter in the milk. Drain the potatoes and mash them or pass them through a potato mill into a bowl. Beat in the rest of the butter and the warm milk and season, if necessary.
    Arrange the mash in dollops just around the rim of the dish, then bake the pie for another 10 minutes or so, or until the mash is a little golden in places. Leave it to stand for 5 or 10 minutes before serving with lemon wedges.

Serves 5

APPLES FOR SAM

1 THICK PORK FILLET, ABOUT 540 G (1 LB 3 OZ),
   TRIMMED OF ALL FAT
2 LARGE EGGS
2 GARLIC CLOVES, VERY FINELY CHOPPED
2 TABLESPOONS CHOPPED PARSLEY
ABOUT 100 G (3½ OZ/1 CUP) DRY BREADCRUMBS
LIGHT OLIVE OIL, FOR FRYING
LEMON WEDGES, TO SERVE

Pork schnitzels

My mother always made piles of these. You can also use veal, if you like. These with bread and some pan-fried chips scattered with fresh herbs is a dream meal — and one that would have made me sing as a child. Lemon veal or this were my best. If there are any at all left the next day, they are lovely in a roll with a few green salad leaves, a squeeze of lemon or lime and, if you like, a small dollop of mayonnaise. Great for a picnic.

Slice the pork into 2 cm (³/4 inch) pieces and then pound the slices flat with a meat mallet to about 2 mm (¹/16 inch) thick. Cut these in half so that they are about 5 cm (2 inches) square, and then put them in a flattish dish.

Whisk the eggs, garlic and parsley together in a small bowl, and season lightly with salt and pepper. Pour over the pork and turn it over with your hands so that all the pieces are coated with egg. Cover with plastic wrap and set aside for about 30 minutes.

Put the breadcrumbs on a plate. Lift the pork out of the egg mixture with a fork and pat both sides into the crumbs, pressing them down with your palms so they stick. Pour enough oil into a large non-stick frying pan to shallow-fry the pork in batches over medium heat until golden and crisp on both sides. (If any crumbs burn in the oil, wipe out the pan and pour in fresh oil.) Lift out onto kitchen paper to drain and then put on a clean platter. Serve with lemon and an extra sprinkling of salt. Good served warm or at room temperature, or even cold from the fridge.

Serves 6

4-5 SLICES SOFT WHITE BREAD, CRUSTS CUT OFF
1 EGG
½ TABLESPOON GRATED PARMESAN CHEESE
4 LAMB CHOPS, TRIMMED
2 TABLESPOONS LIGHT OLIVE OIL
2 TABLESPOONS BUTTER
LEMON WEDGES, TO SERVE

Pan-fried
breaded lamb cutlets

This is just lovely with hand-made chips and ripe tomato salad (page 47), or some sliced bright red tomatoes. You could do as my friend Julia might: start with a big bowl of minestrone, then serve these cutlets. She taught me this way of breading the lamb chops, and that's all you need for a meal, I feel. You could also use thin veal chops here — they tend to be much larger, so just make sure they are completely cooked through.

Put the bread in a blender or processor and pulse to make coarse crumbs. Tip them out onto a flat plate. Whisk the egg and parmesan together and season with salt and pepper if you like. Pour into a flattish bowl.

Gently pound the cutlets to flatten the meat to about 5 mm (¼ inch) thick. Wipe them with a paper towel to get rid of any stray pieces of bone. Dip them in the egg, making sure they are well covered everywhere. Shake off the excess egg and then pat them firmly on both sides in the breadcrumbs.

Heat the oil and butter in a large non-stick frying pan (the exact amount you will need for frying will depend on the size of your pan). Add the cutlets and fry over medium-high heat until they are golden on both sides. Lift them out onto a plate lined with kitchen paper to absorb the excess oil. Serve immediately, with a sprinkling of salt and the lemon wedges.

Serves 2

I loved those Italian restaurants as a child... where they bring you a white plate with a schnitzel, a bit flattened so it almost takes up the whole plate, and a plain lemony-yellow lemon unfancily cut next to it.

2 EGGS
GRATED RIND OF 1 SMALL LEMON
125 G (4¼ OZ/1 CUP) PLAIN (ALL-PURPOSE) FLOUR
1 TEASPOON BAKING POWDER
1 TEASPOON SWEET PAPRIKA
125 ML (4 FL OZ/½ CUP) COLD SPARKLING WATER
LIGHT OLIVE OIL, FOR FRYING
500 G (1 LB 2 OZ) COD OR OTHER FIRM WHITE FISH
   FILLETS, CUT INTO STRIPS
LEMON WEDGES, TO SERVE

Fried fish fillets

You can serve these on their own or with some vegetables that have also been cut into thick sticks, dipped in the batter and fried. Zucchini (courgettes), green beans, artichokes and cauliflower are all lovely like this. I like to serve a bowl of thin chips alongside as well.

Whisk the eggs and lemon rind in a bowl. Sift in the flour, baking powder and paprika and add some salt and pepper. Whisk in the water and continue whisking until the batter is smooth — it will be a fairly thick batter.

Pour about 3–4 cm (1½ inches) of oil into a large frying pan and heat it up enough for shallow-frying.

Dip the strips of fish in the batter, shake off the excess and fry for a few minutes on each side until they are crisp and golden. Pat dry on paper towels and then serve at once, with lemon juice squeezed over the top and some extra salt.

Serves 4

APPLES FOR SAM

ABOUT 60 G (2¼ OZ/½ CUP) PLAIN
  (ALL-PURPOSE) FLOUR
ABOUT 75 G (2½ OZ/¾ CUP) DRY BREADCRUMBS
2 SMALL EGGS
1 TABLESPOON CHOPPED PARSLEY
550 G (1 LB 4 OZ) FISH FILLETS, CUT INTO
  CHUNKS
3-4 TABLESPOONS OLIVE OIL
LEMON WEDGES, TO SERVE

Baked
fish fillets

Here is a nice and healthy way to cook your fish, in case you worry about
frying in batter too often.

Preheat the oven to 210°C (415°F/Gas 6-7). Spread the flour on one flattish plate
and the breadcrumbs on another one.

Whisk the eggs and parsley together in a shallow bowl and add some salt.
Sprinkle the fish with some salt, too.

Pat the fish chunks in the flour first, then in the egg and finally in the
breadcrumbs, turning to coat them thoroughly each time. Put the fish on a baking
tray and drizzle with a little of the oil. Turn the fish over and drizzle a little more
oil over the top.

Bake the fish in the oven for 10 minutes, then turn the pieces over and bake
for another 5 minutes or so until they are golden and crisp. Serve with an extra
scattering of salt and some lemon juice squeezed over the top.

Serves 4

400 G (14 OZ) POTATOES, PEELED AND CUT INTO
    CHUNKS
250 ML (9 FL OZ/1 CUP) MILK
30 G (1 OZ) BUTTER
2 TABLESPOONS OLIVE OIL
2 GARLIC CLOVES, PEELED BUT LEFT WHOLE
1 SMALL SAGE SPRIG
200 G (7 OZ) COOKED OR TINNED CHICKPEAS,
    DRAINED

Potato & chickpea mash

If you have some cooked chickpeas left over from something else, this is a great nutritious way to serve them to the small ones of our world. If you need to be a bit more spontaneous, just use tinned chickpeas. You can serve this with an extra drizzle or so of olive oil if you like.

Boil the potatoes for 20–25 minutes in salted water until they are soft. Heat the milk and butter in a small pan until the butter melts. Heat the olive oil, garlic and sage in a saucepan over medium heat until you can smell the garlic. Add the chickpeas and sauté for a few minutes so that the flavours of the garlic and sage mingle with the chickpeas. Remove the garlic and sage. Purée the chickpeas with a hand-held blender until they are completely smooth and silky, adding a little of the milk and butter mixture if necessary.

Mash the potatoes or pass through a potato mill into a wide bowl which you can eventually use for serving. Add the remaining milk and butter mixture and mix it in well. Fold in the chickpea purée and taste for salt. Serve warm or at room temperature, drizzled with extra virgin olive oil if you like.

Serves 6

60 G (2¼ OZ) PECANS
180 G (6½ OZ) RAW CASTER (GOLDEN SUPERFINE)
    SUGAR
185 ML (6 FL OZ/¾ CUP) LIGHT OLIVE OIL
1 TEASPOON VANILLA EXTRACT
3 EGGS
280 G (10 OZ) PLAIN (ALL-PURPOSE) FLOUR
1½ TEASPOONS BAKING POWDER
½ TEASPOON BICARBONATE OF SODA (BAKING
    SODA)
½ TEASPOON GROUND CINNAMON
PINCH OF GROUND NUTMEG
360 G (12¾ OZ/ABOUT 3) ZUCCHINI (COURGETTES),
    COARSELY GRATED
2 TEASPOONS GRATED LEMON ZEST

Zucchini bread

You can't really tell that there is a vegetable in here. This is a lovely bread to make in the summer when there is an abundance of zucchini, and it will keep moist for a few days if you wrap it well. I find a slice makes a great snack, even in times of pre-dinner emergency.

Preheat the oven to 180°C (350°F/Gas 4). Butter and flour a 30 x 11 cm (12 x 4 inch) loaf tin. Spread the pecans on a baking tray and toast them in the oven until they are just crisp and lightly roasted (keep a close eye on them so that they don't burn), then remove the tray from the oven and leave them to cool.

Beat the sugar with the oil and vanilla until smooth and then add the eggs one by one, beating well after each addition. Keep on beating until you have a thick, yet light and fluffy batter. Sift in the flour, baking powder, bicarbonate of soda, cinnamon and nutmeg. Add a pinch of salt and the zucchini, several good grinds of black pepper and the lemon zest and fold together well. Coarsely chop the pecans and gently stir through the batter.

Scrape the batter into the tin and bake for 55–60 minutes, or until a skewer poked into the middle of the loaf comes out clean. Leave the tin on a rack to cool for 10 minutes before turning the loaf out onto the rack to cool. Serve warm or at room temperature, buttered if you like. Well wrapped up, this stays moist and soft for days and it toasts well even after it's lost its moistness.

Cuts into 10–12 slices

125 G (4½ OZ) BUTTER
180 G (6½ OZ/1 CUP) DARK BROWN SUGAR
350 G (12 OZ/3 OR 4 MEDIUM) RIPE BANANAS,
    MASHED
2 EGGS
1 TEASPOON VANILLA EXTRACT
1 TEASPOON GROUND CINNAMON
250 G (9 OZ/2 CUPS) PLAIN (ALL-PURPOSE) FLOUR
1 TEASPOON BAKING POWDER
3/4 TEASPOON BICARBONATE OF SODA (BAKING
    SODA)
3 TABLESPOONS WARM MILK

Banana bread

This is my schoolfriend Alexia's recipe: her mum was a fantastic cook and she always made this. It is a healthy snack or breakfast and an excellent way to use up bananas that otherwise might be on their way out. I always end up making this because bananas in my house just never keep the pale waxy complexion that they have in the shops. For some reason they start deteriorating the minute they come home with me. You can add some chopped walnuts or hazelnuts, too, and some cinnamon. Serve it on its own, or even lightly buttered and with your favourite jam.

Preheat the oven to 180°C (350°F/Gas 4) and butter a 30 x 11 cm (12 x 4 inch) loaf tin.
    Cream the butter and sugar until smooth and then whisk in the mashed bananas. Add the eggs, vanilla, cinnamon and a pinch of salt and whisk in well. Sieve in the flour and baking powder and beat until smooth. Mix the bicarbonate of soda into the milk and stir into the batter.
    Scrape the mixture into the tin and bake for about 50 minutes, until the bread is crusty on the top and a skewer poked into the middle comes out clean. Turn out onto a rack to cool.
    Serve warm or cold, plain or toasted with butter, but allow to cool completely before storing in an airtight container, where it will keep well for several days.

Cuts into 10-12 slices

150 G (5½ OZ) SUGAR
150 G (5½ OZ) BUTTER, SOFTENED
2 EGGS
120 G (4¼ OZ) PLAIN (ALL-PURPOSE) FLOUR
1 TEASPOON BICARBONATE OF SODA (BAKING
    SODA)
1 TEASPOON BAKING POWDER
½ TEASPOON GROUND CARDAMOM
½ TEASPOON GROUND CINNAMON
400 G (14 OZ/ABOUT 2) APPLES, PEELED, CORED
    AND COARSELY GRATED
60 G (2¼ OZ) WALNUTS, LIGHTLY TOASTED AND
    ROUGHLY CHOPPED
1 TEASPOON VANILLA EXTRACT

TOPPING:
60 G (2¼ OZ) WALNUTS, FINELY CHOPPED
60 G (2¼ OZ) BROWN SUGAR
1 TEASPOON GROUND CINNAMON

Apple bread with sugar & cinnamon topping

I love the name apple bread — it carries me off in my fantasy to some very green hills with chunky plates and jugs of fresh cream, with rosy-cheeked children skipping about here and there. It is perfect for snacks, breakfast, with a meal or as a meal with a few chunks of cheese. And maybe even a small pile of fresh blueberries and indeed another pile of fresh cream would be lovely with it. This keeps for several days, well wrapped up. I find it's an excellent healthy snack to have on hand to give to a suddenly starving child. I often send a bit for school snacks as well as banana bread.

Preheat the oven to 180°C (350°F/Gas 4). Butter and flour a 30 x 11 cm (12 x 4 inch) loaf tin. Beat together the sugar and butter until fluffy. Add the eggs and beat them in well. Sift the flour, bicarbonate of soda, baking powder, cardamom and cinnamon in, and add a pinch of salt. Mix well. Add the apples, walnuts and vanilla and mix those through well. Scrape the mixture into the tin.

For the topping, mix together the walnuts, sugar and cinnamon and then scatter abundantly over the top of the batter. Bake for about 45 minutes, or until the top is crusty brown and a skewer poked into the middle comes out clean. Check after 30 minutes and cover the top with foil if it is already quite brown.

Cool slightly before turning out carefully. Do this over your serving plate so that you don't lose any topping. Serve slightly warm or at room temperature, on its own, with whipped cream or with a simple vanilla ice cream.

Cuts into 10-12 slices

1 EGG
120 G (4¼ OZ) LIGHT BROWN SUGAR
1 TEASPOON VANILLA EXTRACT
80 G (2¾ OZ) BUTTER, SOFTENED
50 G (1¾ OZ) PLAIN (ALL-PURPOSE) FLOUR
50 G (1¾ OZ) WHOLEMEAL (WHOLEWHEAT)
   FLOUR
1 TEASPOON BAKING POWDER
100 G (3½ OZ) QUICK-COOKING OATS
1 TABLESPOON MILK

Oat biscuits

These are plain, healthy and good. You could serve them for breakfast instead of porridge sometimes, with a mug of warm milk.

Preheat the oven to 180°C (350°F/Gas 4) and line a large baking tray with baking paper.

Whip the egg, sugar and vanilla together until the sugar has dissolved. Beat in the butter and then sift in the plain and wholemeal flours and baking powder. Add a pinch of salt and the oats and mix well with a wooden spoon. Stir in the milk. With lightly moistened hands, shape the dough into walnut-sized balls and put them, well spaced, on the baking tray. Flatten them a bit so they look like mini hamburger patties. Bake for about 15 minutes until they are golden around the edges (they might still be a little soft on top). Cool on a wire rack and then keep in your biscuit tin for up to 5 days.

Makes about 25 biscuits

250 ML (9 FL OZ/1 CUP) POURING (SINGLE) CREAM
125 ML (4 FL OZ/1/2 CUP) PURE MAPLE SYRUP
250 ML (9 FL OZ/1 CUP) MILK
1 TEASPOON VANILLA EXTRACT

Maple syrup & vanilla ice cream

I am crazy about this with the pecan butter biscuits (page 358). You could also sauté some chopped walnuts or pecans in butter and then fold them through when the ice cream is just about ready. This will keep for up to a week in the freezer.

Mix together the cream and maple syrup in a bowl or container that has a lid. Whisk in the milk and vanilla. Put the lid on the bowl and put it in the freezer. After an hour give the mixture an energetic whisk with a hand whisk or electric mixer. Put it back in the freezer and then whisk again after another couple of hours. When the ice cream is nearly firm, give one last whisk and put it back in the freezer to set.

Alternatively, pour into your ice cream machine and churn, following the manufacturer's instructions.

Serves 6-8

popsi then

220 G (7³/4 OZ) BUTTER, SOFTENED
70 G (2¹/2 OZ) ICING (CONFECTIONERS') SUGAR, PLUS
    A LITTLE EXTRA FOR DUSTING
1 TEASPOON VANILLA EXTRACT
280 G (10 OZ/2¹/4 CUPS) PLAIN (ALL-PURPOSE) FLOUR
70 G (2¹/2 OZ) PECANS, CHOPPED

ICING:
250 G (9 OZ) ICING (CONFECTIONERS') SUGAR
30 G (1 OZ) BUTTER, SOFTENED
1 TEASPOON VANILLA EXTRACT
2 TABLESPOONS MILK
A FEW DROPS OF FOOD COLOURING

Pecan butter biscuits

These are Stella's (Richard's mum), and I have been hooked since I first tasted them. Made without the icing, they are gorgeous with the maple syrup ice cream (page 355). Although I love the pecans here, you might like to try it with another nut — perhaps walnuts or hazelnuts. This will give you about 40 biscuits. You might like to ice yours with a soft creamy icing tinted with your favourite colour.

Preheat your oven to 190°C (375°F/Gas 5). Cream the butter with the icing sugar and vanilla until it is smooth. Add the flour in four portions, mashing it in well with a wooden spoon after each addition. Mix the nuts through.

Divide the dough into quarters. Dip your fingers in icing sugar and then, from each quarter of dough, roll 10 balls the size of cherry tomatoes. Put on two ungreased baking trays, leaving some space between each ball. Flatten each one a bit, and then dip your thumb in icing sugar and make an indent in each ball. The icing sugar will sit in here and, even if you're not icing the biscuits, it'll look good.

Bake one tray at a time for about 15 minutes or until the biscuits are firm and golden, and slightly darker around the edges. Bake for a few more minutes, if necessary. They are delicate, so carefully lift them off the trays and onto racks to cool. Wait until they are completely cold if you are going to ice them, otherwise store them in a biscuit tin.

To make the icing, cream together the icing sugar, butter, vanilla and milk until completely smooth. You may need to use more or less milk to get a soft, buttery consistency. Add the food colouring, mixing it in well. If you are not ready to ice the biscuits immediately, cover the bowl with a wet paper towel.

Use a small butter knife or a teaspoon to spread the icing quite rustically into and over the indentations in the biscuits. When the icing has hardened a little, store the biscuits in a tin. They keep very well at room temperature.

Makes 40

50 ML (1³/4 FL OZ) MAPLE SYRUP
¹/2 TEASPOON GROUND GINGER
1 TEASPOON GROUND CINNAMON
A PINCH OF GROUND CLOVES
¹/2 TEASPOON GROUND CARDAMOM
100 ML (3¹/2 FL OZ) POURING (SINGLE) CREAM
100 G (3¹/2 OZ) CASTER (SUPERFINE) SUGAR
100 G (3¹/2 OZ) BUTTER, SOFTENED
1 EGG
250 G (9 OZ/2 CUPS) PLAIN (ALL-PURPOSE) FLOUR
1 TEASPOON BAKING POWDER

Gingerbread biscuits

My mother's friend, Iria, gave me this recipe. It smells of Christmas and is typical in Finland, she says. You can make gingerbread men or any shapes you like (and there are many cutters available — trees, bells, hearts, birds, cows, flowers). I think these are lovely to dust with icing sugar, wrap up and put in a beautiful wrapped box for a gift. They are not too spicy — but very Christmassy. If you make holes in the biscuits with a skewer when they have just come out of the oven, you can thread them with ribbon or string and hang them on your tree as decorations.

Put the maple syrup, ginger, cinnamon, cloves and cardamom in a small saucepan over low heat, stirring to dissolve all the spices. Remove from the heat and allow to cool a bit, then stir in the cream with a wooden spoon. Mix well, making sure that nothing is left stuck on the bottom.

Beat the sugar and butter together for a minute or two, until the sugar dissolves. Add the egg. Mix in the flour and baking powder alternately with the maple syrup cream. Mix well with a wooden spoon until the mixture is thick and smooth. Cover the dough with plastic wrap and leave in the fridge for at least 3 hours or even overnight.

Preheat the oven to 190°C (375°F/Gas 5) and line two baking trays with baking paper.

Take lumps of the dough and roll out on a floured surface with a floured rolling pin to about 5 mm (¹/4 inch) thick. Add extra flour as you roll if you find the dough too soft to handle. (You can also make the biscuits very thin if you prefer, and they will then need less time in the oven.) Cut out shapes with your cookie cutters. Put about half the shapes on the baking trays, leaving just a little space between them for spreading. Bake one tray at a time for 12-15 minutes, or until the biscuits are golden with a deeper gold around the edges.

Lift them onto wire racks to cool and use the same trays to bake the rest of the biscuits. (If you are making holes to hang them from your Christmas tree, do that now and then hang them when they harden.) These will keep in a biscuit tin or plastic bag for up to 2 weeks.

Makes about 35 biscuits, depending on the shapes

popsi now

stripes

Pot-roast steak with spinach & omelette
Little spinach and carrot pots
Pomegranate & apple jellies
Vanilla ice cream
Chocolate ice cream
Ice cream sundaes
Chocolate & vanilla milkshakes & double thickshakes
Raspberry ripple ice cream
Chocolate & vanilla marble cake
Chocolate vanilla biscuits
Chocolate toffee nut squares

- memory -

I remember the ice cream man with the box on his bicycle, coming down the road and ringing his bell. The diagonal red and silver stripes in that milky sorbet. Such sweet, chocolatey music... I wish I could have that again. We did that once — got my father to take us up to the shop and bought 20 ice creams and attached them onto our bicycles somehow and rode down the road trying to sell them before they melted — then strewed them, like petals, to our neighbours. And once I took an ice cream to school in my small suitcase and thought to eat it at lunch break. There was such a mess and ripples of laughter from the other small childen.

1 SMALL CELERY STALK
1 SMALL CARROT, PEELED AND ROUGHLY CHOPPED
1 LARGE RED ONION, ROUGHLY CHOPPED
5 TABLESPOONS OLIVE OIL
400 G (14 OZ) TINNED DICED TOMATOES
3 TABLESPOONS CHOPPED PARSLEY
1 GARLIC CLOVE, PEELED AND SQUASHED A BIT
200 G (7 OZ) SPINACH LEAVES, ROUGHLY CHOPPED
20 G ($^{3}/_{4}$ OZ) BUTTER
3 EGGS
2 TABLESPOONS GRATED PARMESAN CHEESE
600 G (1 LB 5 OZ) THICK SLICE OF RUMP STEAK
75 G (2$^{3}/_{4}$ OZ) THINLY SLICED HAM
125 ML (4$^{1}/_{2}$ FL OZ/$^{1}/_{2}$ CUP) RED WINE

Pot-roast steak with spinach & omelette

Ask your butcher to slice the meat in half horizontally, stopping just before he cuts all the way through so that the steak opens out like a book. I love to serve this with buttered noodles and you might even like to add a few peas to the omelette for a spotted effect.

Put the celery, carrot and onion in a processor and pulse until they are finely chopped, or do so by hand. Heat 3 tablespoons of the oil in a flameproof casserole and fry the chopped vegetables over medium heat until they are nicely golden. Add the tomatoes and parsley and cook for about 5 minutes, until the tomatoes collapse and bubble up thickly. Add 250 ml (9 fl oz/1 cup) of hot water, season with salt and keep warm.

Meanwhile, heat 1 tablespoon of oil and the garlic in a 28 cm (11 inch) non-stick frying pan and add the spinach. Cook over medium heat until the spinach wilts, turning it over often so that it cooks evenly. Remove from the pan and season with salt. Drain well.

Wipe out the pan with a paper towel. Add the butter and melt over medium-low heat. Beat the eggs, parmesan and a little salt together and pour into the pan. Swirl the pan so that the egg reaches the side to make a flat omelette. Fry until it is just set, spiking it here and there if necessary so that the uncooked egg runs to the bottom. Remove from the heat.

Lay the steak out flat and cover with a sheet of plastic wrap. Pound with a meat mallet until the steak is 3 mm (^{1}/8 inch) thick all over. Remove the plastic and season the meat with salt and pepper. Slide the omelette from its pan to cover the meat, then spread the spinach on top and cover this with the ham slices. Roll up tightly and tie with string.

Heat the remaining oil in the frying pan and brown the meat on all sides over medium heat, salting the browned parts as you go. Add the wine and cook until it bubbles up, scraping the bits off the bottom of the pan. Put the meat and the winey juices in the casserole dish with the tomato sauce (if the sauce looks as if it needs more liquid, add a little more water), cover and simmer over low heat for about 20 minutes, until the meat is cooked through but still tender. Remove from the heat and leave with the lid on for another 15 minutes before slicing. Serve with the sauce spooned over. Nice with buttered noodles or mashed potatoes.

Serves 4

400 G (14 OZ) CARROTS, PEELED AND CHOPPED
200 G (7 OZ) ENGLISH SPINACH LEAVES
80 G (2³/4 OZ) PARMESAN CHEESE, GRATED
2 EGGS, LIGHTLY BEATEN

BÉCHAMEL SAUCE:
60 G (2¹/4 OZ) BUTTER
40 G (1¹/2 OZ) PLAIN (ALL-PURPOSE) FLOUR
400 ML (14 FL OZ) MILK, WARMED
FRESHLY GROUND NUTMEG

Little spinach & carrot pots

I use little individual pots (about 6 cm/2¹/2 inches wide at the top, 4 cm/1¹/2 inches across the base and 4 cm/1¹/2 inches high). They look good in this size and are perfect servings for all-size humans. These are baked in a bain marie so they stay beautifully moist.

Preheat the oven to 180°C (350°F/Gas 4) and butter ten little 100 ml (3¹/2 fl oz) pudding pots. Cook the carrots in boiling salted water until they are soft. Lift them out with a slotted spoon, purée and put into a bowl. Add the spinach to the boiling carrot water and blanch for a few minutes until it is all wilted and soft. Drain, leave until it has cooled enought to handle and then squeeze out all the excess water. Chop up finely and put in a separate bowl.

To make the béchamel, melt the butter in a small saucepan. Whisk in the flour and cook for a few minutes, stirring constantly, then begin adding the warm milk. It will be immediately absorbed, so work quickly, whisking with one hand while adding ladlefuls of milk with the other. When the sauce seems to be smooth and not too stiff, add salt, pepper and a grating of nutmeg and continue cooking, even after it comes to the boil, for 5 minutes or so, mixing all the time. It should be a very thick and smooth sauce.

Pour off any water that has collected in the bottom of the carrot bowl, then mix in 8 tablespoons of the béchamel along with half of the parmesan. Stir the rest of the béchamel and parmesan into the spinach. Taste each bowl, adding extra salt, pepper or nutmeg if you think it's needed. Add half the beaten eggs to each bowl and mix them in well.

Divide the spinach mixture among the pots. Rap them firmly on the table to flatten the mixture, then divide the carrot purée among the pots. The mixture should just fill the pots.

Put the pots in a roasting tin and add enough hot water to the tin to come halfway up the sides of the pots. Move the tin carefully to the oven and bake for about 45 minutes, or until the pots are puffed, golden and firm. Turn the oven off and leave the tin in the oven for about 10 minutes. Remove the pots from the tin, carefully run a knife around the rims then turn them out onto plates.

Makes 10

VEGETABLE OIL, FOR GREASING
170 ML (5½ FL OZ/²/3 CUP) POMEGRANATE JUICE
 (FROM 2 LARGE POMEGRANATES)
2 TABLESPOONS LEMON JUICE
75 G (2³/4 OZ) CASTER (SUPERFINE) SUGAR
24 G (1 OZ) LEAF GELATINE, OR 6 TEASPOONS
 POWDERED GELATINE
170 ML (5½ FL OZ/²/3 CUP) APPLE JUICE

Pomegranate & apple jellies

When I was a child they recommended jelly and ice cream after tonsil operations because it goes down so well when you have a sore throat. I forget about jelly sometimes and then, when I remember, I make it — because actually it's like giving your child a slice of pure fruit juice. I make it with a good pure-as-possible juice — you can use any flavour you like but you do need colour in your jellies. Serve the jellies plain, or with a small scoop of vanilla or buttermilk ice cream or even a little pile of the actual fruit, served on the side with a dusting of icing sugar. You can just make three pomegranate and three apple jellies and forget about the stripes, if you're short of time.

Brush four 250 ml (9 fl oz/1 cup) moulds with vegetable oil and then wipe out the excess oil with a paper towel. If you're using leaf gelatine, put the pomegranate juice, 1 tablespoon of lemon juice and 50 g (1³/4 oz) of sugar in a saucepan with 3 tablespoons of water. Heat gently, stirring until the sugar dissolves. Put half the gelatine leaves in a bowl of cold water to soften for a couple of minutes. Squeeze out the excess water and add the gelatine to the pan. Stir until it has completely dissolved. (If you're using powdered gelatine, don't put 3 tablespoons of water into the juice pan, but put it in a small bowl and sprinkle the gelatine over it. Leave for a minute or two until it softens and swells and then stir it into the hot juice. Continue stirring until it is completely smooth.)

Put the apple juice in a small saucepan with the remaining lemon juice, remaining sugar and 3 tablespoons of water. Heat gently, stirring until the sugar dissolves. Soak the remaining gelatine leaves in cold water for a couple of minutes and when softened, squeeze them out. Add to the pan of apple juice and stir until the gelatine has completely dissolved. (Once again, you need to change the method slightly if you're using powdered gelatine.)

Divide half of the pomegranate mixture between two of the moulds. Put the remaining mixture to one side, but do not refrigerate. Divide half of the apple mixture between the other two moulds and put what's left aside.

Refrigerate the moulds for about 3 hours until the jellies are almost completely set. Now carefully spoon the rest of the apple mixture on top of the pomegranate jellies and vice versa, so that each jelly has two stripes. (If the jelly has already started to set in the pan, heat it up ever so slightly to just melt it, leave to cool completely and then pour over the set layer.) Put the moulds back in the fridge for at least 4 hours or overnight, until the jellies are set.

To serve, gently pull the jellies away from the sides of the moulds with your fingers. Quickly dip each mould into a bowl of hot water twice (too long and your jelly will dissolve). Turn out onto a plate. If the jelly doesn't want to come away, help it along by slipping your fingers down one side — the whole jelly should then plop onto your plate. Serve plain or with ice cream.

Serves 4

---

3 EGGS
120 G (4¼ OZ) CASTER (SUPERFINE) SUGAR
1 TEASPOON VANILLA EXTRACT
250 ML (9 FL OZ/1 CUP) MILK
1 VANILLA BEAN
500 ML (17 FL OZ/2 CUPS) POURING (SINGLE) CREAM

Vanilla ice cream

This is simple and quick to make and fairly essential for serving with a whole raft of desserts. Or just a scoop of vanilla ice cream alone, I find one of the cleanest and purest foods possible. If you don't have a vanilla bean, just use an extra teaspoon of good vanilla extract. The washed and dried vanilla bean can be popped into a jar of sugar to make vanilla sugar. So next time you need sugar and vanilla, use your vanilla sugar instead.

Whip together the eggs, sugar and vanilla until smooth and creamy. Put the milk in a saucepan. Split the vanilla bean lengthways, scrape the seeds into the milk with the tip of a teaspoon and throw the bean in, too. Heat gently so that the vanilla bean and seeds flavour the milk. Just before the milk comes to the boil, remove it from the heat and whisk a ladleful into the eggs to acclimatize them. Whisk in another ladleful and then tip the whole lot back into the saucepan with the milk. Put it over the lowest possible heat and cook for a minute or so, whisking all the time, just so that the eggs cook through. Remove from the heat, whisk in the cream and pour into a bowl or container that has a lid. Leave to cool completely, whisking now and then while it cools so that you get the maximum flavour from the vanilla bean. Remove the vanilla bean and rinse and dry it for another use.

Put the lid on the bowl and put it in the freezer. After an hour give the mixture an energetic whisk with a hand whisk or electric mixer. Put it back in the freezer and then whisk again after another couple of hours. When the ice cream is nearly firm, give one last whisk and put it back in the freezer to set.

Alternatively, pour into your ice cream machine and churn, following the manufacturer's instructions.

Makes 1.25 litres (44 fl oz/5 cups)

200 G (7 OZ) DARK (SEMI-SWEET) CHOCOLATE,
    ROUGHLY CHOPPED
375 ML (13 FL OZ/1½ CUPS) MILK
3 EGG YOLKS
100 G (3½ OZ) CASTER (SUPERFINE) SUGAR
1 TEASPOON VANILLA EXTRACT
250 ML (9 FL OZ/1 CUP) POURING (SINGLE) CREAM

Chocolate ice cream

This is rich and beautiful. It makes me incredibly happy to have a scoop of beautiful chocolate and a scoop of beautiful vanilla next to each other. I don't like ice cream to be too sweet, and the chocolate you use will be important in determining the amount of sugar. Use the best-quality chocolate you can buy. You might even like to try this one day with a couple of spoonfuls of cocoa powder stirred in for an even richer hit of chocolate. Save the whites in the freezer for pavlova or meringues — you never know when you'll need them.

Put the chocolate and milk in a heavy-based saucepan over low heat, whisking often until it has all melted together. Take care that it doesn't stick and burn. Meanwhile, whisk the egg yolks with the sugar and vanilla in a bowl until thick and creamy. Whisk in a ladleful of the warm chocolate milk to acclimatize the eggs. Whisk in another ladleful and then tip the whole lot back into the saucepan and put it over the lowest possible heat. Cook for a minute or so, whisking all the time, just so that the eggs cook through. Remove from the heat. Whisk in the cream and pour into a bowl or container that has a lid. Leave to cool completely and then put the lid on the bowl and put it in the freezer. After an hour give the mixture an energetic whisk with a hand whisk or electric mixer. Put it back in the freezer and then whisk again after another couple of hours. When the ice cream is nearly firm, give one last whisk and put it back in the freezer to set.

Alternatively, pour into your ice cream machine and churn, following the manufacturer's instructions.

Makes 1.25 litres (44 fl oz/5 cups)

FOR EACH SUNDAE:
3 TABLESPOONS BERRY SYRUP (PAGE 15), FRUIT
 SAUCE (PAGES 54 AND 107) OR CHOCOLATE
 OR TOFFEE SAUCE (PAGES 321 AND 247)
2 SCOOPS ICE CREAM
3-4 TABLESPOONS LIGHTLY WHIPPED CREAM

Ice cream sundaes

Once you know your family's favourite flavours, you can really have fun here. Serve these in a big bowl or glass for a very special treat, with your own home-made chocolate, toffee or fruit sauce and freshly whipped cream. One scoop chocolate, one scoop vanilla, one scoop maple syrup ice cream (page 355) with chocolate sauce is also good. You can also make sorbet sundaes (mango, pomegranate and strawberry) with a little whipped cream. And you can also scatter some chopped nuts over the cream and add chunks of fresh fruit, too. You can go quite over the top, as long as there are not too many kids seated and waiting.

Drizzle a little of the sauce or syrup around the side of a sundae bowl or dessert glass so that it sticks there. Put the ice cream in the bottom, top with the cream and drizzle the syrup or sauce over the top. Leave it for a few minutes for the syrup to run down through the cream and ice cream, then serve before the ice cream melts too much.

Makes 1

My children like to have a scoop of chocolate and a scoop of vanilla. And I watch them stirring and staring into their bowls through the various stripes and streaks of brown and white that finally settle into beige soup. It flings me right back in time to my childhood.

FOR EACH MILKSHAKE:
2 SCOOPS CHOCOLATE OR VANILLA ICE CREAM
    (PAGES 376 AND 374)
250 ML (9 FL OZ/1 CUP) MILK
3 TABLESPOONS CHOCOLATE FUDGE SAUCE OR MARS
    BAR SAUCE (PAGE 321)

FOR EACH DOUBLE THICKSHAKE:
3 SCOOPS CHOCOLATE OR VANILLA ICE CREAM
    (PAGES 376 AND 374)
3 TABLESPOONS CHOCOLATE FUDGE SAUCE OR MARS
    BAR SAUCE (PAGE 321)

Chocolate & vanilla milkshakes & double thickshakes

I loved these when I was growing up. I like to make them chocolate or vanilla — both with some chocolate sauce drizzled so that it is stuck around the side of the glass and has to be scraped off with a spoon. Vanilla ice cream with some berry sauce (page 54) dribbled around the glass is also good, or strawberry sorbet (page 59) instead of vanilla ice cream.

If you don't have a special milkshake machine, move the ice cream from the freezer to the fridge 5 minutes or so beforehand so that it is slightly softened and easy to whisk.

Whisk the ice cream in a bowl until it is soft and creamy. You can do this by hand, or with a hand-held blender. Add the milk and whisk until smooth and frothy.

Trickle most of the sauce around a tall glass so that it clings to the side and then pour in the milkshake. Drizzle the last of the sauce on top and serve at once, with straws (everything always tastes delicious with straws).

Serves 1

DOUBLE THICKSHAKE: Whisk the softened ice cream with a hand-held blender until it is soft and creamy.

Trickle most of the sauce around a tall glass so that it clings to the side and then pour in the thickshake. Drizzle the last of the sauce on top and serve at once, with straws and a long teaspoon.

Serves 1

ICE CREAM:
250 ML (9 FL OZ/1 CUP) MILK
3 EGGS
120 G (4¼ OZ) CASTER (SUPERFINE) SUGAR
1 TEASPOON VANILLA EXTRACT
500 ML (17 FL OZ/2 CUPS) POURING (SINGLE) CREAM

RASPBERRY PUREE:
40 G (1½ OZ) CASTER (SUPERFINE) SUGAR
JUICE OF HALF A LEMON
250 G (9 OZ) RASPBERRIES

Raspberry ripple ice cream

Try to use fresh raspberries here, but frozen will do if you can't find any. Sometimes I love a tiny scoop of this with a tiny scoop of strawberry sorbet and a tiny scoop of vanilla ice cream. Just on its own or with a couple of vanilla biscuits on the side.

For the ice cream, heat the milk gently in a saucepan. Whisk the eggs, sugar and vanilla extract together in a bowl until they are smooth and creamy. Just before the milk comes to the boil, remove it from the heat and whisk a ladleful into the eggs to acclimatize them. Whisk in another ladleful and then pour the eggs and milk back into the saucepan. Turn down the heat to its lowest and cook for a minute or so, whisking all the time, just to cook the eggs through. Remove from the heat, whisk in the cream and pour into a bowl that has a lid. Leave to cool completely, whisking now and then while it cools.

Put the lid on the bowl and put it in the freezer. After an hour, remove the bowl from the freezer and give the mix an energetic whisk with a hand whisk or electric mixer and then put it back in the freezer. Whisk again after another couple of hours. Put it back in the freezer until it is nearly firm.

Meanwhile, make the raspberry purée. Put the sugar, lemon juice and 125 ml (4 fl oz/½ cup) of water in a small saucepan and bring to the boil. Simmer over low heat for about 5 minutes until it has reduced a bit. Take it off the heat, add the raspberries and then purée until smooth. Strain the purée through a fine sieve to catch all the seeds. Cool completely.

Swirl the purée through the ice cream with a spoon. Make a few more swirls, folds and pirouettes but not so many that the purée starts to blend in with the ice cream. Cover the bowl again and return to the freezer to set completely.

Alternatively, pour the ice cream mixture into an ice cream machine and churn following the manufacturer's instructions. When it is ready, transfer to a freezer container and then add the raspberry purée and make your swirls.

Take out of the freezer a few minutes before serving so that it is not rock hard.

Makes 1.5 litres (52 fl oz/6 cups)

250 G (9 OZ) BUTTER, SOFTENED
280 G (10 OZ/1¼ CUPS) CASTER (SUPERFINE) SUGAR
4 EGGS
280 G (10 OZ/2¼ CUPS) PLAIN (ALL-PURPOSE) FLOUR
1½ TEASPOONS BAKING POWDER
150 ML (5 FL OZ) POURING (SINGLE) CREAM
1 TEASPOON VANILLA EXTRACT
2 TABLESPOONS UNSWEETENED COCOA POWDER

Chocolate & vanilla marble cake

This is a recipe from my mother's Finnish friend, Iria. She and my mum say that every Finn has their own recipe for a classic stripey 'tiger cake'. You can also make this with just vanilla and have a plain sponge cake — good for filling with jam and cream or covering with a chocolate icing — but most people love to see the two different colours in the cake. Children enjoy helping with this — they love licking the beaters and the chocolate and vanilla bowls.

Preheat the oven to 180°C (350°F/Gas 4). Grease and flour a 24 cm (9½ inch) springform cake tin or a small bundt tin.

Beat the butter and sugar together until pale and creamy. Add the eggs one at a time, beating well after each one goes in. Sift in the flour and baking powder and beat well, then beat in the cream so that you have a fluffy mixture. Divide the batter between two bowls, putting more than half into one bowl. To this add the vanilla and beat it in well. Sift the cocoa into the other half, whisking it in completely.

Dollop most of the vanilla batter into the greased tin (you don't have to entirely cover the bottom). Then dollop the chocolate batter in here and there, followed by the remaining few tablespoons of the vanilla batter. Use a skewer or the tip of a teaspoon to make a few swirls so that the two batters become a bit stripey. You don't want them mixing together, but distinct white and brown patches swirling into each other.

Bake for 50-60 minutes, or until a skewer poked into the centre comes out clean. Cool in the tin before turning out.

Makes one 24 cm (9½ inch) cake

APPLES FOR SAM

180 G (6½ OZ) BUTTER, SOFTENED
150 G (5½ OZ) CASTER (SUPERFINE) SUGAR
1 EGG
1 TEASPOON VANILLA EXTRACT
240 G (8¾ OZ) PLAIN (ALL-PURPOSE) FLOUR
20 G (¾ OZ) UNSWEETENED COCOA POWDER

Chocolate & vanilla biscuits

These are lovely and easy, and something that kids can make from beginning to end, as long as you don't worry too much how they turn out. They could also be good to use for making and shaping Christmas decorations — you could make white or brown faces with eyes, mouth, hair, even white and brown plaits... You might like to add some ground cinnamon, anise, cardamom or other spices to the dough.

Mash together the butter and sugar in a bowl with a wooden spoon. Add a pinch of salt and all but 20 g (¾ oz) of the flour and work them in. Whisk the egg with the vanilla and add this to the bowl, mixing it all well. Now knead it quickly, gently and thoroughly.

Divide the dough in half. Add the cocoa to one half, kneading it in thoroughly. Knead the remaining 20 g (¾ oz) of flour into the other half. Pat both doughs down into flattish discs, cover separately with plastic wrap and refrigerate for about 30 minutes.

Preheat the oven to 180°C (350°F/Gas 4).

On a lightly floured surface, roll out the doughs separately to a thickness of about a few millimetres, depending on what you decide to make. You can cut out circles, squares and Christmas shapes with a biscuit cutter, cut free-form shapes with a small blunt knife, or make plaits by folding strips of each colour over each other and pressing the ends together. Put on baking trays lined with baking paper, allowing a little room for the biscuits to spread. Bake for 12-15 minutes, or until they are crisp.

Makes plenty!

225 G (8 OZ/2¼ CUPS) PECANS OR WALNUTS,
  ROUGHLY CHOPPED
450 G (1 LB) BUTTER
1 TEASPOON VANILLA EXTRACT
500 G (1 LB 2 OZ/2¼ CUPS) SUGAR
250 G (9 OZ) DARK (SEMI-SWEET)
  CHOCOLATE, CHOPPED

Chocolate toffee nut squares

These are my friend Toni's. She always arrives with a bagful for me and the kids and so she finally showed me how to make them. You don't have to cut them into perfect squares — they are nice broken up into irregular bits. These are lovely wrapped up and taken to a friend as a gift — just as Toni did for me.

Line a 27 x 40 x 2.5 cm (11 x 16 x 1 inch) baking tray with a double thickness of baking paper. Scatter the nuts in and flatten them with the back of a wooden spoon to make a compact even layer.

  Put the butter and vanilla in a heavy-based saucepan and add a pinch of salt and 2 tablespoons of water. Heat until the butter melts and just starts to bubble, then add the sugar. Cook over low heat, stirring almost continuously to prevent it sticking to the bottom, until you have a thick rich toffee-coloured mass that comes away from the side of the pan when stirred — if you have a thermometer it will be at just below 150°C (300°F). It could take up to 20 minutes to get there, depending on your pan and the heat. If the toffee looks like separating at any point, take it off the heat and vigorously beat in 2 tablespoons of hot water to bring it together again, standing back as it may splash up.

  Carefully pour the toffee over the nuts, pouring around the sides first and working your way in to cover all the nuts. Scatter the chocolate as evenly as possible over the hot toffee, then leave it for 5 minutes to soften before spreading it evenly with a spatula. Leave to cool and set completely — in the fridge if it's very hot. Use the baking paper to lift it out of the tin. Break up into pieces and keep in a biscuit tin, or in the fridge if the weather's hot.

Makes about 20 squares

multicolour

Smoothies
Tiny savoury tartlets
Raw vegetables with sauce for dunking
Meat & vegetable soup
Mixed vegetable risotto
Sausage & potato frittata
Meatloaf with roasted vegetables
Roasted zucchini & tomatoes with thyme
Pavlovas with oranges & cherries
Tiny sweet tartlets with crema and fruit
Pandoro birthday cake

- memory -

Our toys might come alive at night, we believed, just like in the stories they had read us. And so we tried not to fall asleep, fighting against our dragging lids and crossing our hearts that we'd wake each other when the excitement began. We never saw that happen, but we could imagine it as we played the next day — skirts flapping, dusty shoes and trying not to crumple the butterfly's wing that we had just saved.

We would sift through our dried flowers and want to help, now and then, in the house with the fun jobs, like snipping away the roses that had finished with their blossoming, or spilling more water or food into our dog's bowl. Washing up the dishes and mopping floors were among our very favourites, along with whisking anything cakey or biscuity and licking the bowl afterwards, and washing our dolls' clothes in a big basin of soapy water outside on the veranda. There were also some dull things that we sometimes got asked to do, but mostly we tried to shuffle away, pretending our ears were blocked. Laying the table was an inbetween kind of job. But tidying up was our worst. We just couldn't see the point of that at all.

PEACH SMOOTHIE:
1 JUICY PEACH, PEELED, STONED AND SLICED
125 G (4½ OZ/½ CUP) GREEK-STYLE NATURAL YOGHURT
125 ML (4 FL OZ/½ CUP) MILK
1 HEAPED TEASPOON HONEY

APRICOT SMOOTHIE:
4 APRICOTS, PEELED, STONED AND CUT INTO CHUNKS
125 ML (4 FL OZ/½ CUP) BUTTERMILK
125 ML (4 FL OZ/½ CUP) MILK
1 TEASPOON HONEY

STRAWBERRY SMOOTHIE:
115 G (4 OZ) STRAWBERRIES, HULLED
125 ML (4 FL OZ/½ CUP) BUTTERMILK
125 ML (4 FL OZ/½ CUP) MILK
1 TEASPOON HONEY

BLUEBERRY AND RASPBERRY SMOOTHIE:
75 G (2¾ OZ) BLUEBERRIES
60 G (2¼ OZ) RASPBERRIES
125 ML (4 FL OZ/½ CUP) MILK
100 G (3½ OZ) GREEK-STYLE NATURAL YOGHURT
1 TEASPOON MAPLE SYRUP

Smoothies

These are wonderful for breakfast or just as a snack. You can use pretty much any fruit you like. My kids love these and like to see a wedge of the fruit on the top of their smoothie glass. Use a nice creamy natural yoghurt and make sure your fruit is ripe and cold before you make these.

Blend all the ingredients until very smooth and frothy, and add more honey or maple syrup if you prefer your smoothie sweeter.

All make 1 large glass

PASTRY CASES:
125 G (4½ OZ) BUTTER, CUT INTO CUBES
250 G (9 OZ/2 CUPS) PLAIN (ALL-PURPOSE) FLOUR
½ TABLESPOON OLIVE OIL

Tiny savoury tartlets

I always make these for birthdays. They are just the right size to pop into a child's mouth. Adults love them, too, and you can be as modern as you like with your fillings. The number of pastry shells you get will depend on the size of your cases. Mine are tiny individual ones, while some are punched into a tray of 12 or 24.

For the pastry, put the butter and flour in a bowl with ½ teaspoon of salt and crumble with your fingers until it is like coarse sand. Add 3 tablespoons of cold water and the oil and work into a loose dough. Knead quickly but gently until smooth, then flatten, cover with plastic wrap and refrigerate for about an hour.
    Preheat the oven to 180°C (350°F/Gas 4) and have ready 45 tiny tart cases that are 4.5 cm (1³/4 inches) across the top and no more than 2 cm (³/4 inch) deep. They don't need to be greased (there is enough butter in the dough).
    Break off small balls of pastry about the size of cherry tomatoes and flatten into the cases with your thumb and forefinger, pressing to a couple of millimetres thick. (If your cases are shallow you could roll out the pastry first, then press into the cases and trim the excess pastry away.) Bake for about 20 minutes, or until golden, and then cool a bit in the cases before gently removing. Leave to cool completely before filling.
    These can be made the day before and kept in an airtight container overnight.

Makes about 40 tartlet cases

FILLING IDEAS:
- soft-boiled eggs mashed with olive oil and chopped parsley;
- avocado mashed with lemon juice and paprika;
- a 320 g (11 oz) tin of tuna in oil mashed with 3 soft-boiled eggs, a chopped spring onion (scallion), 1 tablespoon chopped parsley, 2 tablespoons mayonnaise, the juice of 1 lemon, a pinch of paprika and 2 tablespoons light olive oil.

The tartlets are best with something creamy to balance the pastry. Any soft cheese like mozzarella works well and sometimes I like to use 250 g (9 oz/1 cup) smooth ricotta mixed with 25 g (1 oz) grated parmesan, 1 scant tablespoon olive oil, the juice of half a lemon and a little fresh thyme. I fill all the cases with this, then top with any of the following:
- roasted tomatoes, basil oil, parmesan flakes
- smoked salmon, dill sprigs, a drizzle of lemon juice
- bresaola or prosciutto, torn basil leaves, parmesan flakes.

APPLES FOR SAM

5 TABLESPOONS OLIVE OIL
1 TEASPOON HONEY
½ TEASPOON DIJON MUSTARD
1 TABLESPOON SESAME SEEDS
1 TABLESPOON BALSAMIC VINEGAR
JUICE OF 1 LEMON
1 ROSEMARY SPRIG
1 GARLIC CLOVE, PEELED AND SQUASHED A BIT
1 RED PEPPER (CAPSICUM), CUT INTO THICKISH
   CHUNKS
1 SMALL FENNEL BULB, TRIMMED, HALVED AND CUT
   INTO SLICES
4 INNER CELERY STALKS, CUT INTO STICKS
FIRM INNER LEAVES OF A SMALL ROMAINE
   (COS) LETTUCE
4–5 THICK SLICES BROWN BREAD, CUT INTO CHUNKS

Raw vegetables with sauce for dunking

Use the best-looking, healthiest and most colourful vegetables you can find. You might like to make variations — some mashed-up avocado or a soft creamy cheese for dipping as well. The sauce can be served in individual bowls or just one big communal bowl if it's family.

Put the oil, honey, mustard, sesame seeds and vinegar in a bowl and whisk together well with a fork. Add salt to taste. Squeeze in lemon juice, tasting as you go, and stop when you're happy with the flavour. Add the rosemary and garlic and leave for the flavours to mingle while you prepare the vegetables.

Rinse the vegetables, drain and pat dry. Stack in groups on a platter and pile the bread on too. Serve with the bowl of sauce and a pile of napkins.

Serves 4

500 G (1 LB 2 OZ) STEWING BEEF (SILVERSIDE,
   TOPSIDE)
ABOUT 650 G (1 LB 7 OZ) VERY RIPE TOMATOES
2 LEAFY CELERY STALKS, CHOPPED
3 CARROTS, PEELED AND CHOPPED
1 HANDFUL PARSLEY, ROUGHLY CHOPPED
2 BAY LEAVES
5 ALLSPICE BERRIES
4 SMALLISH ZUCCHINI (COURGETTES), CHOPPED
400 G (14 OZ) POTATOES, PEELED AND CUT INTO
   SMALL CHUNKS
OLIVE OIL, TO SERVE
GRATED PARMESAN CHEESE, TO SERVE

Meat &
vegetable soup

You'll need the largest stockpot you've got to make this nutritious and tasty soup. A bit of everything goes in here and you can take it straight to the table as a complete meal with your favourite bread. You could leave out the meat and use just vegetables, if you like, adding a couple more varieties. I use very lean beef here but, if you like the taste of the fat, make sure you buy a good piece of meat and don't trim it. Keep the cut-up potatoes in a bowl of cold water or cut them up later while the soup is cooking, as they only need to go in for the last 40 minutes. This is an abundant amount of soup that will serve many and still give you leftovers and enough time the next day to make a cake.

Cut up the meat into pieces about the size of Turkish delight, or smaller if you would prefer to find them that way in your bowl later. Put them in a large pot and cover with about 2.5 litres (87 fl oz/10 cups) of cold water. Bring to the boil, skimming the surface until it is clear. Simmer, covered, for about 30 minutes.

   Meanwhile, cut the core out of each tomato and cut a cross on the bottom. Drop them into the boiling meat broth for about 20 seconds, until they wrinkle and the skin starts to come away. Lift them out with a slotted spoon, peel them and chop them up. Add to the meat pot with the celery and carrots and bring back to the boil, skimming the surface again if necessary. Add the parsley, bay leaves and allspice berries, counting how many you put in so you know exactly how many to fish out before serving. Season with salt, lower the heat and simmer for about 1 1/2 hours, uncovered at first until the liquid level reduces a bit, and then covered. Add the zucchini and potatoes about 40 minutes from the end. Taste that there is enough salt and add pepper, if you want. Check the liquid level, adding a little more water towards the end if you prefer it more soupy than stewy. Serve warm, with parmesan and olive oil drizzled over the top of each serving.

Serve 6-8

3 TABLESPOONS OLIVE OIL
1 RED ONION, FINELY CHOPPED
1 LEAFY CELERY STALK, CUT INTO SMALL BLOCKS
100 G (3½ OZ) CARROTS, PEELED AND CUT INTO
    SMALL BLOCKS
200 G (7 OZ) ZUCCHINI (COURGETTES), CUT INTO
    SMALL BLOCKS
80 G (2¾ OZ) GREEN BEANS, TRIMMED, CUT INTO
    3-4 CM (1½ INCH) LENGTHS
1 LARGE RIPE TOMATO, PEELED, DESEEDED AND
    CHOPPED
2 OR 3 BASIL LEAVES, TORN
400 G (14 OZ) RISOTTO RICE
125 ML (4 FL OZ/½ CUP) WHITE WINE
1 HEAPED TABLESPOON CHOPPED PARSLEY
30 G (1 OZ) BUTTER
40 G (1½ OZ) PARMESAN CHEESE, GRATED, PLUS
    EXTRA FOR SERVING

Mixed vegetable risotto

Sometimes I like to serve this a little more liquidy than a normal risotto so that it's a bit soupy when I take it to the table but carries on absorbing liquid. You can add absolutely any other vegetables you like to this basic version. I give the children a large tea cup as well as their plate of risotto, then they can spoon tiny quantities of risotto into the cup, patting it around the edge, so that it cools quicker. Giovanni has always done this since he was a child, so that he doesn't have to wait for ages for his risotto to cool down.

Heat the oil in a wide heavy-based pan suitable for making risotto. Sauté the onion, celery and carrots over medium heat until they are lightly golden and softened. Add the zucchini, beans, tomato and some of the basil and sauté for another 5 minutes or so. Add the rice, sauté for a couple of minutes to coat it with oil, and then pour in the wine. Let it bubble up and then reduce. Add 1 litre (35 fl oz/ 4 cups) of hot water and some salt and pepper and bring to the boil. Lower the heat and simmer for about 20 minutes, stirring now and then.

Towards the end, when it looks like most of the liquid has been absorbed, add another 250 ml (9 fl oz/1 cup) of hot water. Taste to check that there is enough salt. The risotto is ready when the rice is cooked and the dish is still a bit liquidy. Stir in the rest of the basil, the parsley, butter and parmesan and leave with the lid on for a couple of minutes. Serve with extra parmesan.

Serves 5-6

2 SMALL POTATOES, SCRUBBED
5 TABLESPOONS OLIVE OIL
375 G (13 OZ) ITALIAN SAUSAGE, SKINNED AND
    CRUMBLED
1 RED ONION, CHOPPED
1 CARROT, PEELED AND CHOPPED
80 G (2¾ OZ) BUTTON MUSHROOMS, FINELY SLICED
4 TABLESPOONS CHOPPED PARSLEY
6 EGGS, LIGHTLY BEATEN

Sausage &
potato frittata

This is from Richard and Sue, my two American friends, and I like this
for a Sunday breakfast or supper with wholemeal bread. If you think
your children won't enjoy the vegetables here, you could make it with
just the sausage, potatoes and parsley — or anything else you know will
be appreciated.

Boil the potatoes in their skins in lightly salted water until they are tender but not
breaking up. Drain, cool and then cut into chunks, keeping the skins on. Put to one
side for now.

Heat 2 tablespoons of the oil in a 26 cm (10½ inch) non-stick frying pan over
medium heat and fry the sausage meat until it is quite deeply golden, breaking up
clusters with a wooden spoon. Lift out into a bowl with a slotted spoon. Add the
onion to the pan and sauté until golden, then add the carrot. Sauté for 5 minutes
or so, until both become soft and a bit gooey. Add another tablespoon of oil and the
mushrooms and sauté until the mushrooms have given up their water and turned
golden. Season lightly if needed. Spoon the contents of the pan into the bowl with
the sausage.

Preheat the grill (broiler) to medium–high.

Add the last of the oil to the pan and sauté the potatoes until they have a
golden crust in some places. Stir in the parsley and the contents of the sausage
bowl and cook for a minute or two. Reduce the heat to medium–low and pour in
the eggs, shifting everything around with a wooden spoon so that the eggs leak
under here and there. Once the bottom looks softly set, put the pan under the grill
so that the frittata sets just enough to be cut into slices. Don't overdo it though, as
this is nice when it is still a little soft. Serve warm with your favourite bread.

Serves 6–8

80 G (2³⁄4 OZ/ABOUT 4 SLICES) WHITE BREAD,
  CRUSTS REMOVED
125 ML (4 FL OZ/¹⁄2 CUP) MILK
2 LARGE CARROTS, PEELED
2 LARGE ZUCCHINI (COURGETTES), TRIMMED
1 LARGE POTATO, PEELED
1 RED CAPSICUM (PEPPER)
500 G (1 LB 2 OZ) LEAN MINCED (GROUND) BEEF
2 TABLESPOONS CHOPPED PARSLEY
1 GARLIC CLOVE, FINELY CHOPPED
1 HEAPED TABLESPOON GRATED PARMESAN CHEESE
1 EGG, LIGHTLY BEATEN
4 TABLESPOONS OLIVE OIL
100 G (3¹⁄2 OZ) THINLY SLICED PANCETTA
2 SAGE SPRIGS
2 SMALL ROSEMARY SPRIGS
2 GARLIC CLOVES, UNPEELED
1 TABLESPOON PLAIN (ALL-PURPOSE) FLOUR
125 ML (4 FL OZ/¹⁄2 CUP) WHITE WINE

Meatloaf with roasted vegetables

My friend Julia, who is a marvellous cook, showed me this. You could also make it with leftover roast meat — all pulsed up in a processor. Use a large baking tray so that your vegetables can sit quite flat and are not steaming on top of each other. If you prefer, leave out the sauce-making at the end and just serve this with tomato sauce.

Preheat the oven to 180°C (350°F/Gas 4). Soak the bread in the milk for about 15 minutes, squashing it up with your hands so it collapses.

Cut the carrots in half lengthways, then each half into four. Cut the zucchini in half lengthways, then in half again to make chunks. Cut the potato into more or less the same shaped wedges, and the capsicum into strips. Put to one side.

Put the mince in a bowl with the parsley, chopped garlic, parmesan, egg and squashed up bread, and a flat teaspoon of salt. Mix together until smooth, then form a very large loaf like a giant egg.

Drizzle half the olive oil into a large flameproof baking dish and put the meatloaf on top. Cover with overlapping slices of pancetta, tucking them in at the bottom. Scatter the vegetables all around, drizzle them with the rest of the oil and toss with some salt. Tuck the sage, rosemary and garlic under the vegetables. Bake for about 1¹⁄4 hours, turning the vegetables over halfway through. They should be crusty and golden and the bacon crispy. Turn the oven off. Remove the vegetables and meatloaf to a platter, cover with foil and put back in the oven to keep warm.

Put the baking dish on the stovetop over high heat and sprinkle in the flour. Cook, stirring constantly to scrape up all the bits and pieces from the bottom of the dish. Pour in the wine and stir until it has evaporated. Add 250 ml (4 fl oz/1 cup) of hot water, season with salt and cook until the sauce becomes smooth and thickens a bit. Serve with the meatloaf cut into thick slices, and the vegetables.

Serves 6

600 G (1 LB 5 OZ/7 OR 8 SMALL) ZUCCHINI
(COURGETTES)
600 G (1 LB 5 OZ/ABOUT 3 OR 4) CARROTS, PEELED
800 G (1 LB 12 OZ/ABOUT 6) TOMATOES
3 GARLIC CLOVES, FINELY CHOPPED
1 LEAFY CELERY STALK, HALVED LENGTHWAYS
AND THINLY SLICED
3 TABLESPOONS CHOPPED PARSLEY
6 TABLESPOONS OLIVE OIL
6 THYME SPRIGS

Roasted zucchini & tomatoes with thyme

I love this — it is healthy and appetizing; tasty for a side dish, or as a light meal on its own with some bread. It is important that your tomatoes are deep red and beautifully ripe. I particularly like this simple combination, but you can use other herbs instead — perhaps basil or rosemary — and you might like to include some other vegetables, depending on who you are serving and what they like. Red peppers (capsicums), eggplant (aubergines) and potatoes could all be cut up and included here. You'll need one large baking dish of about 25 x 35 cm (10 x 14 inches) where the vegetables can sit quite flat. If you aren't going to serve this immediately, switch off the oven when the vegetables are cooked, but leave the tray in there to cool down completely.

Preheat the oven to 200°C (400°F/Gas 6). Trim the zucchini and slice them diagonally into chunks of about 3 cm (1 1/4 inches): slice once in one direction, and then in the other direction, and so on. Put them in a large baking dish. Slice the carrots diagonally in one direction to give longish strips about 3 mm (1/8 inch) thick. Add to the dish. Cut the tomatoes into wedges (six or eight depending on the size of the tomato) from top to bottom. Put in the dish and add the garlic, celery, parsley and oil. Season quite generously with salt and pepper; roll up your sleeves and mix everything through with your hands. I love doing this, and so do my kids, but you can use a large spoon if you prefer. Bury the thyme sprigs underneath and put the dish in the oven. Bake, uncovered, for 30 minutes, turning the vegetables over once in this time.

Turn the vegetables again, lower the heat to 180°C (350°F/Gas 4) and cook for another 1 1/4 hours, or until the vegetables are golden roasted and moist and the natural sweetness of the tomatoes and carrots have come into being. Turn the vegetables once or twice more during this time, trying not to mash things up, but the tomatoes will invariably be melting and losing their shape. There should be very little liquid left, so you may have to add a few drops of water. Serve hot, or at room temperature.

Serves 6-8

3 LARGE EGG WHITES, AT ROOM TEMPERATURE
1 TEASPOON CORNFLOUR (CORNSTARCH)
230 G (8 OZ/1 CUP) CASTER (SUPERFINE) SUGAR
A FEW DROPS OF VANILLA EXTRACT
½ TEASPOON APPLE OR WHITE WINE CIDER

TO SERVE:
2 ORANGES
24 CHERRIES
250 ML (9 FL OZ/1 CUP) WHIPPING CREAM
1 TABLESPOON ICING (CONFECTIONERS') SUGAR,
  PLUS SOME FOR SERVING

Pavlovas with oranges & cherries

This makes eight small pavlovas, but if you want one big one, just double
the amounts and extend the cooking time by 10 minutes. The egg yolks
can be used for making custard (page 135), or chocolate ice cream
(page 376), or they can be added to an omelette. If you are making a large
pavlova, pile all the meringue into the centre of your lined baking tray and
pat it out to about a 28 cm (11 inch) circle, smoothing the middle of the
top where your cream and fruit will sit. If you want to make 16 small
pavlovas, use two baking trays and switch them around in the oven
halfway through the baking time. And, if you want to, you can make them
even smaller for children and get more out of the mixture. I like this with
oranges and cherries but you can put pretty much any fruit on top with
the cream. A few chopped pistachios always look good, as well.

Preheat the oven to 150°C (300°F/Gas 2) and line a large baking tray with baking
paper. Whisk the egg whites in a large bowl and, once they form white peaks and
start stiffening, add the cornflour. Begin adding the sugar, sprinkling it in a bit at
a time, and keep whisking until you have added it all and everything seems like it
may climb out of the bowl on its own. Whisk in the vanilla and vinegar.
　　Use two tablespoons to form the meringues on the baking tray — make eight
rounded piles that are about 10 cm (4 inches) across, although you could make
them a bit taller, slimmer or more elegant if you like. Flatten the tops slightly, so
that your cream and fruit will have somewhere to sit, and smooth around the sides
with the back of a teaspoon. Cook on the middle shelf of the oven for 40 minutes
or so (check after 10 minutes and lower the temperature a little if the meringues
are colouring). Switch off the oven and leave the pavlovas in for 30-40 minutes to
cool, then remove them from the oven to cool completely. You can then store them
in a tin at room temperature for up to 5 days until you are ready to serve them.
　　To serve, peel the oranges with a sharp knife, taking off all the pith. Cut out the
segments by slicing down either side of the membranes. Halve the cherries and
remove the stones. Whip the cream and icing sugar until peaks form, spoon onto
the pavlovas and scatter with cherries and oranges. Dust with icing sugar to serve.

Serves 8

125 G (4½ OZ) BUTTER, CUT INTO CUBES
40 G (1½ OZ) CASTER (SUPERFINE) SUGAR
250 G (9 OZ/2 CUPS) PLAIN (ALL-PURPOSE) FLOUR
½ TABLESPOON OLIVE OIL

CREMA:
675 ML (23 FL OZ/2⅔ CUPS) MILK
30 G (1 OZ) PLAIN (ALL-PURPOSE) FLOUR
30 G (1 OZ) CORNFLOUR (CORNSTARCH)
125 G (4½ OZ) CASTER (SUPERFINE) SUGAR
3 EGG YOLKS
40 G (1½ OZ) BUTTER
1 TEASPOON VANILLA EXTRACT
125 ML (4 FL OZ/½ CUP) POURING (SINGLE) CREAM

Tiny sweet tartlets with crema & fruit

Top these with fresh fruit such as raspberries, grapes, pomegranate seeds and wild strawberries. If you like, you can make the tart cases and crema the day before, but whisk the cream into the crema just before filling the cases. You will probably have some crema left over, so you could dollop it into pancakes, or eat it with biscuits or just straight off the spoon.

For the pastry, put the butter, sugar and flour in a bowl with a small pinch of salt and crumble with your fingers until it is like coarse sand. Add 3 tablespoons of cold water and the oil and work into a loose dough. Knead quickly but gently until smooth, then flatten, cover with plastic wrap and refrigerate for about an hour.

Preheat the oven to 180°C (350°F/Gas 4) and have ready 45 tiny tart cases that are 4.5 cm (1¾ inches) across the top and no more than 2 cm (¾ inch) deep. They don't need to be greased (there is enough butter in the dough).

Break off small balls of pastry about the size of cherry tomatoes and flatten into the cases with your thumb and forefinger, pressing to a couple of millimetres thick. (If your cases are shallow you could roll out the pastry first, then press into the cases and trim the tops.) Bake for about 20 minutes, or until golden, then cool a bit in the cases before gently removing. Leave to cool completely before filling.

For the crema, put 500 ml (17 fl oz/2 cups) of the milk in a pan and warm it over low heat. Mix the flour, cornflour and sugar together in a bowl. Whisk the remaining milk with the egg yolks, add to the bowl and whisk until smooth. Pour into a saucepan and put over medium-low heat. Gradually stir in the warm milk and keep stirring until it thickens. Add the butter and vanilla and stir until smooth. Remove from the heat and leave it, stirring often as it cools. Cover and keep in the fridge until ready to use.

Just before filling the pastry cases, whip the cream to soft peaks. Give the crema an energetic whisk so there are no lumps then fold the whipped cream through. Dollop a teaspoon or so into each case and top with a bit of fruit. Keep in the fridge if you are not eating them straightaway.

Makes about 45

100 ML (3½ FL OZ) MILK
½ TEASPOON ORANGE FOOD COLOURING
600 G (1 LB 5 OZ) WHITE CHOCOLATE,
   ROUGHLY CHOPPED
1 PANDORO CAKE
SMALL COLOURED SWEETS, LARGER SWEETS
   AND SMALL LOLLIPOPS
BIRTHDAY CANDLES

Pandoro birthday cake

For this you will need one pandoro cake with its beautifully exaggerated form. In an emergency, once, I used this as a cake for Cassia's birthday. I iced it with bright orange chocolate that I dripped over the whole gorgeous pandoro, top and sides, and then stuck sweets into. If you can't find bright orange chocolate, just use white chocolate mixed with orange food colouring. This cake will keep well for a couple of days, so you can make it in advance.

Put the milk and food colouring in a small saucepan and heat until hot but not boiling. Keep warm.

Put the chocolate in a large bowl over a saucepan of boiling water, making sure that the water doesn't touch the bottom of the bowl. Heat, stirring a few times, until the chocolate melts and is quite smooth. Stir in the hot coloured milk and continue heating and stirring until it is all blended in and the chocolate is glossy and smooth.

Put the pandoro on a large serving plate. Quickly cover it with the chocolate, drizzling and spreading it with a spatula as you work. It doesn't have to be perfect — it is lovely exaggerated. Stick the sweets on just before the chocolate sets, positioning the larger and heavier ones closer to the bottom so they don't slide down, and holding them in place until they take hold. Decorate with the lollipops and candles.

Serves many

It's the memories that really make you rich...

I remember stepping out onto our school stage, searching for the faces of those I loved most among all the hundreds of others. The same faces that fed me first and tucked special things into small boxes for me to take to school.

Now, I will sew beads onto feathers for their concerts, encourage them when their tummies are sore from too many sweets and have them wake up to the smell of hot buttered toast.

They crawl along at the pace of tortoises, stopping to admire things I long ago lost time for, chattering in their squeaky notes. Those wonderful calm moments of no rivalry — just going along with the flow and the evergreen jigsaw-puzzling that keeps one family boat from sinking. For how can they all be allowed to row when they want to, and stop when they are tired?

I line them up at night among their dolls and toys and examine their perfect faces and fraying toenails. I love you, mice...

A

a coloured fruit salad 61
angel hair pasta with zucchini,
   mint & feta 186
apples
   apple bread with sugar
     & cinnamon topping 350
   baked cinnamon apples with
     buttermilk ice cream 284
apricot & apple pie, wholemeal
   105
apricot sauce 107

B

baked cinnamon apples with
   buttermilk ice cream 284
baked fish fillets 345
baked fish parcels 275
baked ham & cheese bread
   pudding 149
baked pumpkin with butter
   & brown sugar 97
banana bread 349
barbecued fillet & bread
   spiedini 303
barbecued fish skewers 122
barbecued mixed grill with
   corn 125
beans
   cannellini beans in tomato
     48
   farro & borlotti bean soup
     295
   green bean soufflé loaf 205
   lamb & green bean casserole
     190
beef
   barbecued fillet & bread
     spiedini 303
   beef stew with carrots 92

cottage pie 338
escalopes with ham & cheese
   228
hamburgers 304
meat broth 335
meat canneloni 182
mince & potato croquettes
   227
paillard 194
pot-roast steak with spinach
   & omelette 367
spaghetti with mince 294
steak pie 217
beetroot gnocchi 148
berries
   berry & buttermilk cake
     55
   chocolate & cranberry
     biscuits 58
   cranberry syrup 15
   lemon sandwiches with
     raspberries & cream 139
   meringue with strawberries
     & chocolate 62
   pear & berry crumble 163
   raspberry ripple ice cream
     381
   raspberry sauce 54
   strawberry jam 68
   strawberry sorbet 59
biscuits
   chocolate & cranberry 58
   chocolate & vanilla 387
   gingerbread 358
   jam shortbread 70
   oat biscuits 354
   pecan butter 358
boiled potatoes with parsley
   233
bread
   apple bread with sugar
     & cinnamon topping 350
   banana bread 349
   chocolate loaf 290
   half-moon rolls 213
   mixed brown bread 290
   olive oil focaccia 211

white loaf with honey, butter
& pecans 247
white milk bread/rolls 262
wholemeal focaccia 212
zucchini bread 347
bread dumplings in chicken
broth 328
bread pudding, baked ham
& cheese 149
broccoli
broccoli soup 173
gratinéed 203
sautéed, with tomato 200
broth
chicken 327
meat 335
vegetable 334
brown bread & butter ice
cream 309
brown bread, mixed 290
brown rice risotto with butter
& parmesan 300
brownies 315
buttermilk ice cream 284
butters, fruit 166

C

cabbage salad with oranges
& lemons 89
cakes
berry & buttermilk cake 55
brownies 315
chocolate & vanilla marble
cake 384
chocolate cake with icing
311
honey cake 279
lemon meringue ice cream
cake 141
lemon sandwiches with
raspberries & cream 139
orange juice & olive oil cake
with pine nuts 100

pandoro birthday cake 417
pear butter cake 248
tiny cakes with pink icing
167
vanilla cake 276
calamari, fried 223
cannellini beans in tomato 48
carrots
carrot purée 95
creamy carrots 95
little spinach & carrot pots
371
cauliflower, sautéed 241
celery, gratinéed, with tomato
& parmesan 204
cheese
angel hair pasta with
zucchini, mint & feta 186
cheese pies 216
chicken sautéed with cheese
& milk 128
creamy spinach with feta 199
escalopes with ham & cheese
228
fried mozarella sandwiches
221
ham & cheese bread pudding,
baked 149
ham & cheese omelette 130
macaroni cheese 222
pasta with cheese 270
ricotta gnocchi 266
spinach & ricotta canneloni
179
thin pizza with stracchino
cheese 264
chicken
casserole 39
chicken broth 327
chicken soup 333
croquettes 330
drumsticks & wings with
orange tomato glaze 81
escalopes with lemon &
butter 232
escalopes with parsley &
capers 189

escalopes with tomatoes &
    capers 40
fried buttermilk marinated
    chicken 231
roast chicken & potatoes
    with thyme, lemon & garlic
    236
sautéed with bay leaves &
    juniper berries 235
sautéed with cheese & milk
    128
chips
    pan-fried, with rosemary &
        sage 245
    very thin 240
chocolate
    chocolate & cranberry
        biscuits 58
    chocolate & vanilla biscuits
        387
    chocolate & vanilla marble
        cake 384
    chocolate bread pudding
        320
    chocolate cake with icing 311
    chocolate fudge sauce 321
    chocolate ice cream 376
    chocolate loaf 290
    chocolate milkshake 380
    chocolate pannacotta 310
    chocolate toffee nut squares
        388
    hazelnut chocolate balls 319
    hot chocolate 316
    meringue with strawberries
        & chocolate 62
cottage pie 338
cranberry syrup 15
cream of pumpkin soup 78
creamy spinach with feta 199
crepes
    meat canneloni 182
    spinach & ricotta canneloni
        179
croquettes
    chicken 330
    mince & potato 227

crumble, pear & berry 163
crumpets 250
custard 135
custard squares, fried 136

D

desserts
    baked cinnamon apples with
        buttermilk ice cream 284
    chocolate bread pudding 320
    chocolate pannacotta 310
    fried custard squares 136
    fruit salad, a coloured 61
    Greek yoghurt with
        condensed milk & oranges
        103
    Greek yoghurt with honey,
        cinnamon, pecans &
        pomegranate 159
    lemon rice pudding with
        roasted peaches 282
    lemon sandwiches with
        raspberries & cream 139
    mango sorbet 110
    meringue with strawberries
        & chocolate 67
    pavlovas with oranges
        & cherries 412
    pear & berry crumble 163
    peppermint crisp pie 206
    poached fruit in vanilla
        syrup 158
    pomegranate & apple jellies
        373
    pomegranate sorbet 162
    rosehip semolina puddings
        67
    semolina puddings with
        caramel 249
    wholemeal apricot & apple
        pie 105
    see also ice cream
double thickshakes,
    chocolate/vanilla 380

APPLES FOR SAM

dough, for fun 135
drinks
   double thickshakes 380
   fizzy orange 117
   hot chocolate 316
   lemonade 116
   milkshakes 380
   smoothies 394
dumplings
   bread dumplings in chicken
     broth 328
   mince & rice dumplings with
     dill, egg & lemon sauce 185

eggs
   custard 135
   eggs with bread & butter
     130
   eggs in tomato 49
   ham & cheese omelette 130
   risotto with fried egg 119
   sautéed potatoes with egg
     131
   spaghettini with egg &
     toasted parsley
       breadcrumbs 120
   watercress omelette 198
   zucchini omelette 194
escalopes
   beef, with ham & cheese 228
   chicken, with lemon & butter
     232
   chicken, with parsley &
     capers 189
   chicken, with tomatoes &
     capers 40

farro & borlotti bean soup 295
fish
   baked fish fillets 345
   baked fish parcels 275
   barbecued fish skewers 122
   fish cakes 239
   fish pie 340
   fish soup with poached fish
     to follow 326
   fried fish fillets 344
   pan-fried sole with lemon
     garlic butter 224
   poached fish 326
   sole bundles with spinach
     193
   see also seafood
fizzy orange 117
focaccia
   olive oil 211
   wholemeal 212
fried buttermilk marinated
   chicken 231
fried calamari 223
fried custard squares 136
fried fish fillets 344
fried mozarella sandwiches 221
fried potato halves with
   oregano 242
fried risotto balls 35
frittata, sausage & potato 405
fruit
   apricot sauce 107
   cranberry syrup 15
   fruit butters 166
   fruit salad, a coloured 61
   poached, in vanilla syrup 158
   raspberry sauce 54
fun dough 135

G

gingerbread biscuits 358
gnocchi
 beetroot 148
 ricotta 266
goulash, sausage & potato 79
granola 258
gratinéed broccoli 203
gratinéed celery with tomato
 & parmesan 204
Greek yoghurt
 with condensed milk &
  oranges 103
 with honey, cinnamon, pecans
  & pomegranate 159
green bean soufflé loaf 205
green vegetable soup with egg
 & lemon 176

H

half-moon rolls 213
ham & cheese bread pudding,
 baked 149
ham & cheese omelette 130
hamburger patties 44
hamburgers 304
hazelnut chocolate balls 319
honey cake 279
hot chocolate 316

I

ice cream
 brown bread & butter 309
 buttermilk 284
 chocolate 376
 ice cream sundaes 377
 lemon curd 140
 lemon meringue ice cream
  cake 141
 maple syrup & vanilla 355
 raspberry ripple 381
 vanilla 374
 vanilla yoghurt 280

J

jam shortbread 70
jams
 mandarin 106
 quince 69
 rosehip 66
 strawberry 68

L

la pizza rossa 53
lamb
 barbecued mixed grill with
  corn 125
 lamb & green bean casserole
  190
 pan-fried breaded lamb
  cutlets 343
leek & potato soup 259
legumes
 cannellini beans in tomato 48
 farro & borlotti bean soup
  295
 green bean soufflé loaf 205
 lamb & green bean casserole
  190
 lentil rice 297
 lentil soup 296
 lentils & sausages 298
lemon
 lemon curd ice cream 140
 lemon meringue ice cream
  cake 141

lemon rice pudding with
   roasted peaches 282
lemon sandwiches with
   raspberries & cream 139
lemonade 116
lentils
   lentil rice 297
   lentil soup 296
   lentils & sausages 298
little spinach & carrot pots 371

M

macaroni cheese 222
mandarin jam 106
mango sorbet 110
maple syrup & vanilla ice
   cream 355
Mars Bar sauce 321
mayonnaise 240
meat
   hamburger patties 44
   lentils & sausages 298
   meat & vegetable soup 401
   meat broth 335
   meat canneloni 182
   meat lasagne 32
   meatloaf with roasted
     vegetables 408
   mince & rice dumplings with
     dill, egg & lemon sauce 185
   sausage & potato goulash 79
   spaghetti with meatballs 25
   see also beef; lamb; pork; veal
meatloaf with roasted
   vegetables 408
meringue
   lemon meringue ice cream
     cake 141
   meringue with strawberries
     & chocolate 62
   pavlovas with oranges
     & cherries 412

milkshakes, chocolate/vanilla
   380
mince & potato croquettes 227
mince & rice dumplings with
   dill, egg & lemon sauce 185
mixed brown bread 290
mixed grill, barbecued, with
   corn 125
mixed vegetable risotto 404

O

oat biscuits 354
olive oil focaccia 211
omelettes
   ham & cheese 130
   watercress 198
   zucchini 194
orange juice & olive oil cake
   with pine nuts 100

P

paillard 194
pan-fried breaded lamb cutlets
   343
pan-fried chips with rosemary
   & sage 245
pan-fried sole with lemon garlic
   butter 224
pancakes 253
pandoro birthday cake 417
pasta
   angel hair pasta with
     zucchini, mint & feta 186
   macaroni cheese 222
   meat lasagne 32
   pasta with calamari & peas
     177
   pasta with cheese 270
   pasta in chicken broth 328

pasta with prosciutto, tomato
& oregano 26
pasta with tomato sauce 29
pasta with tuna, tomato
& olives 22
penne with prawns, cream
& tomato 152
penne with tomato, eggplant
& ricotta 21
spaghetti with meatballs 25
spaghetti with mince 294
spaghettini with egg &
toasted parsley
breadcrumbs 120
vermicelli soup with lemon
& butter 18
vermicelli soup with tomato
& basil 17
pavlovas with oranges &
cherries 412
pea & potato mash 195
pear & berry crumble 163
pear butter cake 248
pecan butter biscuits 358
penne
with prawns, cream & tomato
152
with tomato, eggplant &
ricotta 21
peppermint crisp pie 206
pesto, tomato 266
pies
cheese 216
cottage pie 338
fish 340
steak 217
wholemeal apricot & apple
105
pizza
la pizza rossa 53
pumpkin pizza 82
thin pizza with stracchino
cheese 264
poached fruit in vanilla syrup
158
pomegranate & apple jellies
373

pomegranate sorbet 162
pork
pork schnitzels 342
roast rack of pork with fennel
& honey 87
pot-roast steak with spinach
& omelette 367
pot-roasted veal with sage &
garlic 301
potatoes
boiled potatoes with parsley
233
fried potato halves with
oregano 242
leek & potato soup 259
mince & potato croquettes
227
pan-fried chips with rosemary
& sage 245
pea & potato mash 195
potato & chickpea mash 346
potato & yoghurt salad 271
sage & rosemary mashed
potatoes 94
sausage & potato frittata 405
sausage & potato goulash 79
sautéed potatoes with egg
131
very thin chips 240
prawns
penne with prawns, cream
& tomato 152
prawn & spinach brown rice
risotto 154
pumpkin
baked pumpkin with butter
& brown sugar 97
pumpkin fritters 98
pumpkin pizza 82
pumpkin soup, cream of 78

quince jam 69

R

raspberry ripple ice cream 381
raspberry sauce 54
raw vegetables with sauce for
  dunking 400
rice
  brown rice risotto with butter
    & parmesan 300
  fried risotto balls 35
  lemon rice pudding with
    roasted peaches 282
  lentil rice 297
  mixed vegetable risotto 404
  prawn & spinach brown rice
    risotto 154
  rice & vegetable pilaf 38
  risotto with fried egg 119
  tomato risotto 34
  white risotto in spinach broth
    267
ricotta gnocchi 266
ripe tomato salad 47
risotto
  brown rice risotto with butter
    & parmesan 300
  fried risotto balls 35
  mixed vegetable risotto 404
  prawn & spinach brown
    rice risotto 154
  risotto with fried egg 119
  tomato risotto 34
  white risotto in spinach broth
    267
roast chicken & potatoes with
  thyme, lemon & garlic 236
roast rack of pork with fennel
  & honey 87
roast veal with oranges &
  lemons 85
roasted zucchini & tomatoes
  with thyme 411
rosehip jam 66
rosehip semolina puddings 67

S

sage & rosemary mashed
  potatoes 94
salads
  cabbage salad with oranges
    & lemons 89
  potato & yoghurt salad 271
  ripe tomato salad 47
sauces
  apricot 107
  chocolate fudge 321
  dunking 400
  Mars Bar sauce 321
  raspberry 54
  toffee 247
sausage & potato frittata 405
sausage & potato goulash 79
sausages & lentils 298
sautéed broccoli with tomato
  200
sautéed cauliflower 241
sautéed chicken with bay
  leaves & juniper berries 235
sautéed potatoes with egg 131
sautéed tomatoes in olive oil &
  rosemary 46
seafood
  fried calamari 223
  pasta with calamari & peas
    177
  penne with prawns, cream
    & tomato 152
  prawn & spinach brown rice
    risotto 154
  see also fish
semolina puddings with
  caramel 249
semolina soup with butter &
  sage 260
smoothies 394
sole bundles with spinach
  193
sole, pan-fried, with lemon
  garlic butter 224

sorbet
  mango 110
  pomegranate 162
  strawberry 59
soup
  broccoli 173
  chicken 333
  farro & borlotti bean 295
  fish 326
  green vegetable soup with
    egg & lemon 176
  leek & potato 259
  lentil 296
  meat & vegetable 401
  pumpkin, cream of 78
  semolina soup with butter
    & sage 260
  vermicelli soup with lemon
    & butter 18
  vermicelli soup with tomato
    & basil 17
  see also broth
spaghetti
  with meatballs 25
  with mince 294
spaghettini with egg &
  toasted parsley
    breadcrumbs 120
spinach
  creamy spinach with feta 199
  little spinach & carrot pots
    371
  prawn & spinach brown rice
    risotto 154
  spinach & ricotta canneloni
    179
squashed zucchini 202
steak pie 217
strawberry jam 68
strawberry sorbet 59
syrup, cranberry 15

T
----

tarts
  peppermint crisp pie 206
  tiny savoury tartlets 396
  tiny sweet tartlets with crema
    & fruit 414
  wholemeal apricot & apple
    105
thin pizza with stracchino
  cheese 264
tiny cakes with pink icing 167
tiny savoury tartlets 396
tiny sweet tartlets with crema
  & fruit 414
toffee sauce 247
tomato
  cannellini beans in tomato 48
  eggs in tomato 49
  pasta with tomato sauce 29
  ripe tomato salad 47
  sautéed tomatoes in olive oil
    & rosemary 46
  tomato lasagne 31
  tomato pesto 266
  tomato risotto 34
  veal involtini 43
turkey breast with dried
  apricots & pancetta 86

V
----

vanilla cake 276
vanilla ice cream 374
vanilla syrup, poaching 158
vanilla yoghurt ice cream 280
veal
  barbecued mixed grill with
    corn 125
  paillard 194
  pot-roasted veal with sage
    & garlic 301

APPLES FOR SAM

roast veal with oranges & lemons 85

veal involtini 43

vegetables

baked pumpkin with butter & brown sugar 97

beetroot gnocchi 148

boiled potatoes with parsley 233

carrot purée 95

creamy carrots 95

fried potato halves with oregano 242

gratinéed broccoli 203

gratinéed celery with tomato & parmesan 204

green bean soufflé loaf 205

little spinach & carrot pots 371

mixed vegetable risotto 404

pan-fried chips with rosemary & sage 245

pea & potato mash 195

potato & chickpea mash 346

pumpkin fritters 98

raw, with sauce for dunking 400

rice & vegetable pilaf 38

roasted zucchini & tomatoes with thyme 411

sage & rosemary mashed potatoes 94

sautéed broccoli with tomato 200

sautéed cauliflower 241

sautéed tomatoes in olive oil & rosemary 46

squashed zucchini 202

vegetable broth 334

see also salads; soup

vermicelli soup

with lemon & butter 18

with tomato & basil 17

very thin chips 240

W

waffles 251

watercress omelette 198

white loaf with honey, butter & pecans 247

white milk bread or rolls 262

white risotto in spinach broth 267

wholemeal apricot & apple pie 105

wholemeal focaccia 212

Y

yoghurt

Greek yoghurt with condensed milk & oranges 103

Greek yoghurt with honey, cinnamon, pecans & pomegranate 159

potato & yoghurt salad 271

vanilla yoghurt ice cream 280

Z

zucchini

angel hair pasta with zucchini, mint & feta 186

squashed zucchini 202

zucchini bread 347

zucchini omelette 194